What Justices Want

The most sophisticated theories of judicial behavior depict judges as rational actors who strategically pursue multiple goals when making decisions. However, these accounts tend to disregard the possibility that judges have heterogeneous goal preferences – that is, that different judges want different things. Integrating insights from personality psychology and economics, this book proposes a new theory of judicial behavior in which judges strategically pursue multiple goals, but their personality traits determine the relative importance of those goals. This theory is tested by analyzing the behavior of justices who served on the US Supreme Court between 1946 and 2015. Using recent advances in text-based personality measurement, Matthew E. K. Hall evaluates the influence of the "Big Five" personality traits on the justices' behavior during each stage of the Court's decision-making process. *What Justices Want* shows that personality traits directly affect the justices' choices and moderate the influence of goal-related situational factors on justices' behavior.

Matthew E. K. Hall is Associate Professor of Political Science and Law at the University of Notre Dame. He specializes in American political institutions with an emphasis on judicial behavior, elite personality, and policy implementation. His book *The Nature of Supreme Court Power* (Cambridge University Press, 2011) won the C. Herman Pritchett Award for Best Book on Law and Courts from the American Political Science Association.

What Justices Want

Goals and Personality on the US Supreme Court

MATTHEW E. K. HALL
University of Notre Dame

CAMBRIDGE
UNIVERSITY PRESS

CAMBRIDGE
UNIVERSITY PRESS

University Printing House, Cambridge CB2 8BS, United Kingdom

One Liberty Plaza, 20th Floor, New York, NY 10006, USA

477 Williamstown Road, Port Melbourne, VIC 3207, Australia

314–321, 3rd Floor, Plot 3, Splendor Forum, Jasola District Centre, New Delhi – 110025, India

79 Anson Road, #06–04/06, Singapore 079906

Cambridge University Press is part of the University of Cambridge.

It furthers the University's mission by disseminating knowledge in the pursuit of education, learning, and research at the highest international levels of excellence.

www.cambridge.org
Information on this title: www.cambridge.org/9781108472746
DOI: 10.1017/9781108621410

© Matthew E. K. Hall 2018

First published 2018

Printed in the United States of America by Sheridan Books, Inc.

A catalogue record for this publication is available from the British Library.

Library of Congress Cataloging-in-Publication Data
NAMES: Hall, Matthew Eric Kane, author.
TITLE: What justices want : goals and personality on the U.S. Supreme Court /
Matthew E.K. Hall, University of Notre Dame, Indiana.
DESCRIPTION: Cambridge [UK] ; New York, NY : Cambridge University Press, [2018]
IDENTIFIERS: LCCN 2018010098| ISBN 9781108472746 (hardback) |
ISBN 9781108462907 (pbk.)
SUBJECTS: LCSH: United States. Supreme Court–Officials and employees. |
Judges–Selection and appointment–United States.
CLASSIFICATION: LCC KF8748 .H357 2018 | DDC 347.73/2634–dc23
LC record available at https://lccn.loc.gov/2018010098

ISBN 978-1-108-47274-6 Hardback
ISBN 978-1-108-46290-7 Paperback

To Brittany
who always judges my extraverted and neurotic behavior
with openness, conscientiousness,
and sometimes even agreeableness

Contents

Figures

Tables

Acknowledgments

I am indebted to numerous scholars, students, and friends for their wisdom and assistance in developing this project and, ultimately, producing this book. I want to thank Miles Armaly, Eileen Braman, David Campbell, Lee Epstein, Jim Gibson, Micheal Giles, Don Green, Gary Hollibough, Greg Huber, Mark Hurwitz, Jonathon Klingler, Adam Ramey, Timothy Johnson, Geoff Layman, Stefanie Lindquist, Jeff Mondak, and Paul Parker for their thoughtful and constructive feedback on various versions of this project. Special thanks to Amanda Bryan for her detailed feedback and assistance in supplementary data collection. And special thanks to the anonymous reviewers (from Cambridge University Press and another publisher) who offered invaluable suggestions for improving the manuscript. I also want to thank the many research assistants who helped me gather information and code data for this book.

However, most of the credit for this book must go to my wife, Brittany (a personality psychologist by training), who convinced me that personality traits fundamentally influence people's behavior in almost every context. It only took me a few years of hearing this insight to realize that judges might be people too.

Who They Are and What They Want

On November 1, 1962, Estelle Griswold, the executive director of the Planned Parenthood League of Connecticut, and Charles Lee Buxton, the head of obstetrics and gynecology at Yale University, opened a clinic in New Haven, Connecticut. The clinic was one of several that Planned Parenthood had opened in Connecticut over the prior few decades. Like the other clinics, this one's purpose was to provide birth control information to married couples and dispense contraceptives to married women.

Within days of opening the clinic, Griswold and Buxton were arrested for violating an 1879 Connecticut statute, which prohibited any person from using "any drug, medicinal article or instrument for the purpose of preventing conception."[1] Violators could be fined or imprisoned for up to a year, and Connecticut law stated that "[a]ny person who assists, abets, counsels, causes, hires or commands another to commit any offense may be prosecuted and punished as if he were the principal offender."[2] Griswold and Buxton were found guilty as accessories to violating the anti-contraceptive statute and fined $100 each. The Appellate Division of the Circuit Court and the Supreme Court of Errors in Connecticut both affirmed their convictions, so Griswold and Buxton appealed their case to the US Supreme Court.

When Griswold and Buxton opened the clinic in New Haven, they were well aware of the anti-contraceptive statute. In fact, one of their goals in opening the clinic was to provoke a legal action that would allow them to challenge the archaic Connecticut law. Though once fairly common in the United States, Connecticut's 82-year-old ban on contraceptives was one of only two such laws still in place in 1961. In the preceding decades, several doctors and patients had brought challenges to the law, but those challenges had failed on procedural grounds.[3] In the most recent case, *Poe v. Ulman*,[4] Buxton and his patients had asked the Supreme Court to invalidate the statute, but their lawsuit was deemed unripe because the law had not actually been enforced against them. With their arrest and conviction, Griswold and Buxton were now positioned to directly challenge the constitutionality of the anti-contraceptive law.

In their appeal to the Supreme Court, Griswold and Buxton argued that the Connecticut statute violated the constitutional right to privacy. The US Constitution does not explicitly guarantee a right to privacy – indeed, the word "privacy" does not appear anywhere in the Constitution's text. Yet, in the preceding years, several constitutional scholars had come to believe that a right to privacy could be inferred from various constitutional provisions. The First Amendment Free Speech and Free Assembly Clauses protect the "freedom to associate and privacy in one's associations"; the Fourth Amendment Search and Seizure Clause and the Fifth Amendment Self Incrimination Clause protect "the sanctity of a man's home and the privacies of life."[5] The Fourteenth Amendment prohibits the state from depriving a person of "liberty" without "due process of law," and this clause had been interpreted to protect various fundamental personal liberties not explicitly listed in the text. Moreover, the Ninth Amendment says that "[t]he enumeration in the Constitution, of certain rights, shall not be construed to deny or disparage others retained by the people," which suggests the Constitution may indeed protect certain rights not enumerated in the text itself. If so, it may protect a right to privacy that includes the use of contraceptives in a marital relationship. But would the Supreme Court agree with this novel legal theory?

The question raised by *Griswold v. Connecticut* prompted one of the most fundamental, consequential, and enduring debates in American constitutional law. If Griswold and Buxton were right, the Constitution may protect a wide range of private, intimate, and personal behavior that had long been outlawed throughout the United States. How far would such a right to privacy extend? Would it protect contraceptive use outside of marriage? What about other private sexual acts? Would privacy include all intimate decisions related to family and procreation, such as the right to abort a child? What about the right to suicide or drug use? Such an interpretation might spark a revolution in the Constitution's protections for a wide variety of behavior. But it might also empower judges to subject democratic majorities to their will and impose their own values on the public. How would judges decide which rights were truly fundamental? How could one determine if judges were protecting constitutionally enshrined rights or inventing new ones out of whole cloth? On the Court, this critical debate played out between the two most senior justices: Hugo Lafayette Black and William Orville Douglas.

Black and Douglas were similar in many ways. They both had political backgrounds (Black was a US senator; Douglas was chairman of the Securities and Exchange Commission), and both harbored presidential aspirations, even after joining the Court.[6] Both were lifelong Democrats, appointed to the Court by Franklin Roosevelt, and regarded as liberals throughout their careers. Both justices shared a constitutional philosophy in which the Court generally deferred to the government with regard to economic regulations but strictly enforced protections for civil liberties. They were both well known for their strong stance on First Amendment freedoms, and they frequently signed each other's dissenting opinions in free speech cases.[7] Indeed, out of the 2,595 cases that Black and Douglas heard together on the Supreme Court, they voted together almost 80 percent of the time.[8]

Yet, the two long-time allies broke sharply in *Griswold v. Connecticut*. In the Court's conference discussion, Black firmly rejected Griswold's argument: "The right of husband and wife to assemble in bed," he declared, "is a new right of assembly to me."[9] But Douglas disagreed, insisting that the First Amendment protected the freedom of association, and the Court had interpreted that freedom to include a variety of activities on the periphery of association, including the right to travel and the right to send a child to a nonpublic school. The same logic applied here, Douglas argued, because there is nothing more personal than the marital relationship.[10] Douglas's argument won the day: The justices split 7–2 in Griswold's favor, and Chief Justice Earl Warren assigned Douglas to write the opinion of the Court. Douglas's initial draft was brief yet unapologetically bold:

The association of husband and wife is not mentioned in the Constitution, nor in the Bill of Rights ... But it is an association as vital in the life of a man or woman as any other, and perhaps more so ... We deal with a right of association as old as the Bill of Rights, older than our political parties, older than our school system. It is a coming together for better or for worse, hopefully enduring, and intimate to the degree of being sacred.[11]

However, what Douglas's draft offered in rhetorical flourish, it lacked in legal substance – at least in the eyes of Justice William J. Brennan Jr. and his clerk, Paul Posner, who were privately shown a copy of the opinion before it was circulated to the full Court. At Posner's suggestion, Brennan sent Douglas a memo urging him to adopt a broader legal framework to justify the decision:

Instead of expanding the First Amendment right of association to include marriage, why not say that what has been done for the First Amendment can also be done for some of the other fundamental guarantees in the Bill of Rights? In other words, where fundamental rights are concerned, the Bill of Rights guarantees are but expressions or examples of those rights, and do not preclude applications or extensions of those rights to situations unanticipated by the framers.[12]

Douglas followed Brennan's suggestion and revised his draft. The opinion ultimately adopted by the Court held that "specific guarantees in the Bill of Rights have penumbras, formed by emanations from those guarantees that help give them life and substance."[13] The right to privacy, the Court ruled – including the right of married couples to use contraceptives – was among those penumbras. Thus, in two senses, Douglas demonstrated his openness to change in *Griswold*: He was open to changing the Court's jurisprudence to protect the use of contraceptives, and he was open to changing the logic he used to arrive at that conclusion. Justice Black vehemently dissented.

Why did Black and Douglas split in *Griswold*? As one might expect, given his liberal predisposition, Justice Black was no great fan of the Connecticut law. In fact, his dissenting opinion emphasized that he did not believe the law was "wise" or "good" policy. In fact, he "fe[lt] constrained to add that the law is every bit as offensive to me as it is to my Brethren of the majority."[14] In private, he called the law "abhorrent, just viciously evil."[15] However, Black nonetheless rejected the majority's creative logic finding the law unconstitutional: "I like my privacy as well as the next one, but I am nevertheless compelled to admit that government has a right to invade it unless prohibited by some specific constitutional provision."[16] Thus, Black concluded that his fellow justices were changing the Constitution's meaning in order to reject a law of which they personally disapproved. His opinion essentially boiled down to a rejection of such changes:

I realize that many good and able men have eloquently spoken and written, sometimes in rhapsodical strains, about the duty of this Court to keep the Constitution in tune with the times. The idea is that the Constitution must be changed from time to time, and that this Court is charged with a duty to make those changes. For myself, I must, with all deference, reject that philosophy. The Constitution makers knew the need for change, and provided for it. Amendments suggested by the people's elected representatives can be submitted to the people or their selected agents for ratification. That method of change was good for our Fathers, and, being somewhat old-fashioned, I must add it is good enough for me.[17]

The last line was a paraphrase of the traditional Gospel song, "Old-Time Religion" ("Give me that old time religion, it's good enough for me!"). And in that line hides an important clue explaining the clash between Black and Douglas. In order to understand *what they did*, one must understand *who they were*.

Hugo Lafayette Black was born in 1886 in Clay County, Alabama – a poor, rural, and isolated region near the Appalachian foothills. His mother was a thoroughly devout Baptist – indeed, the Bible was the only book she ever read to him.[18] His father had fought for the Confederacy during the Civil War and named his oldest son Robert Lee.[19] Black's father also drank heavily, and the memories of his father's drinking problems instilled in Black a lifelong skepticism toward alcohol.[20] Black attended a small country high school with no library or study facilities,[21] but he was expelled for breaking a switch that a teacher was using to discipline his sister, and he never graduated.[22] Nonetheless, Black attended the new University of Alabama Law School, which had only two professors at the time.[23] After graduating, he was appointed as a local police court judge, elected district attorney, and later worked as a personal injury lawyer.[24] As an adult, Black maintained his religious devotion, serving as a Sunday school teacher and an organist in his Baptist church.[25]

In 1923, Black joined the Ku Klux Klan. He later minimized his participation in the Klan, claiming he "went to a couple of meetings and spoke about liberty," but, in actuality, during his first race for the Senate, Black marched in parades, spoke at numerous meetings, and dressed in full Klan regalia.[26] Although he occasionally protested the Klan's illegal and violent activities, he nonetheless remained a member in the hopes of attaining higher political office.[27] Asked years later by one of his clerks why he had joined, he answered simply: "Why son, if you wanted to be elected to the Senate in Alabama in the 1920s, you'd join the Klan, too."[28]

Despite his limited education – or perhaps because of it – Black relished reading, especially classics, such as Shakespeare, Dickens, Enlightenment philosophies, and the works of the Founding Fathers.[29] "The experience of communing with original texts, along with his childhood reading of the Bible, helped Black develop the rudiments of a strict constructionist judicial philosophy. Judicial subjectivity, he believed, was the greatest evil, and subjectivity could be avoided by forcing judges to study the text and original understanding of the Constitution."[30] His fidelity to the Constitution and to his principles, like his religious faith, was unflinching. Even in negotiations with other justices, Black "felt less free than Douglas to change a position after he made a commitment," and he held steadfastly to his textualist dogma throughout his time on the Bench.[31]

Regardless of their ideological similarities, Black's principled inflexibility and legalistic purity were anathema to Justice Douglas, who "came to see Black as a moralistic prude and lamented what he considered Black's jurisprudential rigidity."[32] And Black's rigid tendencies only became stronger as he grew older. Indeed, his colleagues noted an increasing lack of "openness," "flexibility," and "receptivity to new ideas."[33] While Black was strict, rigid, and dogmatic, Douglas was open, flexible, and creative.

William Orville Douglas was born in 1898 in Otter Tail County, Minnesota. He was raised by his mother to be deeply ambitious, coveting the presidency throughout his lifetime.[34] His political ambition often prompted him to change his policy positions and, in some instances, even details about his own life in hopes of advancing his career. (For example, in his first autobiography, he described the intestinal colic he suffered as a child as an undiagnosed case of polio in hopes that the similarity to Franklin Roosevelt might aid him in a future campaign.[35]) He distinguished himself at Whitman College and then put himself through Columbia Law School. After he graduated, Columbia hired him to teach corporate law, and Douglas soon earned a reputation as the "finest law teacher in America" and a pathbreaking legal scholar.[36] After he joined the Court, many – including Black – viewed him as a borderline genius.[37]

Whereas Black was religious and moralistic, Douglas was brash and scandalous. Despite his professed reverence for the "enduring," "vital," and "sacred" institution of marriage, Douglas was on his third marriage when he penned the opinion in *Griswold*. He had met his current wife two years earlier when she was a 23-year-old college student (Douglas was 64 at the time); within a year, he would leave her for his fourth wife, a 20-year-old waitress he met while vacationing.[38] Indeed, throughout his life, Douglas was prone to incessant womanizing as well as binge drinking and self-destructive behavior. Justice Felix Frankfurter once called him "the most cynical, amoral character" he had ever known.[39]

Douglas's disdain for convention also shaped his professional life. "Douglas was contemptuous of the norms of the Court and of colleagues he considered intellectually slow."[40] His work was marked by "disinterest and carelessness," and some "wondered on occasion whether he was mentally absent."[41] Early in his career, when he was still angling for the vice-presidency and, ultimately, the White House, he often changed his positions, seemingly for political gain. When he abandoned those ambitions after the 1960 election, "Douglas became more romantically aggressive in his defense of the principle that individuals should not blindly follow convention, but should be free to assert themselves in the face of disapproval."[42] Yet, whether he was contorting his principles for political expediency (to the frustration of his colleagues) or rebelliously defending individual liberty (against popular pressures), Douglas was always willing to defy the status quo. He was ever the creative thinker, pressing the envelope of the Court's role in American life. Near the end of his career, he no longer even bothered to pretend that he was constrained by legal precedents or conventional legal norms. In short, whereas Black felt a deep allegiance to consistency, Douglas was always open to change – in wives, in political positions, and, most certainly, in the law.

Thus, upon closer reflection, the split between Black and Douglas in *Griswold* may not be so surprising. The conventional, rigid Black balked at breaking with the Court's tradition because he could not square the right to privacy with his narrow devotion to his "textualist creed."[43] In contrast, Griswold's argument found sympathetic ears in "the freewheeling abstract expressionism represented most flamboyantly by Douglas."[44] In other words, in order to fully understand the divergence between Black and Douglas, one must look beyond their partisan affiliation, political ideology, and institutional context. To fully understand the justices' behavior, one must understand their personalities.

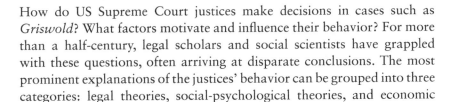

How do US Supreme Court justices make decisions in cases such as *Griswold*? What factors motivate and influence their behavior? For more than a half-century, legal scholars and social scientists have grappled with these questions, often arriving at disparate conclusions. The most prominent explanations of the justices' behavior can be grouped into three categories: legal theories, social-psychological theories, and economic theories.

Legalist Approaches. Traditional legal scholars often describe judicial behavior by reference to a theory known as legalism or formalism. In this view, the act of judging is a technical process in which judges mechanically apply preexisting laws to a set of specific facts in the case before them.[45] As Chief Justice John G. Roberts Jr. explained in his confirmation hearings, judges are like umpires in a baseball game: "Umpires don't make the rules; they apply them ... it's my job to call balls and strikes and not to pitch or bat."[46] Or, as Alexander Hamilton eloquently explained in

The Federalist Papers, "judges possess neither force nor will, but merely judgment."[47]

In most cases, the application of law to facts is relatively straightforward. If the law says the speed limit is 55 miles per hour and a defendant was driving at 60 miles per hour, then the defendant violated the law. However, sometimes judges must answer more complicated legal questions in order to apply the law, especially in cases involving the US Constitution. The meaning of 55 miles per hour might be perfectly clear, but what do phrases like due process, equal protection, or freedom of speech mean? Is the death penalty a cruel and unusual punishment? Does a prayer at a high school graduation constitute an establishment of religion? And what exactly does it mean for Congress to regulate commerce among the several states? In the legalist view, when judges encounter ambiguous legal questions, such as these, they answer by applying a neutral method of interpretation, such as originalism or textualism. Therefore, judges do not exercise independent discretion; they systematically apply a process of legal interpretation based on neutral principles of law.

Legalism offers a fairly accurate description of what *most* judges do *most* of the time. However, Supreme Court justices are not most judges. Of the millions of legal actions filed in the United States each year, only a tiny fraction ever reach the US Supreme Court. In fact, for the last decade, the justices typically hear fewer than a hundred cases each year. Accordingly, they focus their attention on the most contentious cases involving the most important, complex, and ambiguous legal questions. Moreover, the so-called neutral interpretive methods, such as originalism or textualism, generally require substantial subjective interpretation and rarely provide clear answers to any question before the Court. Far from a mechanical process in which judges predictably follow a common legal craft, these methods of interpretation require the justices to use their discretion.

Moreover, all judges – but especially US Supreme Court justices – undoubtedly exercise some discretion on a regular basis. In fact, even the most clear-cut legal questions allow for discretion, and that discretion introduces the possibility of personal bias. Just as a hometown umpire might tend to see a larger strike zone when a rival batter comes to the plate, so too a judge may see special reason for leniency when a sympathetic defendant is charged with speeding. The opportunities for personal biases to influence decision-making are even greater when the legal questions at stake are inherently ambiguous. Thus, it should come as no surprise that the media, commentators, and academics often describe Supreme Court justices as liberal or conservative based on their tendencies to make liberal or conservative decisions. Accordingly, at its core, legalism fails to account for the most basic facts about judging on the US Supreme Court: The justices frequently disagree, they disagree in predictable ways, and (believe it or not) they are human beings who are susceptible to all of the influences and biases that affect other human beings.

Social-Psychological Approaches. The human aspect of judging is the starting point for social-psychological theories of judicial behavior.[48] These theories emphasize the importance of individual differences, such as demographic characteristics,[49] life experiences,[50] role orientations,[51] and ideological attitudes,[52] in shaping judicial decisions. These approaches, though distinct, share a common understanding of how people make choices: Individuals possess distinct characteristics, and they respond to stimuli based on those characteristics. Accordingly, judges' choices are simply idiosyncratic responses to the stimuli presented in the cases they hear.[53]

These individual characteristics may influence judges' decisions in specific and nuanced ways. For example, judges who have daughters may be more sympathetic to plaintiffs in sex discrimination cases than judges who only have sons.[54] But for the most part, judges' individual characteristics are thought to influence their behavior by shaping their ideological policy preferences.[55] That is, certain characteristics, such as judge's race, political party, or religion, tend to be associated with more liberal or conservative policy preferences, and it is these policy preferences that are thought to genuinely drive the judges' decision-making. This "attitudinal" model simplifies the social-psychological approach by arguing that US Supreme Court justices base their decisions solely on their personal policy preferences. The most prominent advocates of this view, Jeffrey Segal and Harold Spaeth, succinctly summarize the attitudinal model: "[Chief Justice William H.] Rehnquist vote[d] the way he [did] because he [was] extremely conservative; [Justice Thurgood] Marshall voted the way he did because he was extremely liberal."[56]

The notion that judges base their decisions on their own policy preferences was once a highly controversial idea in the legal academy, and it is still disputed by some judges, lawyers, and law professors.[57] However, beginning with the legal realist movement in the early twentieth century, numerous scholars have convincingly established that judges do not mechanically apply neutral principles of law to case facts. Instead, judges often make decisions based on the same ideological and policy considerations that motivate legislative and executive decision-makers.[58] In fact, among social scientists studying judicial behavior, the claim that judges make decisions based (at least partially) on a desire to influence policy is now so widely accepted that proponents of the view are sometimes criticized for attacking a straw man.[59]

Nonetheless, the degree to which judges pursue policy goals varies across judges. A variety of factors "dampen the ideological ambitions of lower court judges," including "caseload pressures, the threat of reversal or eventual overruling (and so of not having the last word), desire for promotion, a different case mix, and lower visibility."[60] In contrast, US Supreme Court justices decide which cases to hear, tend to focus on important and controversial cases, cannot be promoted to a higher court, and are far more visible than any other type of judge. Consequently, US Supreme Court justices are the judges most likely to pursue their own ideological preferences.[61]

Yet judges may also vary in attributes that influence their behavior without shaping their policy preferences. Dating back to the early twentieth century, some scholars have argued that judges are influenced by their individual personalities.[62] For example, judges' self-esteem may be associated with judicial activism, the decision to enter politics, or their understanding of a judge's proper role.[63] Judges' birth order may influence their policy preferences and willingness to exercise judicial review by inducing particular childhood roles.[64] And personality traits may be associated with interpersonal influence and leadership styles on courts.[65] Yet, as James Gibson emphasized more than three decades ago, "[t]he amount of attention given personality attributes is not commensurate with the potential influence of these variables."[66] That sentiment still rings true today. In fact, "[s]ince 1980, there has been a slow decline in attention to psychology" in courts-related research.[67]

Economic Approaches. Beginning in the 1990s, economic (sometimes called "strategic") models replaced social-psychological theories as the predominant approach to studying judicial behavior. Economic models depict judges as rational actors who strategically seek to maximize their utility; that is, when confronted with an array of options, judges make the choice they believe will best serve their objectives. This approach offers a comprehensive theory of judicial decision-making. Judges are not simply black boxes who spit out responses to stimuli based on their characteristics; they are rational human beings trying to pursue their goals. Moreover, economic theories highlight the interdependent nature of judicial behavior. Supreme Court justices do not naively pursue their policy goals; they rationally anticipate the actions of their fellow justices, lower court judges, the president, Congress, and other social and political actors. Taking all of this information into account, the justices then strategically choose the option they believe will best serve their goals.[68] Therefore, in order to understand a judge's behavior, one must understand the judge's goals, options, and constraints.

Most economic accounts of judicial behavior assume that US Supreme Court justices pursue only one goal with regard to their professional decision-making: a desire to influence policy. Accordingly, the economic account usually offers only a minor revision to the attitudinal model: The justices' decisions are driven by their policy preferences *after accounting for their strategic context.* However, many studies contemplate the possibility of alternative motivations influencing judicial behavior. For example, Supreme Court justices may strive to attain prestige and celebrity, maintain collegial relations with their fellow justices, or conserve time for leisure and other nonjudicial activities.[69] In other words, the justices may not be single-minded policy seekers; instead, they may pursue a variety of goals as they make decisions. These recent studies offer a more sophisticated and probably more realistic view of how justices actually think and behave.

But even these enhanced strategic accounts overlook a critical factor influencing judicial behavior: the individual differences among judges (apart from differences in their policy preferences) that were the focus of early social-psychological approaches. Most economic models assume that every justice's goals and strategic calculations are identical to those of every other justice. Yet, social-psychological theories (as well as simple common sense) suggest that different judges may prioritize different goals. Indeed, the field of behavioral economics has challenged traditional economic decision models by incorporating various psychological factors that may influence rational decision-making, including personality traits.[70] Accordingly, individual judges may vary a great deal in the value they attach to particular goals. Most judges probably make decisions based on their ideological preferences, but they may vary in the degree to which they view that behavior as appropriate. Similarly, some judges may care a great deal about harmonious relations with their colleagues, but others may thrive on conflict and competition.

In short, the most sophisticated theories of judicial behavior view judges as rational actors who strategically pursue multiple goals when making decisions. However, these accounts tend to disregard the possibility that goal preferences vary among judges. In contrast, I propose a psychoeconomic approach to studying Supreme Court behavior, which suggests that justices strategically pursue their goals, but *different justices want different things.*

The Psychoeconomic Approach. My psychoeconomic approach is based on the assumption that the justices' behavior depends on *who they are* and *what they want.* I call the approach "psychoeconomic" because it integrates insights from both psychology and economics. First, I draw on personality psychology to assess the individual personality differences among Supreme Court justices. These personality traits reflect the justices' different goal preferences – that is, the value they attach to particular goals. Second, I incorporate these personality traits into an economic model of behavior. I argue that justices strategically pursue multiple goals, and their personality traits determine the relative importance of those goals.

In the next chapter, I develop my psychoeconomic account. I begin by summarizing the predominant economic theory of judicial behavior, which is focused on the justices' goals (i.e., what they want) and their strategic pursuit of those goals. Next, I summarize insights from personality psychology, which emphasize the importance of individual differences among the justices (i.e., who they are), particularly heterogeneous goal preferences (i.e., different justices want different things). Finally, I incorporate these personality traits into a comprehensive theory of Supreme Court behavior. In Chapter 3, I explain my approach to measuring the justices' personality traits based on their written language.

The remainder of this book employs the psychoeconomic approach in a series of empirical analyses to explain the justices' behavior in each stage of a Supreme Court case. Chapter 4 describes the agenda-setting stage, in which the justices decide whether to grant certiorari (that is, the justices officially decide whether to hear a case). Chapter 5 examines the assignment of a justice to author the opinion of the Court. Chapter 6 examines the justices' bargaining behavior as they negotiate over opinion content through intra-Court memoranda. Chapter 7 describes the justices' final votes on a case's merits (i.e., which party wins and which party loses), and Chapter 8 examines the decision to file a separate opinion. Finally, Chapter 9 summarizes my empirical findings and offers insights for the future study of personality and political behavior.

2

Goals and Personality

Explaining the behavior of US Supreme Court justices requires an understanding of the justices' goals. That is, in order to understand *what justices do*, we must understand *what justices want*, and what justices want depends on *who the justices are*. I start from the premise that judges are real people, not legalistic automatons or single-minded ideologues. As such, they are motivated by multiple goals. That is, when justices make decisions, they care about more than one objective, and they make decisions with those multiple objectives in mind. Moreover, because judges are people, they are motivated by many of the same goals that motivate most people in their personal and professional lives.

For example, consider a group of college students enrolled in a typical academic course. What do the students want? Most students probably want to succeed in the course, although different students may have different ideas of what success means – some students may want an "A"; others may be content to pass. But they have other desires as well. Most students would prefer to learn interesting material rather than study a dull topic. Some students hope to impress the professor and earn a letter of recommendation. Others may enjoy interacting with their classmates in discussions and group projects. Some may even want to meet new friends through the class. And, of course, every student probably wants to limit the amount of time and energy they devote to the course so they can work on other courses, participate in extracurricular activities, and enjoy leisure time. In short, college students pursue multiple goals; therefore, any time students make decisions, multiple motivations influence their choices. When selecting a partner for a class project, a student might consider their potential partner's intelligence, scheduling availability, or even sense of humor because each of these qualities may help the student achieve various goals, such as academic success, convenience, or enjoyment.

The same principle applies to Supreme Court justices. Of course, given the Court's elite and exclusive status, the justices likely share more similarities than students in a random college class. (They may be more comparable to students in an advanced graduate course at a prestigious university.) But Supreme Court justices, like almost any group of people, also pursue multiple goals, and they often consider more than one goal when making choices. In fact, like most people, justices probably care about so many different goals that no single list could possibly be comprehensive. Nonetheless, scholars have identified the most important judicial goals – those goals that are shared by a substantial number of judges and have a significant impact on their professional behavior. For example, prior studies have found that judges care about influencing policy, attaining prestige, conserving effort, and maintaining collegial relationships with other judges.[1]

Many scholars of judicial behavior assume that all judges have the same goals – as if every judge cares about the same things and places the same weight on each of those objectives. A few scholars acknowledge that judges likely differ in the values they attach to different goals,[2] but these scholars usually ignore varying goal preferences for fear "[t]he enterprise would devolve into 'what-the-judge-ate-for-breakfast' accounts, with goals 'so numerous and relating to outcomes in so complex a manner as to obscure the actual basis for decision.'"[3] "The importance of individual differences," these scholars argue, "is dampened" by "group constraints"[4] and superceded by "institutional preferences."[5] Disregard for varying goal preferences is particularly pernicious in studies of the US Supreme Court, which often assume that the justices' institutional context renders non-policy goals irrelevant.[6]

But, of course, the assumption that all Supreme Court justices pursue identical goals is unrealistic. Just as all humans (even in a specialized professional context) vary in their personal values and motivations, different judges undoubtedly prioritize different goals. Any comprehensive theory of judicial behavior must account for these individual differences in the judges' goals in order to fully understand the choices judges make. Accordingly, I adopt a "psychoeconomic" approach to studying judicial behavior, which posits that judges have heterogeneous goal preferences; that is, judges vary in their propensity to seek certain goals. Therefore, a full understanding of judicial behavior requires an examination of the individual characteristics that make judges different from one another. Humans are generally rational actors who make strategic choices in pursuit of their goals; however, humans also vary in their individual characteristics, and these varying characteristics prompt some individuals to prefer certain goals over others. Judges are no different: They generally pursue their goals, but they vary in their goal preferences. Therefore, in order to establish *what justices want*, we must first determine *who they are*. In other words, we must understand the judges' personalities.

THE BIG FIVE AS GOAL PREFERENCES

The study of personality as it relates to political phenomena has enjoyed a revival in recent years. Most of this research employs the five-factor model (also called the Big Five), which gained prominence among psychologists over the last two decades. The Big Five are based on extensive studies in which subjects were asked to rate how well specific adjectives or phrases describe themselves or others. Researchers then used factor analysis to identified the broad trait domains that underlie these responses.[7] Most analyses identify five predominant traits: extraversion, conscientiousness, agreeableness, neuroticism (or its inverse, emotional stability), and openness. The same Big Five traits have also been empirically derived from natural language by proponents of the lexical school of personality psychology.[8] The five-factor model has been replicated in a variety of languages and contexts,[9] and the literature suggests the Big Five are heritable,[10] highly stable after the age of thirty, and extremely stable after the age of fifty.[11] Moreover, the Big Five has been used to predict important life outcomes in a wide variety of domains,[12] and, between 2005 and 2009, it appeared in psychology publications nearly eight times as frequently as the previously dominant sixteen personality factor (16P) and Big Three typologies combined.[13]

"The Big Five taxonomy has opened a promising new frontier in research on political attitudes and behavior."[14] Among the mass public, the Big Five are associated with ideology, partisanship, and political participation.[15] More recently, social scientists have employed the Big Five to study the behavior of political elites, including state legislators and members of Congress.[16] This research suggests the Big Five are critical predictors of political behavior across a variety of contexts. Moreover, numerous historical and biographical accounts emphasize the importance of judges' personalities.[17] Therefore, the systematic study of judges' personality traits may be particularly useful for explaining their behavior.

Accordingly, this book offers the first comprehensive, systematic examination of the Big Five personality traits and their influence on the behavior of US Supreme Court justices. Due to the nature of this enterprise, the analyses that follow are inherently exploratory in many respects. My hope is that future researchers will continue to investigate the empirical and theoretical links between the Big Five and judicial behavior. However, as an initial foray into this vast and fertile research area, I also propose a novel theoretical framework with which to incorporate the Big Five into traditional models of judicial behavior.

More specifically, I argue that personality traits can help explain judges' behavior by reflecting their goal preferences. The Big Five describe individuals' global personalities, that is, "their enduring emotional, interpersonal, experiential, attitudinal, and motivational styles."[18] These "dispositional traits are believed to be stable aspects of individuals that shape how they respond to the vast array of stimuli they encounter in the world."[19] In other words, personality traits indicate individuals' characteristic styles of interacting with their environments – their perceptions, attitudes, and preferences with respect to particular goals.[20] By describing the Big Five as goal preferences, I focus on their "motivational properties": "Talkative people want to talk, sympathetic people want to help; ergo, at least some traits have motivational properties."[21] Other approaches to personality (as well as some popular conceptions of personality) depict traits as simple behavioral patterns; however, the motivational approach is consistent with these alternative views[22] and offers three important advantages.

First, the preeminent personality scholars subscribe to the Five Factor Theory (not to be confused with the five-factor model), which depicts personality traits as "abstract dispositions" that "define the individual's potential and direction" rather than mere "act frequencies" or "consistencies in behavior."[23] Thus, treating personality traits as motivational properties is consistent with the views of leading personality psychologists and provides a theoretical grounding for the role of traits in shaping behavior. In contrast, viewing traits as simple behavioral patterns offers no theoretical explanation for why traits are associated with those behaviors.

Second, the Five Factor Theory provides a theoretical foundation for constructing a judge's utility function. Most judicial scholars provide little rationale for focusing on some possible goals while ignoring others;

instead, they typically assemble an ad hoc list of goals based on the judicial behavior literature, insights from economics, or intuition.[24] In contrast, drawing on the Five Factor Theory, I propose a nearly universal utility function – that is, a set of goals pursued in varying degrees by virtually every human being in virtually every social context. Specifically, because the Big Five reflect individuals' "endogenous basic tendencies," which are "rooted in evolved human biology,"[25] I assume that these basic tendencies reflect potential sources of utility across contexts. For example, as described below, extraversion reflects a person's preference for influence and attention. Thus, the existence of this basic tendency suggests that – at least on average – humans generally gain utility from influence and attention.

Finally, and most importantly, the motivational approach facilitates the incorporation of personality traits into economic choice models. In other words, the Big Five can serve as valid proxies for individual goal preferences in an economic utility model because these traits reflect the relative weight that individuals place on different goals.[26] Therefore, we can use the judges' personality traits to predict their behavior as they prioritize various goals. For example, the existence of the extraversion tendency suggests that humans generally tend to value influence and attention, but the degree to which they do so varies depending on their extraversion.

Of course, portraying personality traits as goal preferences may inadvertently detract from the richness of the theoretical construct. Personality traits may also reflect a number of individual characteristics beyond preferences, such as capacities or constraints.[27] For example, extraverted individuals may not only prefer to attract attention; they may also be especially proficient at doing so. I do not mean to deny that these different components of personality traits exist, and I will occasionally note their relevance when discussing particular forms of judicial behavior. However, I argue that conceptualizing traits as goal preferences ultimately offers more advantages for the study of judicial behavior by facilitating the incorporation of traits into economic models of behavior.

In the following sections, I describe the Big Five factors and their relationship to the justices' goal preferences.

EXTRAVERSION: A PREFERENCE FOR INFLUENCE AND ATTENTION

"Extraversion implies an energetic approach to the social and material world."[28] This trait incorporates two "aspects." The first is called assertiveness or agency, which reflects "social dominance and the

enjoyment of leadership roles, assertiveness, exhibitionism, and a subjective sense of potency in accomplishing goals"; the second aspect is
called sociability or enthusiasm, which indicates "[t]he degree to which a
person needs attention and social interaction."[29] In other words, highly
extraverted individuals tend to be both assertive and sociable, and these
two tendencies are found together so frequently that they both constitute
aspects of the same broad trait. Therefore, a person's extraversion reflects
the degree to which that person prioritizes influence and attention.
Highly extraverted individuals tend to influence others (because they are
dominant and assertive), and they tend to interact with others and seek
out prominence (because they are sociable and gregarious). In contrast,
less extraverted individuals tend to avoid exerting influence and seeking
attention.

Like most people, Supreme Court justices are social creatures operating
in a social world. As such, it is no surprise that they also value both
influence and attention. That is, justices generally value exerting influence
over others and attracting attention from others.

Influence. Justices generally want to influence the Court's case law – that
is, the body of legal doctrine that the Court creates, which governs lower-
court judges as binding precedent. By shaping the Court's case law, the
justices can influence the behavior of lower-court judges, lawyers, public
officials, and the American people. Moreover, a justice's desire to influence
law and policy may actually encompass a variety of more basic motivations. Indeed, influencing law and policy may indirectly help justices attain
personal satisfaction, prestige, and notoriety.[30]

The primary mechanism through which Supreme Court justices exert
influence is through interactions with other justices. Because the Court
generally operates under majority rule, the justices' capacity to shape
legal and policy outcomes depends on their ability to influence one
another and, ultimately, build majority coalitions. Consequently, justices
often strive to persuade, pressure, or otherwise manipulate each other's
behavior through oral arguments, the conference discussion, bargaining
memos, or informal conversations. Frequent intra-Court interactions can
also build respectful relationships, which may facilitate future coalition
building. Interactions also help justices acquire information about their
colleagues' preferences, intentions, and plans; this information may aid
justices' ability to act strategically in order to advance their legal and
policy goals.[31]

But, of course, influencing other justices through social interactions
consumes valuable time and energy, and justices may prefer to conserve

that effort for other tasks. Intra-Court bargaining and debate may also hinder collegial relations if other justices feel unduly pressured. Politicking may even offend other justices and hinder future coalition building. Finally, striving to influence other justices may cause personal stress and frustration that could otherwise be avoided, and some justices may feel uncomfortable with assertive and dominant behavior. Accordingly, justices must balance the benefits of influencing one another against these countervailing considerations.

Attention. Justices also value attention from various judicial audiences, including their fellow justices, lower-court judges, lawyers, academics, public officials, the media, and the public.[32] First, many scholars have recognized a judge's "*need* to turn to others for social interaction."[33] Judges are human beings, and human beings are social creatures who generally value interacting with others.[34] The desire for social interaction is particularly relevant for judges because their career requires an unusual level of isolation and limited interaction with others.[35] Judges are expected to maintain a professional distance from lawyers and the parties in their courts in order to maintain objectivity. Often, the only peers with whom judges can freely and regularly interact are other judges. US Supreme Court justice may be particularly isolated due to their elite status and the small number of justices of equal rank. Accordingly, many Supreme Court justices enjoy interacting with and attracting attention from their fellow justices as part of their daily jobs.

However, social interactions may also come with costs. Interactions take up time and energy, which means they can distract justices from their judicial work and leisure time. Interactions may also cause stress or conflict. Some justices may actually prefer social isolation – in fact, the isolating nature of a judge's job may have partially attracted them to a judicial career in the first place. Finally, the longer judges serve on the bench, the more they acclimate to social isolation,[36] and Supreme Court justices have generally had long judicial careers. Accordingly, justices must balance their desire for social interaction against the possible benefits of isolation.

More broadly, justices also value attention beyond acquiring it from those they interact with on a daily basis. For example, judges tend to value prestige among their fellow jurists and legal practitioners, admiration among legal academics, prominence in history books, and celebrity in the media and among the public.[37] This desire for prestige, prominence, and popularity often prompts Supreme Court justices to seek out opportunities to speak in public, lecture at universities, publish academic articles, and author popular books. It may also prompt justices to follow popular opinion when making decisions.[38]

But, while some justices actively pursue these opportunities, others spurn the spotlight and jealously guard their privacy. For example, Justice David H. Souter was sometimes dubbed "a misfit or a loner" because he preferred "hiking, sailing, time with old friends, [and] reading history" to the activities normally associated with Supreme Court justices in this "media saturated age."[39] Thus, justices must balance their desire for attention against the benefits associated with privacy and anonymity.

Extraversion Summary. In sum, Supreme Court justices generally desire influence and attention. However, the justices must balance these desires against the potential costs associated with assuming leadership roles and sacrificing privacy. Different justices balance these goals in different ways: Some adopt an assertive, sociable, and prominent persona, while others keep to themselves and avoid public scrutiny. The degree to which justices prioritize influence and attention is reflected by the Big Five factor *extraversion*.

Therefore, I expect justice extraversion to be positively associated with behaviors that exert influence over other justices, such as authoring majority opinions and circulating opinion drafts. I also expect justice extraversion to be positively associated with behaviors that attract attention from judicial audiences, such as (again) authoring opinions and following popular preferences, especially in cases that have already attracted attention from relevant audiences.

CONSCIENTIOUSNESS: A PREFERENCE FOR INDUSTRIOUSNESS AND DUTIFULNESS

"Conscientiousness describes socially prescribed impulse control that facilitates task- and goal-directed behavior, such as thinking before acting, delaying gratification, following norms and rules, and planning, organizing, and prioritizing tasks."[40] This broad trait also incorporates several interrelated facets, which can be grouped into two "aspects." The first aspect is called industriousness or achievement-striving, and reflects a "need for achievement and commitment to work"; the second aspect is called dutifulness or orderliness, and reflects "[t]he degree to which a person is willing to comply with conventional rules, norms, and standards" and is "governed by conscience."[41] In other words, highly conscientious individuals tend to work hard and fulfill their duties, and these two tendencies are found together so frequently that they both constitute aspects of the same broad trait. Highly conscientious individuals tend to expend more effort in their work (because they are industrious and achievement-striving), and they tend to follow rules and norms (because they are governed by conscience). In contrast, less conscientious individuals tend to avoid expending effort and shirk their duties.

Supreme Court justices obviously strive to fulfill the responsibilities associated with their positions. That is, justices generally want to do the things they are supposed to do. A justice's responsibilities encompass two related, yet distinct, sets of obligations, which map onto the two aspects of conscientiousness: the obligation to complete job-related tasks and the duty to follow legal norms.

Industriousness. At the simplest level, an appointment to the Supreme Court is a job, and, like any other job, it comes with expectations for completing job-related tasks. Accordingly, a justice's responsibilities obviously include assisting in the Court's practical, day-to-day functioning. Supreme Court justices are expected to show up for work, participate in oral arguments and conferences, read briefs and case materials, write their share of majority opinions, and generally contribute to the Court's deliberative process. Failure to meet these obligations may incur a variety of negative consequences. At the extreme, a justice who seriously neglected his or her responsibilities could theoretically face the threat of impeachment. More minor delinquency could damage a justice's reputation or hinder the justice's ability to pursue other goals. For example, failure to properly research a case might provoke criticism from colleagues, academics, or the media. Failure to craft a strong majority opinion may prompt other justices to withdraw their support. And failure to competently assist in the Court's judicial work may sully relations with other justices. In contrast, reliably performing these tasks in an efficient and effective manner should avoid such embarrassments and yield a sense of professional accomplishment. Accordingly, justices generally strive to fulfill their basic professional obligations.

However, judges – like most humans – undoubtedly gain satisfaction through nonprofessional activities, such as enjoying leisure, spending time with friends and family, and earning outside income.[42] Judges may also gain satisfaction by engaging in extrajudicial activities that enhance their prestige or celebrity, such as writing, teaching, or lecturing.[43] Therefore, judges often seek to minimize the effort (both time and energy) they devote to judicial work in order to maximize these external satisfactions.[44] In other words, just like workers in any context, Supreme Court justices try to avoid expending effort in their jobs. But this desire to avoid job-related effort obviously lies in tension with their responsibility to fulfill their work obligations. Every hour spent reading a brief is an hour not spent with friends or family. Accordingly, justices must balance their industriousness against their effort aversion.

Dutifulness. Upon their confirmation to the bench, Supreme Court justices swear an oath to uphold the US Constitution and the laws of the United States. Their professional duty also includes an obligation to fulfill that oath. Moreover, though not technically required, the vast majority of Supreme Court justices attended law school, practiced law, and served as a judge in a lower court before their appointment to the High Court. Consequently, most justices have been thoroughly socialized into the legal culture for decades, and this culture strongly promotes the rule of law and the understanding that all lawyers and judges have a professional obligation to follow legal norms. For example, legal factors such as statutory text, precedent, or case facts often constrain the options that justices view as realistically available and normatively acceptable.[45]

Perhaps the most important judicial duty is the obligation to faithfully follow the law rather than pursuing particular policy objectives. Scholars of judicial behavior have long understood that justices tend to promote their preferred legal policies, and, consequently, they tend to make decisions that are consistent with their own ideological beliefs. That is, liberal justices tend to support liberal policies, and conservative justices tend to support conservative policies.[46]

However, a justice's desire to pursue policy objectives undoubtedly conflicts with the duty to follow legal rules and norms. Judges are expected to base their decisions on neutral principles of law and an unbiased reading of the facts, and legal norms strongly condemn judges who interject their personal policy preferences into the decision-making process. To be sure, lawyers and judges often disagree about what it means to follow the law. They might, for example, disagree about the proper method of constitutional or statutory interpretation and, consequently, arrive at divergent conclusions about a law's meaning. But few lawyers or judges would deny that they have a professional responsibility to comply with legal norms and follow the law as they best understand it. Moreover, this sense of judicial duty appears to strongly influence the justices' behavior.[47]

Accordingly, the degree to which justices try to align policy with their personal preferences is moderated by their beliefs about how judges ought to make decisions. Scholars have long recognized that the influence of judges' policy preferences is "tempered by what they think they ought to do," and these understandings of appropriate judicial behavior are shaped by individual judges "reacting in a variety of distinctive ways to the expectations they experience."[48] Consequently, the influence of legal norms (such as adherence to precedent or judicial restraint) on decision-making varies across justices.[49] Therefore, justices must also balance their dutifulness against their personal policy objectives.

Of course, legal norms also vary across different courts. For example, judges on the US Courts of Appeals describe their interactions as governed by strong norms of consensus and collegiality, both of which discourage justices from airing their disagreements through dissent or separate opinions.[50] And the low dissent rates on these courts suggest that these norms strongly influence the judges' behavior.[51] The US Supreme Court also once operated under a strong norm of consensus.[52] However, due in part to the failure of the chief justices' social leadership, this norm of consensus collapsed in the 1940s, and dissent rates on the Court have skyrocketed since.[53] In fact, modern norms on the High Court may actually encourage dissensus. As Justice John Paul Stevens once described, "[t]here is a duty to explain your position if it isn't the same as the majority ... and it's just part of my thinking about what a judge should do."[54] Similarly, "[n]o matter how insignificant the disagreement," Justice John Marshall Harlan II[55] always "felt compelled to spell out his views for the sake of intellectual honesty."[56] Moreover, consensual opinions often include more ambiguous language as justices bargain over opinion content and accommodate each others' suggestions.[57] For example, in Chapter 6, I describe a case in which Chief Justice Warren Earl Burger pressed the Court into a consensual opinion rather than honestly expressing his own views. The result was a confusing and contradictory opinion that promoted Burger's policy preferences, yet obscured his true disagreement with his colleagues. In other words, the justices' duty may compel them to express divergent views rather than muddle a majority opinion with compromised language. Therefore, on the modern Supreme Court, justices may often feel a duty to express honest disagreement through a dissenting vote or separate opinion rather than striving to influence the content of the Court's opinion as a member of the majority.

Conscientiousness Summary. In sum, Supreme Court justices generally strive to fulfill their professional responsibilities. However, they must balance their industriousness against their effort aversion, and they must balance their dutifulness against their policy objectives. Different justices balance these goals in different ways: Some prioritize fulfilling their responsibilities, while others shirk their duties. The degree to which justices prioritize industriousness and dutifulness is reflected by the Big Five factor *conscientiousness*.

Therefore, I expect justice conscientiousness to be positively associated with behaviors that require substantial effort, such as writing bargaining memos and opinion drafts. I also expect justice conscientiousness to be positively associated with behaviors that fulfill judicial duties, such as resisting the temptation to pursue policy objectives and expressing honest disagreement.

AGREEABLENESS: A PREFERENCE FOR SOCIAL HARMONY AND ALTRUISM

"Agreeableness contrasts a prosocial and communal orientation toward others with antagonism."[58] This trait can also be divided into two aspects. The first aspect is called politeness, meaning "[t]he degree to which a person needs pleasant and harmonious relations with others"; the second aspect is called compassion, which reflects "the more humane aspects of humanity – characteristics such as altruism, nurturance, caring, and emotional support."[59] Thus, highly agreeable individuals tend to cooperate with others (because they value harmonious relations), and they tend to show compassion toward others (because they are caring and nurturing). In contrast, less agreeable individuals are less likely to cooperate with others or show compassion for those in need.

Supreme Court justices also value social harmony and altruism. Human beings generally desire affection, warmth, and caring, and many people pursue these goals beyond their personal lives, including through their professional careers. Accordingly, Supreme Court justices value social harmony among their peers and coworkers, as well as altruism toward disadvantaged members of society.

Social Harmony. First, justices value harmonious relations with their coworkers, particularly their fellow justices. As discussed above, justices value social interactions in general; however, humans tend to prefer friendly social interactions more than contentious encounters. Therefore, regardless of how frequently the justices interact with their colleagues, they generally prefer that those interactions are warm and pleasant. Harmonious relationships with coworkers, employers, and employees are a critical determinant of job satisfaction across professions. Similarly, judges' job satisfaction depends in large part on their ability to get along with their colleagues and avoid antagonistic interactions. Accordingly, it is no surprise that judges value collegial relations among their fellow justices and strive to maintain social harmony with their peers on the bench.[60]

However, promoting social harmony on the Court often comes at considerable cost. Usually, the best way to get along with other justices is to compromise rather than prioritize one's personal goals and strategic opportunities. In many situations, justices may prefer to incur collegiality costs in lieu of making such sacrifices. Moreover, some justices may thrive on conflict and excel in competitive environments. These justices may actually seek out disharmony as a means of promoting their individual interests or expressing individual views. Therefore, Supreme Court justices must weigh the benefits of social harmony against these competing considerations.

Altruism. Justices also value social harmony beyond their immediate, personal interactions; that is, they value the welfare of those less fortunate than themselves in the broader society and, consequently, often strive to promote social justice. This use of judicial power can provide numerous personal benefits, including a sense of personal satisfaction and accomplishment, an enhanced reputation, and (occasionally) a place in history. For example, Justice John Marshall Harlan I is remembered by historians and legal academics for his opposition to Jim Crow laws in *Plessy v. Ferguson*. Similarly, Chief Justice Earl Warren achieved fame for authoring the Court's opinion in *Brown v. Board of Education*. Therefore, justices may sometimes make decisions with the goal of trying to help people beyond their immediate social world, particularly disadvantaged members of society.

But even helping the less fortunate comes at a price. Supreme Court justices are supposed to make decisions based on neutral principles of law rather than their personal sympathies or social values. They are expected to objectively follow the law, and the law sometimes compels results that hurt disadvantaged members of society. Therefore, actively promoting broader social welfare might conflict with a justice's professional obligation to maintain objectivity. It might also attract criticism from the media, academics, and other justices who condemn this brand of "judicial activism." Trying to use judicial power to help others might also strain relations on the Court if other justices insist on dispassionately following legal standards. Promoting social welfare could even endanger a justice's career; indeed, for years after the *Brown* decision, Southern highways were littered with signs that read "Impeach Earl Warren," and dozens of congressmen signed the Southern Manifesto condemning Warren's decision. Accordingly, justices must weigh their desire to promote social welfare against their professional and ethical obligation to maintain objectivity.

Agreeableness Summary. In sum, Supreme Court justices generally value social harmony and altruism, but they must balance these goals against their desire for individuality and objectivity (i.e., the costs associated with cooperation and judicial activism). The degree to which justices prioritize social harmony and altruism is reflected by the Big Five factor *agreeableness.*

Therefore, I expect justice agreeableness to be positively associated with behaviors that promote social harmony on the Court, such as supporting other justices. I also expect justice agreeableness to be positively associated with behaviors that help disadvantaged members of society, such as supporting liberal rulings.

NEUROTICISM: A PREFERENCE FOR LOSS AVOIDANCE AND NEGATIVITY EXPRESSION

"Neuroticism contrasts emotional stability and even-temperedness with negative emotionality, such as feeling anxious, nervous, sad, and tense."[61] This trait can also be divided into two general aspects. The first aspect is called withdrawal, which reflects "[t]he degree to which a person experiences the world as threatening and beyond control,"[62] and, consequently, tends to retreat from risky activities and exposure to loss due to anxiety and fearfulness.[63] The second aspect is called volatility, which reflects the "tendency to experience distress ... [and] chronic negative effects,"[64] such as anger, irritability, and instability. Highly neurotic individuals tend to be both withdrawn and volatile; that is, they deal with negative emotionality by trying to avoid unpleasant situations or expressing negativity to others. Therefore, highly neurotic individuals tend to focus on costs and avoid risks (because they are anxious, fearful, and easily embarrassed), and they tend to express negativity (because they are irritable and easily upset). In contrast, less-neurotic individuals pursue risky, but potentially beneficial, opportunities while restraining expressions of negativity.

Supreme Court justices are also susceptible to feelings of negativity that accompany various forms of loss, such as failure, criticism, and embarrassment. And, like most people, Supreme Court justices generally respond to potential negativity by striving to avoid the loss (e.g., by withdrawing from risky situations) or expressing negativity (e.g., in the form of anger or frustration).

Loss Avoidance. First, "losses and disadvantages have greater impact on preferences than gains and advantages."[65] This general human tendency toward loss aversion causes individuals to irrationally focus on the negative aspects of experiences rather than the positive aspects, even in riskless choices. This focus on negativity causes loss-averse individuals to fear loss more than an equal gain, prefer the current state of affairs to any change (status-quo bias), and value objects they currently possess more than identical objects they do not possess (the endowment effect).[66] Loss aversion also leads to a related human tendency called risk aversion. When individuals decide whether to take a risk, they typically do so by weighing the potential costs and benefits. Loss-averse individuals tend to place greater weight on potential losses than on potential gains. In fact, prior studies suggest that loss aversion causes humans to weigh losses roughly twice as heavily as they do gains.[67] Thus, the general tendency toward loss avoidance causes most people to avoid loss and withdraw from risky situations.

Of course, federal judges with lifetime tenure and high fixed salaries are well insulated from many common forms of loss, such as losing their job or receiving a pay cut. But they may, nonetheless, face other types of potential loss. As Judge John R. Brown of the Fifth Circuit explains, "Lifetime tenure insulates judges from anxiety over worldly cares for body and home and family. But it does not protect them from the unconscious urge for the approbation of their fellow men."[68] In other words, because judges are insulated from many common forms of loss, they tend to focus on reputational and interpersonal losses, such as the embarrassment, stress, and anxiety associated with criticism from peers, academics, or the public. Accordingly, justices generally strive to avoid these reputational losses by withdrawing from activities that attract potential criticism.

But loss aversion is an inherently irrational psychological phenomenon. Many decisions involve both gains and losses, and focusing primarily on losses or potential losses leads individuals to make irrational choices and withdraw from beneficial situations. Among Supreme Court justices, focusing on potential reputational losses may lead justices to undervalue valuable opportunities. For example, authoring the Court's majority opinion may involve a certain degree of stress and criticism as the opinion author negotiates among the members of the majority coalition. But majority opinion assignments also offer increased policy influence and prestige, and these benefits may outweigh the costs associated with the stress of leadership. In fact, justices often seek out activities that involve the risk of criticism or embarrassment in order to to gain prominence, prestige, and celebrity.[69] Therefore, Supreme Court justices must weigh the costs of potential criticism against the benefits associated with these risky activities.

Negativity Expression. Second, justices, also like all humans, tend to value negativity expression.[70] When they are mad, they want yell; when they are irritated, they want to snap; when they are sad, they want to mope. In other words, the stress and negativity that justices feel as a result of incurring loss (as well as the tension and anxiety justices feel when contemplating potential losses) tends to boil over into anger, frustration, and depression; justices (like all people) value the opportunity to express those emotions. As a result, justices sometimes argue during the conference discussion, circulate acerbic memos, and author caustic dissenting opinions. And such behavior may yield benefits. For example, aggressive argumentation may pressure other justices to change their behavior, and biting dissents may earn a justice accolades from Court observers who share the justice's frustrations. If nothing else, venting negative emotions may make a justice feel better in the moment.

But, of course, negativity expression can also incur costs for a justice. Expressing hostility on the Court may damage a justice's collegial relationships with his or her colleagues, and publicly expressing anxiety or negativity may damage a justice's reputation. Accordingly, justices must weigh their desire to express negativity against these associated costs.

Neuroticism Summary. In sum, Supreme Court justices generally value loss avoidance and negativity expression. But they must balance these goals against the benefits associated with risk-taking and self-control. The degree to which justices value loss avoidance and negativity expression is reflected by the Big Five factor *neuroticism*.

Therefore, I expect justice neuroticism to be positively associated with behaviors that avoid potential criticism, such as supporting the federal government and filing fewer separate opinions. I also expect justice neuroticism to be positively associated with behaviors that express negativity toward other justices, such as circulating opinion suggestions.

OPENNESS: A PREFERENCE FOR INTELLECTUALISM AND CHANGE

"Openness to Experience (vs. closed-mindedness) describes the breadth, depth, originality, and complexity of an individual's mental and experiential life," and is sometimes defined as "[t]he degree to which a person needs intellectual stimulation, change, and variety."[71] This trait (sometimes called openness/intellect) can also be divided into two aspects. The intellect aspect reflects an individual's interest in philosophical discussions, abstract ideas, and complex problems; the openness aspect reflects the degree to which a person enjoys change, variety, and new experiences.[72] Highly open justices tend to seek out opportunities to intellectually engage with different ideas (because they enjoy abstract, philosophical concepts), and they tend to be more open to changing traditions, practices, and their own opinions (because they value variety and new experiences).

Supreme Court justices clearly value various intellectual qualities of their work. Just as most people prefer engaging and varied work, so too justices value the intellectually stimulating aspects of their jobs, as well as variety and flexibility in their judicial work. More specifically, justices enjoy both intellectualism and change.

Intellectualism. First, many judges were attracted to judicial careers due, at least in part, to an intellectual interest in the law and the various philosophical and technical questions involved in resolving legal disputes. Therefore, judges generally enjoy thinking, talking, and writing about the legal disputes they hear, especially those they find particularly intriguing.[73] Cases that reach the Supreme Court often involve especially interesting and controversial legal issues; in fact, the Court's rules specifically state that the justices should consider whether a case poses an "important question of federal law" when deciding whether to hear the case in the first place.[74] Undoubtedly, many justices genuinely enjoy resolving these important legal questions because they enjoy intellectual engagement with new and complex ideas. Therefore, justices should generally gain satisfaction from reading briefs, listening to oral arguments, discussing cases with colleagues and clerks, writing judicial opinions, and contributing to legal development through active engagement in the Court's intellectual activities.

However, engaging in these activities comes at considerable cost. Resolving difficult intellectual challenges requires time and energy and may cause stress and anxiety for the justices. Intellectual engagement may also attract more attention from peers, academics, and the public and, thus, pose the threat of negative attention. Therefore, justices must weigh the benefits of engaging in the Court's intellectual conversation against these potential costs.

Change. Second, many people value change, variety, and new experiences in daily life. A judge's preference for change manifests itself in several ways. First, many judges value variety in their case work. Lower-court judges are often required to hear numerous disputes on very similar issues, which creates monotony and boredom. In contrast, appellate judges tend to hear more varied and interesting cases that have risen up the judicial hierarchy due to their distinct nature. Because the Supreme Court controls its own docket, the justices can strongly influence the variety of legal issues they hear, and justices generally value the ability to hear new and different cases. However, even within those cases that reach the High Court, some justices may prefer to work on a variety of case types rather than focus on a particular specialty. Second, some judges are open to changing their own views on a case as they learn more details, conduct legal research, and deliberate with other judges.[75] This quality should make them less predictable, more engaged in the Court's dialogue, and more open to persuasion. And finally, some judges tend to be more open-minded about rethinking settled law. Accordingly, some judges should be more willing to overturn precedent and change legal doctrine.

But pursuing change also incurs significant costs. Hearing a wide variety of cases requires the justices to invest more time and energy into researching different statutes, precedents, and legal rules. Shifting positions on a case may frustrate colleagues and upset stable coalitions. And, perhaps most importantly, the rule of law requires the consistent application of legal doctrine; therefore, judges may undermine stability in the law if they change legal precedent. Accordingly, justices must weigh their interest in change and variety against the advantages associated with stability, continuity, and consistency.

Openness. In sum, Supreme Court justices generally value intellectualism and change, but they must balance these goals against the benefits of simplicity and consistency. The degree to which justices prioritize intellectualism and change is reflected by the Big Five factor *openness*.

Therefore, I expect justice openness to be positively associated with behaviors that intellectually engage with different ideas, such as circulating bargaining memos and authoring opinions on a variety of legal issues. I also expect openness to be positively associated with behaviors that involve change, such as altering legal precedent and compromising during the bargaining process.

THE PSYCHOECONOMIC APPROACH

To summarize, my psychoeconomic approach draws on both the Five Factor Theory of personality psychology and economic (i.e., strategic) accounts of judicial behavior. First, Five Factor Theory posits that the Big Five personality traits are "abstract dispositions" that "define the individual's potential and direction."[76] Because these traits are "'relatively' stable, person-specific determinants of behavior," they can be understood as individual goal preferences,[77] and, as described in this chapter, each Big Five factor reflects individual preferences with respect to specific goals. Table 2.1 presents the Big Five, their definitions, and associated characteristics. The last column lists the specific goal preferences reflected by each trait.

Next, drawing on rational choice theory, I postulate that these goal preferences (or basic dispositions) comprise the elements of a universal utility function – that is, a set of goals pursued in varying degrees by virtually every human being in virtually every social context. Thus, the psychoeconomic approach posits that individuals maximize their utility by pursuing multiple goals (influence/attention, industriousness/dutifulness, social harmony/altruism, loss aversion/negativity expression, and intellectualism/change). However, the value of these goals varies depending on individual traits. Indeed, some individuals may place very little value on some goals and much greater value on others, depending on their personality traits.

I then apply this general theory of human behavior to US Supreme Court justices. On the psychoeconomic account, Supreme Court justices

TABLE 2.1 *The Big Five as goal preferences*

Trait	Aspects	Characteristics	Goal Preferences
Extraversion	Assertiveness	Agency, Dominance	Influence
	Enthusiasm	Gregariousness, Attention Seeking	Attention
Conscientiousness	Industriousness	Competence, Achievement Striving	Industriousness
	Orderliness	Rule Compliance, Order	Dutifulness
Agreeableness	Politeness	Friendliness, Cooperation	Social harmony
	Compassion	Sympathy, Generosity	Altruism
Neuroticism	Withdrawal	Anxiety, Vulnerability	Loss avoidance
	Volatility	Hostility, Irritability	Negativity expression
Openness	Intellect	Intellectual Stimulation, Ideas	Intellectualism
	Openness	Variety, Imagination	Change

Note. Table reports the main aspects and specific characteristics associated with each Big Five factor.[78] The last column indicates the goal preferences reflected by each factor.

make decisions in pursuit of various goals, and their individual personality traits determine the relative importance of those goals for each justice. In order to further develop my theoretical expectations, I first identify general categories of behavior that are likely to reflect each goal preference. Drawing together the key points from the preceding discussion, I advance the following propositions regarding the justices' behavior:

- More extraverted justices are more likely to engage in behaviors that influence other justices and attract attention from judicial audiences.
- More conscientious justices are more likely to engage in behaviors that require substantial effort and fulfill their judicial duties.
- More agreeable justices are more likely to engage in behaviors that promote social harmony on the Court and support disadvantaged members of society.
- More neurotic justices are more likely to engage in behaviors that avoid potential criticism and express negativity toward other justices.
- More open justices are more likely to engage in behaviors that intellectually engage with different ideas and promote change (both legal change and change in their own views).

In the chapters that follow, I derive testable hypotheses from these general propositions. Specifically, I link these broad goal preferences to specific judicial behaviors in the context of US Supreme Court decision-making (i.e., voting to grant cert, assigning the majority opinion, circulating bargaining memos, casting a dissenting vote, and filing a separate opinion). These hypotheses will generally take one of two forms.

First, a goal preference may prompt justices to engage in more or less of a specific behavior. Here, the critical theoretical task is to explain why the specific behavior tends to promote or undermine the relevant goals. For example, in Chapter 8, I test the relationship between the justices' personality traits and their propensity to file separate opinions. I argue that filing a separate opinion promotes industriousness (because researching and writing a separate opinion requires substantial effort) and dutifulness (because filing a separate opinion fulfills a justice's duty to express honest disagreement). Therefore, the decision to file a separate opinion should be partially driven by a preference for industriousness/dutifulness. Accordingly, I hypothesize that a justices' conscientiousness is positively associated with filing separate opinions. (Notice that I could have developed the same hypothesis by linking separate opinions to *either* industriousness *or* dutifulness. Linking the behavior to both goals merely strengthens my argument.) Hypotheses such as this one (involving direct relationships between traits and behavior) depend on my assertion that the specific behavior (e.g., filing a separate opinion) promotes or undermines the relevant goals (e.g., industriousness and dutifulness).

Of course, not every Big Five trait is associated with every judicial behavior examined in this book. Thus, I do not develop a separate hypothesis for every possible trait-behavior combination. However, consistent with standard practice in the psychology literature, I control for each Big Five trait in all of my statistical models. In a few situations, I discuss unhypothesized relationships in detail because I anticipate disagreement with my theoretical expectations. For example, in Chapter 6, I note that some readers might expect to find a relationship between conscientiousness and a justice's propensity to circulate majority opinion drafts. Therefore, I explain why I did not expect to find that potential relationship so that readers can evaluate my reasoning. However, in other situations I simply state that I see no theoretical link between the relevant behavior and goal preference. For example, I see no theoretical link between dissenting on the merits and a preference for intellectualism or change, and I simply note that point without comment. Critical readers should consider for themselves whether they believe I should expect such a relationship and, if so, consider the lack of empirical support for such a relationship as evidence against my theory.

Second, goal preferences may prompt a justice to engage in more or less of a specific behavior *under certain conditions.* Here, the theoretical task is more complicated. I must first establish that justices tend to engage in a certain behavior more frequently under certain conditions. Then, I must explain why those conditions tend to promote or undermine the relevant goals. For example, in Chapter 7, I summarize the common finding in the literature that a justice is more likely to dissent when the Court's decision runs counter to his or her ideology. Next, I argue that judges have a professional duty to resist their ideological impulses when making decisions, i.e., following ideological biases undermines a justice's professional duty. Therefore, I hypothesize that the influence of a justice's ideology on his or her dissent behavior should be weaker for more conscientious justices (who value dutifulness). Hypotheses such as this one (involving conditional relationships) depend on my assertion that the underlying effect (e.g., the effect of ideology on dissent) promotes or undermines the relevant goals (e.g., dutifulness).

Although the propositions above provide clear guidance for formulating most of my hypotheses, some judicial behaviors have an ambiguous relationship to certain goal preferences. In these situations, I generally expect the conflicting tendencies to cancel out and predict a null relationship. For example, as I explain in Chapter 5, it is unclear whether chief justices should be more or less likely to assign majority opinions to justices who prefer social harmony. These justices may tend to facilitate pleasant negotiations over opinion content, but they may also be unwilling to aggressively marshal the Court in order to form a majority coalition. Therefore, I expect and find a null relationship between agreeableness and majority opinion assignments from the chief justice. (Though I do find a conditional effect between agreeableness and the size of the majority coalition.)

As I describe in greater detail in the empirical chapters, I test these direct and conditional hypotheses using data on Supreme Court justices. One advantage of studying these justices is the plethora of available data on their behavior. The extensive data used in most of my analyses provide sufficient statistical power to identify even small statistically significant relationships. However, because my goal is to identify empirical relationships that are both statistically significant and substantively meaningful, it is important to stipulate a priori a standard for evaluating substantively meaningful effects. I base my standard of substantive significance on the nearly universal view that ideological preferences influence judicial behavior; indeed, the influence of ideology is a focal point of many – if not most – studies of judicial behavior.[79] Therefore, in each chapter, I compare the relationship between personality traits and judicial behavior to the relationship between the justices' ideological preferences and their behavior. If personality is indeed an important influence on justices' choices, the size of these relationships should be at least somewhat comparable.

Of course, testing these hypotheses requires valid measures of justices' Big Five personality traits. In the next chapter, I explain the personality measures that I use throughout this book. Then, in the succeeding chapters, I develop and test specific hypotheses regarding justices' goal preferences and behavior on the US Supreme Court.

3

Measuring Justice Personality

A challenging obstacle to studying personality on the Supreme Court is developing valid and reliable measures of justices' traits. Traditionally, psychologists measure personality traits by administering a questionnaire that "consists of a list of adjectives [e.g., 'temperamental'] or phrases [e.g., 'Sometimes I do things on impulse that I later regret'] and asks the respondent to rate how well each adjective or phrase describes the individual whose personality is being rated – typically the respondent."[1] Unfortunately, this approach is impractical for measuring the personalities of political elites, such as Supreme Court justices, because it is often infeasible to gain access to justices or close informants (especially for those who are deceased). Moreover, justices and their close informants may be especially susceptible to socially desirable responding (i.e., reporting overly positive descriptions[2]) for fear of damaging the justices' reputations.

Therefore, instead of using questionnaires, I employ estimates of the justices' personality traits developed in collaboration with Gary Hollibaugh, Jonathon Klingler, and Adam Ramey.[3] We estimated the justices' personality traits using a textual analysis program called the Personality Recognizer. The use of language to capture individual differences (among various psychological constructs) has been validated in a series of experiments using *Linguistic Inquiry and Word Count* (LIWC) and other computerized textual analysis methods.[4] Similarly, the Personality Recognizer was developed by Francois Mairesse and colleagues using James W. Pennebaker and Laura L. King's corpus of over 1.9 million words from laboratory experiments.[5] By comparing written essays to self-assessed personality ratings, the program's creators

35

trained machine learning models to accurately estimate personality scores for each of the Big Five factors based on written language. In other words, individuals with certain personality traits tend to use certain types of language; therefore, a person's language can be used to estimate their personality traits. For example, the use of third-person nouns and references to people are positively associated with extraversion, while words related to occupation, work, and school, as well as prepositions, future tense verbs, and words longer than six letters, are all associated with conscientiousness.

My coauthors and I used the Personality Recognizer to estimate personality scores for US Supreme Court justices based on their written opinions. The use of written opinions offers several advantages. Almost every justice has written numerous opinions, which are readily available, and all of these opinions were written in comparable contexts. In contrast, other potential sources of the justices' language are limited and problematic. For example, many justices wrote opinions while sitting as lower-court judges, and others wrote legal briefs in prior professional positions (e.g., as the solicitor general). However, many justices did not serve in these roles before their appointment; therefore, these prior writings are not consistently available for many justices. Similarly, some justices spoke before Congress during their confirmation hearings, but many did not, and the nature of these hearings has varied a great deal. Some justices have delivered numerous public speeches, but most have not, and the speeches that are available vary widely in context, audience, and purpose. Finally, most current justices ask questions during oral arguments; however, prior to the 1970s, justices rarely spoke during oral arguments, and, prior to 2004, justices were not individually identified in oral argument transcripts.[6]

One might adopt an approach that analyzes the justices' language from various sources simultaneously (e.g., speeches by those who gave them, lower-court opinions by those who wrote them).[7] However, personality scores estimated based on multiple types of language would be susceptible to bias if justices tend to use different types of language in different contexts – a possibility that is exceedingly likely. For example, references to television and the use of curse words are both negatively associated with conscientiousness. However, one might also suspect that justices are more likely to use such references when giving a speech than when writing a formal legal opinion. If so, those justices for whom speeches are available may appear less conscientious in any analysis that includes both speeches and formal opinions.

Accordingly, formal written opinions are the only comprehensive, consistent, and routinized source of the justices' language. Moreover, this approach is consistent with prior research that uses the language in formal legal opinions to assess attributes of Supreme Court justices.[8]

MEASUREMENT CHALLENGES

Nonetheless, the use of written opinions to estimate the justices' personality traits raises some notable concerns. First, most justices rely to some degree on their clerks to assist in drafting opinions. Of course, law clerks generally deny exerting influence over opinion content – either due to a sense of professional courtesy or personal modesty. For example, Chief Justice William H. Rehnquist described the opinions of Justice Robert H. Jackson, for whom he clerked, as "unquestionably the Justice's own, both in form and substance" and said that Jackson "neither needed nor used ghost writers."[9] Nonetheless, it is well known that many justices rely heavily on clerks for creating initial opinion drafts; moreover, opinions drafted with the assistance of the same clerk tend to share many stylistic similarities, suggesting that clerks do tend to influence opinion language.[10] Accordingly, an analysis of the justices' opinions may reflect the personalities of the justices' clerks in addition to the personalities of the justices themselves. However, two factors alleviate this potential concern.

First, analyses of the justices' opinions suggest that, regardless of the clerks' influence, the justices themselves retain primary control over opinion language, including the opinion's style. Specifically, the premier study of clerk influence finds that "opinions drafted by different clerks for the same justice [are] significantly more homogeneous than different-justice pairs but not significantly less homogeneous than same-clerk pairs."[11] In other words, opinions drafted by the same clerk do share stylistic similarities; however, opinions drafted by different clerks for the same justice also share stylistic similarities, and these two levels of similarity are statistically indistinguishable. Only those opinions drafted for different justices exhibit significantly less similarity.

Second, even if clerks do influence opinion language, their influence should be limited to the time they serve as clerk – usually a single term. My coauthors and I estimated personality traits based on opinions from every term a justice served on the Court.[12] (We assumed the scores are static across time because personality traits are highly stable after the age of thirty and extremely stable after the age of fifty.[13]) Consequently, any effect of the clerks' personalities should simply add noise to the data as each new clerk skews the writing style in a new direction. The only way clerk influence might bias the scores is if a justice consistently selected clerks with similar personality traits (which may itself reflect the justice's personality).

Another potential concern is that Supreme Court opinions often include language that was not written by the opinion author or that justice's clerks. For example, many opinions are the product of considerable negotiation among the justices. Justices sometimes ask other members of the Court to add, remove, or revise certain language in their opinions – especially majority opinions[14] – and these requests are frequently accommodated.[15] (I examine the influence of personality traits on this bargaining process in Chapter 7.) Additionally, "majority opinions tend to be relatively stylized and formulaic,"[16] and they "routinely and boringly" recite case facts and procedural history.[17] In a similar vein, dissenting opinions[18] are often written as rival majority opinions and, therefore, share many of these problematic characteristics.

In order to minimize appropriated and stylized language, my coauthors and I examined only the justices' concurring opinions (both regular and special concurrences).[19] This focus on concurrences reflects Judge Frank Coffin's description of the "feeling of unjudicial glee as one shucks off the normal restraints of writing for a panel and proceeds to thrust and parry with gay abandon."[20] This approach is also consistent with prior text-based measures of justice characteristics that use language from separate opinions.[21] Concurrences are especially well-suited for these analyses because the author of a concurring opinion has little incentive to accommodate the views of other justices. In contrast, majority opinion authors must maintain the support of at least five justices in order to set precedent, and they generally prefer to minimize separate opinions by compromising with other justices. Similarly, the authors of dissenting opinions often strive to unite the dissenters behind a single opinion or lure a justice in the majority to defect.

A third concern – mentioned above – is that, if justices use different language in different types of writings (such as concurring opinions versus dissenting opinions), personality scores based on multiple sources may be endogenous to their behavior. For example, if justices use less agreeable language in dissents than in concurrences, those who write more dissents would appear less agreeable. Therefore, if language from dissents and concurrences were both used to generate personality scores, any relationship between those scores and dissent behavior may simply reflect the measurement process. Thus, the exclusive use of concurrences minimizes this possibility of bias in the measures. Because only concurrences were examined, a justice's propensity to write a concurrence only affects the quantity of language that was examined for each justice; it does not affect the content of that language.[22] Therefore, the personality scores reflect differences in the language justices use in their concurring opinions, not their propensity to write concurring opinions in the first place.

Finally, a skeptical reader might worry that the application of the Personality Recognizer to formal legal writing is inappropriate because the program was trained using informal, unstructured essays written by undergraduate students. However, several factors mitigate this concern. First, the artificial uniformity of legal writing should obscure individual writing styles and make it more difficult to uncover the justices' true personality traits. Therefore, the application of the program to legal writing should bias the results against finding any effects and provide conservative tests for my theory. Second, my coauthors and I found that the distributions of linguistic features in our opinion corpus were similar to those in Mairesse et al.'s training data. The correlation between the mean LIWC category usage from the Pennebaker and King data and the mean usages in their corpus is approximately 0.991, and Spearman's ρ is about 0.789.[23] In other words, the justices' use of linguistic features does not differ substantially from Mairesse et al.'s laboratory writers. Our estimates were also precise. The width of the scores' 95 percent bootstrapped confidence intervals are typically about one standard deviation, meaning the 95 percent intervals are approximately the point estimate plus or minus one half standard deviation. Thus, we concluded that readers can have confidence in the estimates. Lastly, the Personality Recognizer has been employed to measure personality traits in a wide variety of contexts. For example, Ramey, Klinger, and Hollibough have used the program to estimate personality scores for members of the US Congress based on their floor speeches.[24] They find, consistent with their theoretical expectations, that these scores are strongly associated with a variety of congressional behaviors.

SUPREME COURT INDIVIDUAL PERSONALITY ESTIMATES

Therefore, my coauthors and I utilized the Personality Recognizer to generate Supreme Court Individual Personality Estimates (SCIPEs) for the 34 justices serving during the 1946 through 2015 terms. Our SCIPEs are based on every concurring opinion that each justice wrote in every term they served on the Court.[25] To create these estimates, we first processed the language through the 2001 versions of both LIWC and the *MRC Psycholinguistic Database* (MRCPD) in order to collect word counts and proportions across all LIWC and MRCPD categories. We then standardized these results and inserted them into Mairesse et al.'s pretrained models.[26] Finally, we generated 95 percent confidence intervals using 1,000 sentence-level bootstrap replications.[27] Specifically, we assumed that each justice j uses N_j sentences during their tenure. For each justice, we resampled N_j sentences with replacement from our corpus of language during their career.[28]

Figure 3.1 presents the SCIPEs and the 95 percent bootstrapped confidence intervals for each justice-trait (e.g., Justice Antonin Scalia's SCIPE for conscientiousness) on the trait-specific scale. (Note that the scores for Justices Elena Kagan and Charles Evans Whittaker have larger confidence intervals because their scores were based on relatively smaller samples of text.) Because these scores were calculated based on the justices' opinion language, any description of the justices' personality traits relative to the general population would be inappropriate. Instead, these scores should

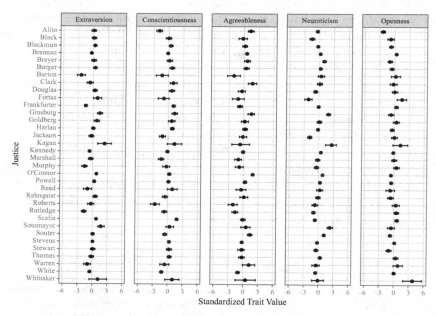

FIGURE 3.1 SCIPEs and 95% confidence intervals

Note: Horizontal lines indicate 95% bootstrapped confidence intervals be understood as reflecting the justices' relative standing on each trait compared to the other justices. Accordingly, in all of the analyses in this book, I use standardized values of the justices' SCIPEs,[29] and I refer to the justices' standing on each trait in a relative sense. For example, I will refer to justices with SCIPEs one standard deviation above and below the mean on extraversion as "more" and "less" extraverted, and some of my figures will refer to these levels as "high" and "low" extraversion. However, both of these terminologies should be understood only as relative comparisons to other justices.

SCIPES AND FACE VALIDITY

If SCIPEs accurately capture the actual personality traits of Supreme Court justices, then these scores should correspond to qualitative accounts of justices' personalities by biographers, historians, and reporters who have interviewed the justices, as well as those who knew them, extensively read their writings, and investigated their behavior both on and off the Court. Therefore, I assess the face validity of SCIPEs by comparing them to qualitative assessments of justices' personalities, which is a common practice when validating new personality measures in the absence of self-reports.[30] To do so, I focus on the three justices with the highest and lowest scores on each of the Big Five factors (i.e., six justices on each trait, thirty justice-trait combinations in all) and compare these assessments to biographical, historical, and media reports of the justices' personalities.

Extraversion. The most extraverted justices identified in the sample – those who should value influence and attention – are Justices Kagan, Sonia Sotomayor, and Ruth Bader Ginsburg. These SCIPEs are supported by historical and biographical accounts of the justices. A profile of Kagan in New York Magazine described her as "a classic extrovert[31]... a glad-hander and a shmoozer."[32] Another author called her "an extrovert, happy to shmooze with anyone."[33] Similarly, one summary of Sotomayor's autobiography explains that "[t]he nation's first Latina justice is also its most extroverted; not only does she ask far more questions during oral arguments than her predecessor, David H. Souter, but she also has refused to indulge the court's pose of Olympian detachment."[34] The most surprising member of this group is Justice Ginsburg, who is sometimes described as shy or reserved.[35] However, as one of her law clerks explains, "Justice Ginsburg has a reputation for being reserved. This is true. But she is also warm and engaging once you get to know her and she has a wonderful and surprising sense of humor."[36] She also "asks lots of questions" during oral arguments, sometimes dominates discussions,[37] and has been known to make a lawyer's argument for him when he faltered.[38] Indeed, for all the talk of her reserved nature, she is one of the most prominent justices on the Court, often admiringly referred to as "the Notorious RBG"— a "firebrand" who appears on countless t-shirts, Halloween costumes, and internet memes.[39] And, during the 2016 presidential election, Ginsburg was the only justice to publicly comment on Donald Trump's unusual candidacy – comments she may have intended to influence the election and which certainly attracted lots of attention from the media, elected officials, and the public.[40] (Moreover, Ginsburg's reputation as shy and reserved is likely a product of her neuroticism, as I discuss below.)

Justices Harold H. Burton, Wiley B. Rutledge, and Frank Murphy are the least extraverted justices in the sample. Burton was described as a "quiet, unassuming" justice,[41] and Rutledge "was rarely seen as an extrovert,"[42] in part because he was "modest"[43] and "seemed to have no ego."[44] Finally, Murphy's biography describes him as "quiet in manner," with the motto "speak softly and hit hard."[45] Thus, these accounts strongly support the SCIPEs for extraversion.

Conscientiousness. The most conscientious justices, who should be industrious and dutiful, are Justices Scalia, Ginsburg, and Kagan. Scalia, with the highest score on conscientiousness, has been called a "conscientious" and "hard-working" justice[46] whose opinions are "carefully wrought" and "highly principled."[47] Ginsburg "pride[s] herself on her professional tone,"[48] devotes great care and attention to her draft opinions, and often works through the day and night.[49] Similarly, Kagan is committed to professional norms, such as resisting the influence of personal political preferences,[50] and, as solicitor general, there "were no complaints about Kagan's work ethic. She was in the office seven days a week. One of her briefs went through fifty-four drafts."[51]

Chief Justice John G. Roberts Jr. and Justices Samuel A. Alito Jr. and Thurgood Marshall score the lowest in conscientiousness. Roberts often relies on his impressive memory rather than bringing notes or cautiously preparing,[52] and he has been criticized as an "agenda-driven" justice,[53] who tries to "push his own ideological agenda" and "help the Republican Party."[54] Alito has similarly been criticized for making decisions based on achieving a desirable outcome rather than following a legal philosophy,[55] and, for years, he appointed clerks who had worked for him on the Third Circuit in order to avoid the effort of interviewing new candidates.[56] Finally, Marshall "did not take his studies seriously" while in school[57] and, while on the Court, often did not prepare for oral arguments or conference.[58] He also tended to buck legal norms in favor of his policy preferences: "He often criticized his colleagues' use of legal formalism that could obscure the real world and the real people affected by their decisions."[59] Thus, these accounts of the justices' conscientiousness also support the validity of SCIPEs.

Agreeableness. Justices Sandra Day O'Connor, Tom C. Clark, and Ginsburg score the highest in agreeableness, meaning that they should value social harmony and sympathy toward the disadvantaged. O'Connor had a "predilection for compromise,"[60] "loved the idea of shaking hands with a colleague and having that human contact,"[61] and pushed a tradition of all the justices eating lunch together.[62] Justice Potter Stewart described Clark's relationships with his colleagues as "very, very amicable and cordial – very friendly,"[63] and Clark was known for his "warmth" and a "broad smile that lit up his face and put people at ease immediately."[64] Ginsburg's friends describe her as "warm" and "gentle"; "when you enter her chambers, you become part of her family."[65] She "offers a depth of warmth and kindness grounded in sensitive emotional awareness"[66] and "often noted proudly that she and Souter, unlike the rest of their colleagues, never engaged in caustic or bitter commentary in their dissenting opinions."[67]

The justices with the lowest SCIPEs for agreeableness are Chief Justice Roberts and Justices Rutledge and Burton. Roberts has been described as a "caustic conservative" who is "intensely competitive"[68] and sometimes addresses lawyers with a sharp tone.[69] Moreover, Roberts believes "the Court should almost always defer to the existing power relationships in society [and has consistently] sided with the prosecution over the defendant, the state over the condemned, the executive branch over the legislative, and the corporate defendant over the individual plaintiff,"[70] suggesting a lack of sympathy for disadvantaged members of society. Rutledge, though a man of "natural kindness,"[71] was also "independent and stubborn."[72] He "stood against the tide, in dissent in the most controversial Supreme Court cases of his day"[73] and "showed great independence," occasionally filing a separate concurrence "even when he agreed with the majority result."[74]

However, the historical and bibliographical accounts regarding Justice Burton offer, at best, mixed support for his low agreeableness score. Burton certainly showed little sympathy or concern for disadvantaged members of society. Instead, Burton tried "above all to be dispassionate, to avoid emotional involvement in cases."[75] Accordingly,

he showed little devotion to civil rights issues and generally opposed civil
liberties claimants.[76] Indeed, Burton dissented alone in the first civil rights
case he heard on the Court, supporting the rights of states to create their
own segregation laws, which was "hardly a promising debut by Burton
from the African American standpoint."[77] Thus, he appears to have been
low on the altruism aspect of agreeableness. Yet, "Burton's personality
was surely the least abrasive on the Court,"[78] and "one of his special
contributions was his ability to get on well with all the other justices."[79]
Accordingly, these accounts do not firmly support the claim that Justice
Burton was particularly disagreeable with regard to social harmony.

Fortunately, Burton appears to be an outlier with regard to SPICEs
misidentifying disagreeable justices. The fourth- and fifth-least agreeable
justices are Justices Abe Fortas and Marshall. Fortas would often offer
"vehement and vicious" comments that "served only to antagonize his
enemies,"[80] and Thurgood Marshall was a man of "fierce candor"[81] who
felt "the frustrations of being an outsider, both personally and ideologically"[82] and took pleasure from making some of his colleagues uncomfortable.[83] Therefore, these accounts generally – but imperfectly – support
the validity of SCIPEs for agreeableness.

Neuroticism. Justices Kagan, Sotomayor, and Ginsburg received the
highest SCIPEs on neuroticism, indicating a tendency to withdraw and
express negativity. As dean of Harvard Law School, Elena Kagan was
known to "lose her temper," and some were "afraid of her."[84] During
her time in the Clinton administration, she often used "blisteringly frank
language" and was not afraid to show her temper, occasionally blowing
up during disagreements.[85] "By many accounts, as a child Sotomayor
was quiet and even withdrawn and listless."[86] "[A]s a freshman, she felt
sometimes intimidated by others ... Sotomayor felt what she's called a
'chasm' between herself and her classmates, and was unsure of herself in
this new world ... Sotomayor was also plagued by her own self doubts as
to whether she belonged at Princeton."[87] As a judge, some were concerned
she was "kind of a bully on the bench,"[88] and her first dissent on the
Supreme Court was called "angry and pointed."[89] Ginsburg is also often
withdrawn, described as "shy" or "timid."[90] Her cautious style causes
her to pause at length while she carefully ponders her words,[91] she is
"meticulously overprepared,"[92] and she sometimes expresses irritation[93]
or even "evident fury."[94]

The attentive reader might notice with some concern that the three
justices who scored highest on extraversion also scored the highest on
neuroticism, and all three of these justices are female. Additionally, two of

the three most conscientious justices and two of the three most agreeable justices were also female – a remarkable pattern given that only four of the thirty-four justices in the sample were women. However, rather than a troubling artifact of the measurement process, this pattern actually reinforces the validity of SCIPEs. The personality psychology literature has found that "explicit personality assessments consistently document that women report higher levels of extraversion, neuroticism, agreeableness and conscientiousness on the Big Five personality dimensions."[95] Therefore, these gender-related patterns are to be expected and may support the view that women on high courts tend to speak in a "different voice."[96] Moreover, these patterns do not extend beyond female justices. For example, the fourth-most neurotic justice, Souter, is near the median on extraversion.[97]

The least neurotic justices include Justices Fortas, Jackson, and Hugo Lafayette Black. Fortas was known as a man with "superb confidence" who "seemed to cut through life like a boat that slips through the water without leaving a wake."[98] Jackson was known as "extraordinarily self-confident."[99] "His manner toward lawyers was never pugnacious [or] hostile," and "he was no man to be awed by the size of an opponent. The stronger they were, the more he seemed to relish the chance to take them on."[100] Black had a "manifestly unshakable assurance in his fundamental views," "exuded confidence" even in elementary school,[101] and usually kept his temper in "close control."[102] Thus, these accounts of the justices' neuroticism also support the validity of SCIPEs.

Openness. Justices Whittaker, Fortas, and Kagan scored the highest in openness, suggesting a preference for intellectualism and change. Whittaker was a "vacillating justice" whose "vote was generally up in the air."[103] Although he enjoyed debating fine legal points,[104] "he just didn't have the power of decision," and "his indecisiveness became legend in the Warren Court."[105] Fortas was an amateur musician with refined tastes who played in a string quartet, collected antiques, enjoyed gourmet food and fine wines, and showed a strong interest in academic subjects such as psychology.[106] Fortas was also so willing to change his legal and policy positions that his clerks came to see him as a "wheeler-dealer," who was "totally unprincipled, and intellectually dishonest."[107] As dean of Harvard Law School, Kagan was a "famously excellent teacher," and "her enthusiasm for debate, for the give-and-take of intellectual life on campus, was real."[108] In the official announcement of her nomination, President Obama emphasized "her openness to a wide variety of viewpoints."[109]

The least-open justices in the sample are Justices Alito, Stewart, and Stephen G. Breyer. Upon his arrival in Washington, DC, in 2006, Alito "reinvented himself as a culture warrior" against 1960s-style liberalism,[110] and on the Court he strongly resisted change, registering as one of the most pro-precedent justices.[111] Stewart was a "steady" justice who generally prioritized tradition, a "slow evolution" of the law, and consistency in his opinions.[112] Breyer also repeatedly emphasized the importance of *stare decisis* (the principle of adhering to precedent) and discouraged the Court from taking radical steps.[113] Thus, these descriptions support SCIPEs for openness.

Face Validity Summary. Historical and biographical accounts of the Supreme Court justices strongly support the face validity of SCIPEs in twenty-nine out of the thirty most extreme justice-trait combinations (the exception being mixed findings regarding Justice Burton's low score on agreeableness). On the one hand, this test of face validity was stringent – demanding thirty separate confirmations involving personality traits that are not widely understood or discussed by most Court observers. On the other hand, a critical reader might argue that, given the wealth of writings about the justices, almost any depiction of a justice's traits could find support from some source (though, as we saw with Justice Burton, that is not always the case). Such criticisms are undoubtedly legitimate and, consequently, these face validity tests are inherently limited. Ultimately, the strength of this charge must be evaluated by the reader guaging the persuasiveness of the preceding sections.

However, in another respect, such a critique is entirely consistent with the methodological approach adopted in this book. Qualitative assessments of personality traits – especially the traits of polarizing, inaccessible, and complicated elites – may be highly unreliable. Such assessments often depend heavily on isolated (and possibly unrepresentative) incidents and subjective (likely biased) reports by close informants or the justices themselves. And these problems may be exacerbated as descriptions are interpreted by reporters and scholars with their own biases. Indeed, many alternative approaches to assessing the justices' personalities (such as canvassing Supreme Court litigants or biographers) would suffer from the same deficiencies. At its core, my project is intended to circumvent reliance on such qualitative assessments by utilizing unbiased and systematic personality estimates. SCIPEs are undoubtedly imperfect estimates of justices' traits, but, at the very least, this textual analysis procedure avoids the problems of subjectivity and interpretive bias inherent to many qualitative approaches. With that in mind, I turn to a more systematic test of SCIPEs' validity.

SCIPES AND CONVERGENT VALIDITY

To further assess the validity of these scores, my coauthors and I examined whether the relationships between SCIPEs and judicial ideology are consistent with those found in the political psychology literature, much of which indicates that liberalism is positively associated with openness and neuroticism and negatively associated with conscientiousness.[114] Evidence for the other traits are more mixed. For example, Mondak et al. found that liberalism was not associated with extraversion and only weakly associated with agreeableness.[115] Yet, among elites, Ramey et al. found positive relationships between liberalism and both extraversion and agreeableness.[116]

My coauthors and I used these findings to test the validity of SCIPEs. We examined Martin–Quinn ideology scores[117] and the proportion of cases in each term in which a justice voted in the "liberal" direction.[118] The independent variables are SCIPEs, along with justices' gender and age, as the latter have well-known correlates with personality traits. We estimated two types of models: linear models with the Martin–Quinn scores as the dependent variable and binomial logit models with the proportion of cases in which each justice voted in the liberal direction as the dependent variable.[119] All models include random intercepts for justice and term, as well as justice-specific random slopes for traits. Models 2 and 4 also include term-specific random slopes for traits. Our results are reproduced in Table 3.1.

Consistent with prior research, openness and neuroticism are positively associated with liberalism, and (in the Martin–Quinn Scores models) conscientiousness is negatively associated with liberalism. Also consistent with prior studies, the results for extraversion and agreeableness are less conclusive, but there is some evidence that agreeableness is positively associated with liberalism. Overall, the results are consistent with the literature and strongly support SCIPEs' convergent validity.

SUMMARY

Altogether, SCIPEs appear to be valid estimates of justices' personality traits. Of course, SCIPEs are, at best, only imperfect estimates; responses to questionnaires might yield more precise measures of traits, though such responses would also entail their own set of problematic biases (selection bias due to underreporting, social desirability bias, etc.). However, to the extent that SCIPEs reflect only imperfect estimates of the justices' actual personality traits, the analyses that follow provide conservative tests of

TABLE 3.1 *Justice personality and ideology*

	Martin–Quinn Scores		Proportion Liberal Votes	
	(1)	(2)	(3)	(4)
Extraversion	−0.01	0.18	−0.22*	−0.03
	(0.36)	(0.36)	(0.10)	(0.08)
Conscientiousness	−0.40*	−0.50*	0.04	−0.07
	(0.12)	(0.13)	(0.16)	(0.07)
Agreeableness	0.07	0.13	0.07	0.09*
	(0.22)	(0.24)	(0.10)	(0.04)
Neuroticism	1.01*	1.10*	−0.21	0.35*
	(0.20)	(0.20)	(0.13)	(0.08)
Openness	0.86*	0.86*	0.31*	0.31*
	(0.15)	(0.18)	(0.10)	(0.10)
Female	−1.31*	−1.55*	−0.27	−0.60*
	(0.44)	(0.40)	(0.23)	(0.09)
Age/100	−5.33	−9.90*	−1.64	−3.45*
	(4.05)	(3.37)	(1.31)	(1.55)
Age²/10,000	9.54*	13.44*	1.72	3.28*
	(3.04)	(2.53)	(0.99)	(1.18)
Constant	−0.42	0.76	0.61	0.88
	(1.37)	(1.15)	(0.44)	(0.53)
Bayesian Information Criterion	1,652.17	1,718.01	4,321.66	4,405.54
Log Likelihood	−723.21	−691.83	−2,061.17	−2,038.81
Number of observations	620	620	620	620

Note: The dependent variable in the "Martin–Quinn Scores" models is each justice's term-specific Martin–Quinn ideology score inverted so that positive values indicate higher degrees of liberalism. The dependent variable in the "Proportion Liberal Votes" model is the proportion of cases in which each justice voted in the liberal direction during each term. Observations are at the justice-term level. All models include random intercepts for justice and term, as well as justice-specific random slopes for traits. Models 2 and 4 also include term-specific random slopes for traits.
Standard errors in parentheses. *$p < 0.05$; two-tailed test.

my theory. Nonetheless, despite the inherent imprecision in these scores, throughout this book I find strong evidence that SCIPEs are associated with a variety of Supreme Court behaviors. Specifically, in the chapters that follow, I examine the role of the justices' personalities in shaping their choices with regard to agenda setting (Chapter 4), opinion assignments (Chapter 5), intra-Court bargaining (Chapter 6), voting on the merits (Chapter 7), and separate opinion filing (Chapter 8).

Moreover, for those readers who remain skeptical of SCIPEs' validity, one might treat the early chapters of this book (4–6) as extended tests of their predictive validity. That is, if SCIPEs are valid measures of the justices' personality traits, they should predict the justices' behavior in theoretically expected ways when making internal decisions (e.g., voting to grant cert or circulating intra-Court bargaining memos). After establishing SCIPEs' predictive validity in these early chapters, I then proceed to test the influence of the justices' personality traits in public contexts (e.g., the final vote on the merits and separate opinion filing).

4

Agenda Setting

In 1954, the Supreme Court issued its landmark decision in *Brown v. Board of Education*, ruling that racially segregated schools are unconstitutional. In the decision's wake, Southern states and localities initiated a variety of policies designed to avoid desegregation without openly defying the Court's ruling. One of the most popular methods of resisting desegregation was the adoption of a pupil placement plan, which granted local officials "practically unreviewable discretion" to assign individual students to local schools. These laws authorized school administrators to place students in specific schools based on a wide variety of racially neutral criteria, such as residence, psychological fitness, scholastic aptitude, health, and moral standards. Because placement plans allowed so many factors to be considered in student assignment, it was nearly impossible to prove that a specific student's assignment to a specific school was racially motivated. And, because the plans purported to utilize individual treatment, it was extremely difficult to bring a class-action suit challenging these laws.[1]

When the parents of African American students in Sumter City, South Carolina, did bring a suit challenging a pupil placement plan, the South Carolina legislature erected an additional legal hurdle designed to impede their case. After a trial court initially denied relief to the parents in 1956, the legislature passed a new law prescribing additional administrative remedies for such lawsuits. Consequently, when the parents appealed their case to the Fourth Circuit Court of Appeals in *Hood v. Board of Trustees*, the federal court denied the appeal on the grounds that they had not yet exhausted their options under state law.[2] Dissatisfied with the Fourth

Circuit's ruling, the parents filed a petition for a writ of certiorari to the US Supreme Court. They argued that, rather than offering a potential remedy, the new South Carolina law was actually a transparent device with which the state hoped to evade judicial oversight and enforcement of the *Brown* decision.[3]

The Fourth Circuit's ruling in *Hood* was well-grounded in the law: Petitioners must generally exhaust their options in state court before appealing to a federal court for relief. Nonetheless, several justices wanted to grant the petition in order to stop South Carolina from thwarting the *Brown* mandate. Justice John Marshall Harlan II disagreed and circulated a memorandum urging his colleagues to deny certiorari:

> In effect, what we are being asked to do is to take judicial notice that South Carolina in all probability intends to use this statute as a means of evading the *Segregation Cases*. For my part, I think this would be a most unwise and lawless thing for the Court to do. Apart from all else it would fly in the face of the established tenet that this Court will not prematurely adjudicate cases presenting abstract, hypothetical, or remote questions ... Moreover, it is settled law that this Court will not look behind a statute to inquire into the propriety of the motives of the legislature.[4]

At first blush, Harlan's opposition to granting cert in *Hood* might seem surprising. Harlan had a fairly strong record on civil rights. The prior year, he had joined the Court's opinion in *Brown v. Board of Education II*, implementing the Court's desegregation order. In fact, according to one of Chief Justice Earl Warren's clerks, Harlan contributed the most forceful sentence in that decision.[5] In the following years, he would join most of the Court's decisions enforcing racial equality and even author the majority opinion in *NAACP v. Alabama* (which stopped the State of Alabama from subpoenaing the NAACP's membership lists).[6]

But Harlan is also remembered as "the ultimate professional"[7] and perhaps the "foremost practitioner of the Wechslerian ideal," espoused by renowned law professor Herbert Wechsler, "that the main constituent of the judicial process is precisely that it must be genuinely principled ... reaching judgment on analysis and reasons quite transcending the immediate result that is achieved."[8] Accordingly, Harlan insisted that "sound law reform should rest on sure-footed legal principle, and not proceed from legally unoriented, albeit socially praiseworthy, impulse."[9] Thus, Harlan thought the Court should adhere to its traditional powers and functions "as much [in] a case where a lower court decision has gone against colored folks as it does [in] one where the decision has been in their favor."[10]

Driven by his firm commitment to his professional responsibilities and principled reasoning, Harlan persuaded his colleagues to deny the petition for certiorari; only Chief Justice Warren and Justice William O. Douglas voted to grant cert.[11]

≈

The US Supreme Court sits atop an enormous and active judicial system. Almost every case heard by the High Court was previously heard in a lower court. Ordinarily, either a state court or a federal district court functions as the trial court, which hears a case for the first time and determines questions of fact. In contrast, the Supreme Court and other intermediate courts generally serve as appellate courts, which hear appeals from trial courts and determine questions of law. Therefore, in most cases, one of the two parties before the Court has prevailed in a lower court (sometimes in several lower courts), and the losing party is asking the Supreme Court to reverse that lower court's decision.

As the highest court in the US judiciary, the Supreme Court can potentially hear any case that originates in any court in the nation, including both state and federal courts. The vast majority of legal cases in the United States originate in state courts. In 2016, more than eighty-four million cases were initiated in the fifty states, the District of Columbia, and Puerto Rico. After exhausting the options in their state judicial systems, losing parties can ask the Supreme Court to review the case in order to examine questions of federal law. Additionally, every year, hundreds of thousands of cases enter the federal judicial system through one of the ninety-four US District Courts around the country (more than 350,000 cases in 2016).[12] Parties that lose in a federal district court have the right to appeal their cases to one of the twelve regional US Courts of Appeals, and, in 2016, more than 60,000 cases were appealed to these intermediate appellate courts.[13] Parties who lose in the Courts of Appeals can then ask to have their cases heard by the Supreme Court.

Although every case filed in a US court has the potential to reach the Supreme Court, very few cases have the right to do so. (A very small number of cases reach the Court through an appeal as a matter of right. Additionally, the High Court has original jurisdiction in some cases, e.g., when one state sues another state). Instead, almost all cases that reach the Supreme Court do so through a process called certiorari (or simply "cert"). Once a party has exhausted their other legal options (in some cases, before they have done so), the party can petition the Supreme Court for a writ of certiorari – literally, an order from the Supreme Court for a lower court to deliver its record in a case so that the High Court can review the decision. But the justices can choose to grant or deny this request. In other words, Supreme Court justices mostly control their own docket: They decide which cases they hear and which cases they do not.

Every year the Court receives around 7,000 petitions for a writ of certiorari. More than 5,000 of these petitions are unpaid, meaning that the filer received a waiver and did not have to pay the Court's filing fee. Most unpaid petitions are from prisoners in state or federal prison, and these petitions rarely raise issues of substantial legal merit. The Court typically receives around 1,500 paid petitions each year, which usually present more pressing legal questions. The justices' clerks initially screen the cert petitions looking for cases the justices may want to hear. Most justices participate in the "cert pool," which means all of their clerks work together to sort through the petitions. The clerks make recommendations for which cases should be on the discuss list – a list of cases in which the justices consider granting cert. Any justice can add a case to the discuss list, but no justice can remove a case from the list.

Each week, the justices meet in conference to consider granting cert to cases on the discuss list. The Court operates under the "rule of four," meaning that the Court will hear a case if any four justices vote to grant the petition for a writ of certiorari (i.e., vote to grant cert). In other words, the Court can agree to hear a case even if a majority of justices oppose granting cert. However, despite the rule of four, the justices are hesitant to hear most cases. In the last few decades, the Court has granted cert in fewer than one hundred of the thousands of cert petitions filed each year.

The justices' ability to control their own agenda is critically important for several reasons. First, docket control allows justices to focus on particularly important, controversial, and interesting cases while avoiding routine disputes with obvious resolutions or little consequence. Thus, docket control allows the Court to operate effectively without becoming overrun with frivolous appeals. Second, the justices' agenda-setting power allows them to focus on legal, political, and social issues they want to resolve while avoiding legal questions they would rather not address. Accordingly, the selection of cases is highly consequential, and the justices often disagree about which cases to hear.

CERT VOTES

The Court's official rules indicate two criteria the justices are supposed to consider when deciding whether or not to grant certiorari and hear a case. First, the justices are supposed to consider granting cert in cases that involve conflicts between the different US Courts of Appeals. For example, if the Court of Appeals for the First Circuit interprets a federal law to mean one thing, but the Second Circuit disagrees, a conflict exists between these two circuits. In such an instance, the meaning of federal law is actually different in one part of the country than it is in another part of the country. One of the Supreme Court's most important functions is to resolve these circuit conflicts in order to reconcile these inconsistencies in the interpretation of federal law. It is not always entirely clear whether a circuit conflict exists, and the justices sometimes prefer to let legal issues "percolate" in the lower courts for a while so they can make more informed decisions.[14] Nonetheless, when a clear conflict occurs between two circuits, the justices are much more likely to grant cert and resolve the conflict.[15]

Second, the justices are supposed to grant cert in cases that raise "an important question of federal law."[16] Obviously, this rule is rather ambiguous, and justices often disagree about which legal questions are truly important. Nonetheless, the best available evidence suggests that justices do tend to grant cert in cases that raise more salient and consequential legal issues. For example, justices are more likely to vote in favor of granting cert in cases that were summarized in the legal periodical *U.S. Law Week*, cases in which the lower court chose to invalidate a federal law, and cases in which more outside parties filed amicus curie ("friend of the court") briefs.[17]

The ambiguity in this second rule enables the justices to consider other strategic factors when making cert decisions. For example, the justices are more likely to grant cert when the solicitor general supports doing so,[18] which suggests the justices either respect the solicitor's expertise or generally defer to the executive branch when deciding whether to hear a case. The justices may also consider each other's preferences when casting cert votes. Of particular importance, justices are more likely grant cert when their own ideological preferences align with the likely outcome of the case (e.g., a liberal justice is more likely to cast a grant vote if the other justices' ideological preferences make a liberal outcome more likely).[19] However, the discretion afforded to justices in determining which cases to hear suggests that their cert decisions may also be driven by their personalities.

Cert Vote Hypotheses. In addition to these traditional explanations, the psychoeconomic approach posits that the justices' personality traits also influence the Court's agenda setting. Specifically, drawing on the theory developed in Chapter 2, I propose the following hypotheses related to cert votes:

- The positive influence of amici attention on grant votes is stronger for more-extroverted justices because granting cert in these cases attracts attention from judicial audiences.
- More-conscientious justices are less likely to cast a grant vote because pursuing policy objectives violates their judicial duty.
- The positive influence of other justices' votes on grant votes is stronger for more-agreeable justices because voting with other justices promotes social harmony on the Court.
- More-neurotic justices are less likely to cast a grant vote because granting cert exposes justices to potential criticism. Additionally, the positive influence of the US government supporting cert on grant votes is stronger for more-neurotic justices because supporting the US government avoids potential criticism.
- More-open justices are more likely to cast a grant vote because granting cert provides an opportunity to intellectually engage with different ideas and promote legal change.

Below I describe the empirical model I used to test these hypotheses. I then develop each hypothesis in more detail and report the findings of the empirical tests.

The Cert Vote Model. In order to evaluate the role of personality traits in shaping the justices' agenda-setting behavior, I replicate Ryan Black and Ryan Owen's analysis of cert voting on the US Supreme Court.[20] Black and Owens examined a random sample of 358 paid non-death-penalty petitions coming out of a federal court of appeals that made the Supreme Court's discuss list from the 1986 through 1993 terms ($N = 3,002$; in the sections that follow, recall that all predicted probabilities of justices voting to grant cert refer to paid petitions that made the discuss list, hence the relatively high probability of justices voting to grant cert in this limited sample). Following their analysis, the dependent variable is the vote by each of the twelve justices serving during this time period on whether to grant a petition for certiorari (1 = grant; 0 = deny).[21] Of course, the restricted nature of this data implies a commensurate limitation in the generalizability of my findings. Specifically, readers should proceed with great caution before applying my conclusions to death penalty cases, in forma pauperis petitions, cases emanating from state courts, or cases falling outside of this time frame.

The model controls for several variables that capture potential influences on cert voting, including justice characteristics (the justices' ideological preferences and indicators for the chief justice and freshman justices), characteristics of the lower-court decision (indicators for media attention, the presence of inter-circuit conflict, and whether the lower court reversed the court below it, published its opinion, invalidated a law on constitutional grounds, sat en banc, and included a dissent), and characteristics of the petition to the Supreme Court (the term-standardized number of amicus briefs filed, as well as indicators for the number of grant votes cast by other justices and the solicitor general's position). I also include the justices' SCIPEs for the Big Five (standardized within this sample of justices), as well as the interaction terms described below. (See Appendix A for a full description of the model.)

JUSTICE TRAITS AND CERT VOTES

Figure 4.1 summarizes the results of the cert vote model. The figure reports the marginal effects of the justices' personality traits on the probability of casting a grant vote, as well as the effects of all statistically significant control variables. As a point of reference, the average predicted probability of a justice casting a vote to grant cert is .31, and this probability is influenced by both legal and ideological factors. For example, the presence of strong inter-circuit conflict is associated with a .09 increase in the probability of a grant vote (from .28 to .37). And a justice being ideologically closer to the predicted policy location of the Supreme Court's merits decision than to the status quo policy is associated with a .07 increase in the probability of a grant vote (from .26 to .33).

The justices' personality traits are also strongly associated with their cert votes, and the magnitude of these effects rivals or exceeds that of several legal, institutional, and ideological influences on cert voting. For example, the effects of a justice's conscientiousness ($-.09$) and neuroticism ($-.09$) on cert voting are both comparable in magnitude to the effect of a justice's ideological preferences ($+.07$).[22] In other words, each of these personality traits explains as much variation in the justices' cert voting as do their ideologies. Given the extensive attention paid to the role of the justices' ideological preferences in shaping their behavior, this comparison is particularly noteworthy.

Extraversion and Cert Votes. The relationship between justice extraversion and cert votes is likely a complicated one. On the one hand, hearing cases inherently creates opportunities for justices to influence

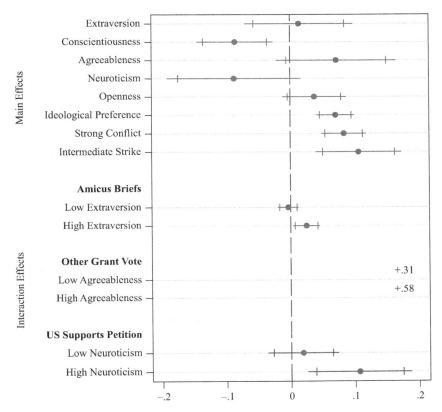

FIGURE 4.1 Marginal effects on agenda setting

Note: Figure reports the marginal effects of a one standard deviation increase in each continuous variable (and one-unit increase in each dichotomous variable) on the probability of a justice voting to grant cert. Horizontal bars indicate 95% confidence intervals and vertical spikes indicate 90% confidence intervals. Predicted probabilities and marginal effects are based on a multilevel logistic regression model with random intercepts for 12 justices. The full model is reported in Appendix A.

each other and attract attention from judicial audiences. On the other hand, hearing more cases does not mean that any particular justice will be able to exert more influence over his or her colleagues. Nor does it guarantee that the Court will attract more attention from judicial audiences. Hearing a few high-profile controversies might actually attract more attention than granting cert in many inconsequential cases. In fact, hearing numerous cases may even undermine attention to the Court as these cases compete against each other for media, elite, and lower-court attention. Therefore, I neither expect nor find any direct relationship between extraversion and cert votes.

However, personality traits may also condition the influence of other factors on the justices' behavior. That is, many situational factors influence justices' cert voting, but the influence of these factors may vary depending on justices' goal preferences. For example, petitions that reach the Supreme Court vary widely in their potential to attract attention. Some petitions relate to complex and esoteric areas of law of little interest to the general public. But others present cases with the potential for the justices to exert tremendous political influence and attract intense public attention. Indeed, some of these petitions have already attracted attention from interest groups, political actors, or legal academics who filed amicus curie ("friend of the court") briefs hoping to influence the Court's cert decision. Such petitions are strong signals that a case is of interest beyond the immediate parties involved, and the Court's ruling in the case may have far-reaching effects, potentially enhancing the justices' reputation and prestige.

I measure the attention each cert petition received from amicus groups by calculating the number of amicus briefs filed in each case before cert was granted, standardized within the term the case was filed. Justices are generally more likely to vote to grant cert in cases in which amicus groups file more briefs. On average, the probability of a justice casting a grant vote in cases with low versus high amici attention (i.e., the minimum or zero briefs versus two standard deviations above the minimum or about three briefs) is .30 versus .32. Thus, justices appear to pay some attention to amicus signals and, on average, seek out the opportunity to attract attention by deciding these salient cases.

However, the effect of amicus briefs on cert votes should vary across justices with different personality traits. Justices who value the opportunity to attract attention from judicial audiences should be especially likely to grant cert when multiple parties file amicus briefs because deciding these cases is likely to attract additional attention. Therefore, the positive influence of amici attention on grant votes should be stronger for more extraverted justices (who value attention).

Figure 4.2 illustrates the relationship between amici attention and the propensity of justices at different levels of extraversion to cast grant votes. The upper panel presents the predicted probability of a grant vote in cases with low versus high amici attention. The lower panel presents the effect of amici attention on the probability of a grant vote. For more-extraverted justices, an increase from low to high amici attention is associated with

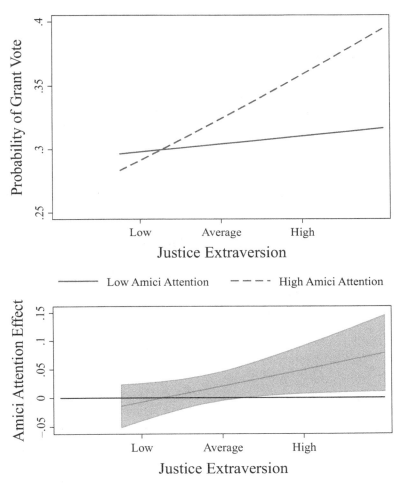

FIGURE 4.2 The effect of amici attention on cert votes at varying levels of extraversion

Note: The upper panel presents the predicted probability of a vote to grant cert in cases with low versus high amici attention (i.e., the minimum versus two standard deviations above the minimum). The lower panel presents the marginal effects of amici attention with 95% confidence intervals. Predicted probabilities and marginal effects are based on a multilevel logistic regression model with random intercepts for 12 justices. The full model is reported in Appendix A.

a .05 increase in the probability of a grant vote (from .31 to .36). For less-extraverted justices, the same increase in amicus attention is not associated with grant votes. Thus, amicus briefs appear to encourage grant votes but only for more extraverted justices.

Conscientiousness and Cert Votes. As described with regard to *Hood v. Board of Trustees*, cert petitions sometimes force the justices to choose between their professional duty and their desire to pursue policy objectives in specific cases. A variety of jurisdictional and procedural rules limit the types of cases that the Supreme Court is supposed to hear. Moreover, a variety of legal norms discourage the justices from hearing a case unless it presents an appropriate vehicle through which to consider an important legal question. Consequently, the Court receives numerous petitions in which the justices may disagree with the lower court's verdict, yet their professional duty demands that they deny cert. For the most part, the justices adhere to these rules and norms; if they did not, their docket might become overrun with cases. However, in borderline situations, some justices may be tempted to bend the rules and accept a case in an effort to rectify a perceived injustice in the lower court. Those justices who strictly adhere to their professional duties should resist this temptation. Therefore, more-conscientious justices (who value dutifulness) should be less likely to vote in favor of granting cert.

A preference for industriousness might lead justices to cast more or fewer cert votes. Conscientious justices might vote to grant cert more often because they are more willing to exert the effort required to handle a larger caseload. However, the industriousness aspect of conscientiousness is also associated with deliberation, perfectionism, and cautiousness.[23] In other words, a preference for industriousness would not necessarily lead justices to hear more cases; instead, it might prompt them to expend more effort on the cases they do hear. In fact, a preference for industriousness might lead justices to hear fewer cases so that they can devote more time and energy to each case. Given these possibilities, one might expect a preference for industriousness to have either a positive or negative effect on cert votes; however, when considered together with the influence of dutifulness, I still expect more conscientious justices to cast fewer grant votes.

Figure 4.1 illustrates the strong negative relationship between the justices' conscientiousness and their propensity to cast votes to grant cert. The probability of a grant vote is .38 for less-conscientious justices and .22 for more-conscientious justices. Thus, more-conscientious justices are more than 40 percent less likely than less-conscientious justices to cast a grant vote, which presumably reflects their propensity to strictly adhere to the rules and norms that limit the Court's docket.

Agreeableness and Cert Votes. Casting a vote to grant cert is not directly connected to social harmony or altruism. That is, casting a grant vote is not necessarily good or bad for harmonious relations on the Court, nor does it necessarily help or hurt the disadvantaged.[24] Therefore, I neither expect nor find any direct association between agreeableness and grant votes.

However, Supreme Court justices do not base their decisions solely on their own characteristics and the characteristics of the case in front of them. They also base their decisions on the behavior and anticipated behavior of those around them: Congress, the president, the public, lower-court judges, and – most importantly – other Supreme Court justices.[25] The justices' behavior during the certiorari process is no different: The justices influence each other's behavior, and that influence is sometimes critically important in determining cert votes. In general, I expect a justice's cert vote to be positively associated with the votes of other justices. That is, a justice should be more likely to vote to grant cert when other justices do so.

Of course, the relationship between one justice voting to grant cert and another justice doing the same does not necessarily prove that one justice influenced the other. The justices are examining the same case, and a relationship between their voting behavior may simply indicate that they tend to agree on which cases deserve cert. For example, if two justices both vote to grant cert in a case involving a circuit conflict, it does not necessarily mean that one justice influenced the other; they may have both been influenced by the presence of the conflict. However, if the relationship between a justice's cert votes and the other justices' cert votes varies across justices with different personality traits, it may indicate that justices are influencing each other in different ways.

Specifically, justices who care more about social harmony on the Court should care more about the behavior of their fellow justices. Frequent disagreement with other justices may undermine a sense of common goals, shared values, and professional detachment on the Court. Moreover, specific cases of disagreement may lead to confrontations or other forms of negativity among the justices (e.g., when justices disagree on the merits vote, they tend to incur collegiality costs).[26] Justices who care more about social harmony on the Court should be sensitive to these concerns and pay more attention to the behavior (and anticipated behavior) of their fellow justices. Therefore, the positive influence of other justices' grant votes on a justice's grant vote should be stronger for more-agreeable justices (who value social harmony).

Figure 4.3 illustrates the relationship between the number of grant votes cast by other justices and the propensity of justices at different

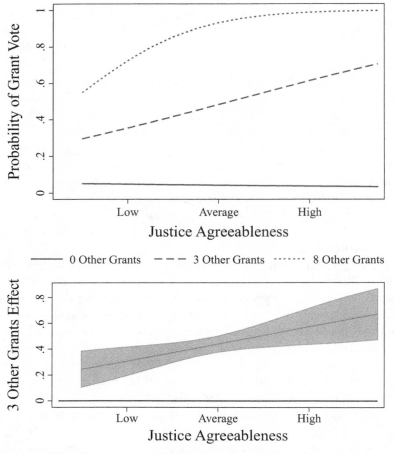

FIGURE 4.3 The effect of other justices' votes to grant cert on grant votes at varying levels of agreeableness

Note: The upper panel presents the predicted probability of a vote to grant cert in cases with zero versus three versus eight votes to grant cert by other justices on the Court. The lower panel presents the marginal effects of three other grant votes with 95% confidence intervals. Predicted probabilities and marginal effects are based on a multilevel logistic regression model with random intercepts for 12 justices. The full model is reported in Appendix A.

levels of agreeableness to cast a grant vote.[27] (For this analysis, I disregard voting order on the Court under the assumption that justices can predict each others' votes with a high degree of accuracy based on past voting behavior, oral arguments, and the conference discussion. However, I have also run this model using only the number of grant votes cast by justices with more seniority, who generally vote first. That model yields similar results.) The upper panel presents the predicted probability of a grant vote in cases with zero versus three versus eight other grant votes. The lower panel presents the effect of three additional grant votes by other justices on the probability of a grant vote.

Regardless of a justice's agreeableness, the probability of voting to grant cert when no other justice does so is fairly low (less than .05). When three other justices cast grant votes, a justice faces a critical decision: A fourth grant vote would satisfy the rule of four and cause the Court to hear the case. Unsurprisingly, justices are more likely to cast a grant vote when three other justices do so; however, this effect is much larger for more-agreeable justices. For less-agreeable justices, the presence of three other grant votes is associated with a .30 increase in the probability of a grant vote (from .05 to .35). For more-agreeable justices, three other grant votes is associated with a .57 increase in the probability of a grant vote (from .04 to .61).[28] Thus, the influence of other grant votes on a justice's vote to grant cert is nearly twice as strong for more- versus less-agreeable justices.

Neuroticism and Cert Votes. Granting cert inevitably involves both costs and benefits for Supreme Court justices. Hearing more cases may enhance justices' influence over law, policy, and society, and it may provide justices with a sense of professional fulfillment. However, reading briefs, hearing arguments, and writing opinions takes time and energy, and the process often involves social pressure, conflict, and stress. Granting cert also inherently involves risks. High-profile cases often attract media scrutiny, complex cases may draw criticism from law professors, lower-court judges, and legal practitioners, and highly controversial cases may cause serious rifts among the justices or prompt rebukes from other branches of government.[29] Serious mistakes could even jeopardize the Court's legitimacy in the eyes of the public.[30] Of course, taking these risks might garner accolades from peers and Court-watchers, earn a justice professional prestige, or even improve our legal system.[31] As justices weigh the potential costs and benefits associated with granting cert, justices who prefer to avoid losses should place more weight on the potential costs and, consequently, vote to deny cert. Therefore, more-neurotic justices (who value loss avoidance) should be less likely to cast a grant vote.

Figure 4.1 illustrates the strong negative relationship between justice neuroticism and grant votes. The probability of a grant vote is .37 for less-neurotic justices and .21 for more-neurotic justices. Thus, more-neurotic justices are about 45 percent less likely than less-neurotic justices to cast a grant vote, which presumably reflects their tendency to avoid the costs and risks associated with hearing cases.

Justices should also be more likely to vote in favor of granting cert when the US government supports granting the petition. The federal government expresses its support for granting cert in two ways. First, in many cases, the government itself filed the petition requesting cert. Second, even when the federal government is not a party to a case, it sometimes files an amicus curie brief urging the Court to grant cert. The justices tend to follow the US government's recommendations due in part to separation of powers considerations. That is, the justices may fear nonimplementation of their decisions, rebukes from the elected branches of government, or popular criticism and, consequently, pay special heed when the government urges them to hear a particular case.[32] Additionally, the solicitor general (who represents the federal government before the Court) has been described as a "Tenth Justice": an agent of the Court who plays a special role by screening cases and advocating positions that advance the Court's institutional goals.[33] Therefore, the justices may follow the solicitor's recommendations based on the assumption that the solicitor is protecting the Court's interests, and disregard for those recommendations may lead to institutional problems in the future (e.g., legal inconsistencies, diminished respect for the Court). Therefore, justices should be more likely to vote in favor of cert when the US government supports a petition, in part because ignoring the federal government may provoke criticism, sanctions, or other institutional problems.[34] And, as expected, the probability of a justice casting a grant vote increases by .05 when the US government supports a cert petition (from .30 to .35). The federal government opposing cert is not associated with cert votes, possibly because denying cert tends to be the Court's default decision.

However, the threat of criticism, sanctions, and institutional problems associated with disregarding the federal government likely has different effects on different justices. Those justices who place greater value on avoiding such negative consequences should tend to grant cert when the US government supports a petition; those justices who are willing to bear these risks should be less likely to vote in favor of cert in these cases. Therefore, the positive influence of the US government supporting cert on grant votes should be stronger for more-neurotic justices (who value loss avoidance).

Figure 4.4 illustrates the relationship between US government support for a cert petition, justice neuroticism, and grant votes. The upper panel

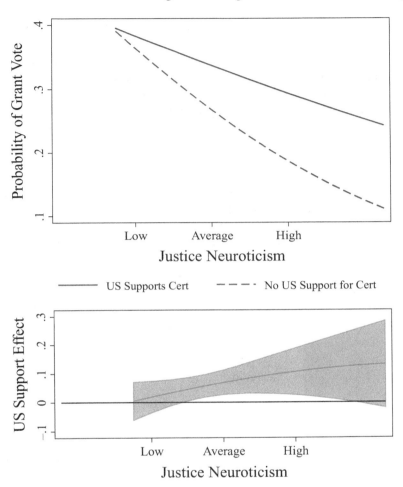

FIGURE 4.4 The effect of US support for cert on grant votes at varying levels of justice neuroticism

Note: The upper panel presents the predicted probability of a vote to grant cert in cases with and without US support for the petition. The lower panel presents the marginal effects of US support with 95% confidence intervals. Predicted probabilities and marginal effects are based on a multilevel logistic regression model with random intercepts for 12 justices. The full model is reported in Appendix A.

presents the predicted probability of a grant vote in cases in which the federal government did versus did not support a cert petition. (Predicted probabilities of a grant vote in cases in which the US government opposed a cert petition are statistically indistinguishable from those in which the

US government was not involved.) The lower panel presents the effect of the federal government's support on the probability of a grant vote. For more-neurotic justices, US support is associated with a .10 increase in the probability of a grant vote (from .19 to .29); for less-neurotic justices, the association between US support and grant votes is statistically indistinguishable from zero. Thus, federal support for a cert petition appears to influence cert voting but only for more-neurotic justices. (I also test the interaction between justice neuroticism and the US government opposing cert; however, such opposition is not associated with cert votes, regardless of justice neuroticism.)

Openness and Cert Votes. Every cert petition filed in the Court presents an opportunity for the justices to engage with a legal question in the context of a specific factual situation. Disposing of these cases by reading briefs, hearing arguments, and writing opinions is often an intellectually stimulating process, and each case presents a potentially new and different legal question as a result of its unique factual background. Accordingly, every time the Court agrees hear a case, justices have an opportunity to intellectually engage with new legal issues. Therefore, more-open justices (who value intellectualism and change) should be more likely to cast a grant vote. Figure 4.1 illustrates the positive relationship between justice openness and grant votes; however, this relationship falls short of conventional levels of statistical significance ($p = .07$; one-tailed test).

PERSONALITY AND AGENDA SETTING

To summarize, the justices' personality traits have a strong and direct association with their cert votes. Justices who are more conscientious and more neurotic are less likely to vote in favor of granting cert, and justices who are more open may be more likely to vote in favor of granting cert, even after controlling for numerous other influences on cert decisions. These findings suggest that justices who value dutifulness and loss avoidance are less likely to support hearing a case, while those who value intellectualism and change may be more likely to do so.

The justices' personality traits also condition other influences on their cert voting. On average, justices are more likely to vote in favor of granting cert when outside parties file amicus curiae briefs, when more of their colleagues vote to grant cert, and when the US government supports the cert petition. However, the influence of these situational factors depends on the justices' personality traits. For more-extraverted justices, amicus briefs are strongly associated with grant votes; however, less-extraverted justices do not appear to respond to amicus briefs. Additionally, the association between a justice's grant vote and grant votes by other justices is substantially stronger for more-agreeable justices. And, finally, only more-neurotic justices tend to follow cert recommendations from the federal government. These findings suggest that the influence of amici attention, other justices' votes, and the federal government's support for cert depends on the justices' preference for attention, social harmony, and loss avoidance, respectively.

At the beginning of this chapter, I described Justice Harlan's opposition to granting cert in *Hood* as an example of a justice's personality shaping his agenda-setting behavior (specifically, Harlan's conscientiousness prompted him to follow legal norms and deny cert rather than pursue his policy objectives). The empirical findings in this chapter suggest that the importance of personality traits extends well beyond that specific example. Indeed, the justices' personality traits appear to strongly influence their agenda-setting behavior in a variety of ways. Accordingly, the justices' personalities may ultimately play a pivotal role in determining which cases are heard by the US Supreme Court, and any analysis of agenda setting that fails to account for these factors is likely incomplete.

5

Opinion Assignments

In 1947, the US Supreme Court considered a challenge to a New York tax on transportation utilities in *Central Greyhound Lines v. Mealey*. The State of New York had levied a two percent tax on the gross income of all utilities operating in the state, including common carriers such as Central Greyhound Lines. Because the Constitution delegates to Congress the power to tax interstate commerce, the tax applied only to buses moving within the state of New York; transportation between New York and other states was not subject to the tax. However, the State Tax Commission held that the utilities tax applied to the transportation of passengers between two points in New York even if substantial portions of the transportation utilized highways in other states. Central Greyhound Lines challenged the constitutionality of the tax as applied to a route between two points in New York because 43.53 percent of the route passed through New Jersey and Pennsylvania and therefore might be considered interstate commerce.

In the Court's conference discussion, a majority of justices supported upholding the New York tax, and the opinion of the Court was assigned to Justice Frank Murphy. Majority opinion assignments were rare for Justice Murphy. "Neither [Chief Justice Harlan Fiske] Stone nor [Chief Justice Fred M.] Vinson had much confidence in his work. Accordingly, he received few opinions in important cases from either chief justice"; in fact, the opinion in *Central Greyhound* had been his "sole assignment to date" during the 1947 term.[1] The other justices viewed him as "lazy and unsophisticated in the law" (Justice Felix Frankfurter once wrote to another justice, "[T]he short of the matter is that today you would no more heed Murphy's tripe than you would be seen naked at Dupont Circle at high noon tomorrow").[2] Murphy "lacked the intellectual drive and the patience to structure the central juridical options of his time," and he even doubted his own technical competence.[3] Most importantly, Murphy was deficient in the social and leadership skills necessary to persuade his colleagues and marshal the Court: He "seldom spoke in public," his assets were "all highly personal rather than 'lawyerly,'" and "he lacked the charisma, and perhaps the cunning, to build a political coalition capable of sustaining reform movements and of surviving himself."[4]

Unsurprisingly, Murphy's assignment to write the majority opinion in *Central Greyhound* proved ill-fated. A few weeks later, he sent a note to Chief Justice Vinson reporting the results of his efforts: "I have done my best to write an opinion acceptable to the majority who voted as I did at conference. I have failed in this task and a majority has now voted the other way."[5] Ultimately, the Court reversed the Tax Commission's decision and held that the state could only tax the receipts from transportation apportioned as to the mileage that occurred within New York's borders. The vote was six to three with Justice Murphy in dissent.

After the Supreme Court grants a petition for certiorari and agrees to hear a case, the parties present arguments to the Court in two forms. First, the lawyers for each party submit written briefs stating their arguments and reply briefs responding to the other party's arguments. Second, the parties present oral arguments to the Court, during which the justices can interrupt to ask the lawyers questions. Outside parties can also submit amicus curie briefs in an effort to persuade the justices. After reading all of these briefs and hearing oral arguments, the justices meet in conference to discuss the merits of the case.[6] The initial vote in the Court's conference forms a preliminary majority coalition that will usually end up deciding which party prevails in the case.

However, the majority coalition must craft an opinion to articulate the reasoning behind its decision. In most cases, this task is assigned to a specific justice who drafts the opinion of the Court (usually a majority opinion).[7] The majority opinion author then circulates the draft opinion among the other justices. The author's goal is to write an opinion that attracts support from at least five members of the Court and consequently sets binding legal precedent.

"At its most basic level, opinion assignment in the Supreme Court is critical because the majority opinion sets the law of the land and precedent for future cases."[8] That is, the vote on the merits of a case (discussed in

Chapter 7) only decides which party wins the case. It is the content of
the Court's opinion that guides lower courts in interpreting the law and
sets precedent that must be followed by lower courts and the Supreme
Court in future cases. Consequently, the most important product that the
Supreme Court produces is the content of its majority opinions.

The opinion assignment process is particularly important because the
author of the Court's majority opinion exercises disproportionate influence over the opinion's content[9] as well as the opinion's legal clarity,
which affects its interpretation by lower courts.[10] The key to the opinion
author's influence is his or her status as the first mover in crafting the
opinion.[11] By virtue of the opinion assignment, the opinion author has the
responsibility to propose an initial version of the majority opinion, which
other justices must either accept or reject. Those who object to the content
of the majority opinion may try to exert influence over that opinion by
bargaining with the opinion author (see Chapter 6) or expressing their
disagreement by writing or joining a separate opinion (see Chapter 8).
However, bargaining and separate opinion writing impose both effort
costs and collegiality costs on the justices engaged in those activities (i.e.,
both activities consume time and energy, and both activities tend to frustrate other justices). Therefore, if a justice disagrees with the content of
the majority opinion, he or she must weigh these costs against the desire to
exert influence over the opinion (by bargaining) or express disagreement
(by writing or joining a separate opinion). The result is that many justices
ultimately accept the opinion proposed by the majority opinion author
despite some minor disagreements with its content.

OPINION ASSIGNMENTS

The factors influencing which justice is assigned to write the majority
opinion depend on which justice controls the assignment. When the chief
justice is in the majority coalition, the chief assigns a member of the
coalition (possibly himself) to author the opinion. When the chief makes
up part of the minority (about 16% of cases), the senior associate justice
(SAJ) in the majority assigns the opinion.

When assigning the majority opinion author, the chief justice often
prioritizes the Court's institutional concerns and other justices' preferences rather than his own personal priorities.[12] Indeed, prior studies have
emphasized that "both policy advantage *and* organizational needs are
important to the chief's opinion assignment calculus.[13]" For example,
chief justices tend to "distribute the Court's workload evenly among

the justices" in order to promote a norm of equity on the Court.[14] This equity norm ensures that the justices share both the increased influence and the increased workload associated with majority opinion assignments. Chief justices also "encourage specialization by assigning similar cases to the same justice" in an effort to improve the quality of the Court's opinions.[15] Higher-quality opinions might enhance the Court's legitimacy, reduce legal ambiguity, and minimize the necessity for future litigation. This practice also satisfies justices who especially enjoy certain areas of law or want to develop a reputation for expertise on a particular legal topic.

Finally, "[b]ecause Court rules lessen the precedential value of plurality, rather than majority, opinions," chiefs often assign the majority opinion with an eye toward uniting a majority coalition.[16] That is, if the majority coalition is small or fragile, the chief may deliberately assign the opinion to a justice who is more likely to maintain the support of at least five justices. Often, chief justices hoping to preserve a majority coalition select potential swing justices as opinion authors; i.e., the chief assigns the majority opinion to the justice most likely to abandon the coalition if he or she were dissatisfied with the opinion's content. However, the chief may also select opinion authors who are more likely to maintain a working majority through persuasion, charm, or other personal attributes.

In contrast to chief justices, SAJs tend to put less emphasis on the Court's institutional interests or the concerns of other justices. Consequently, when assigning the majority opinion, the SAJ is free to pursue his or her own goals. Most prominently, the SAJ may try to use the opinion assignment power to advance his or her policy preferences. Obviously, the SAJ could do so by assigning the opinion to him- or herself. However, self-assignments come with considerable costs: They require the SAJ to expend effort researching and writing the opinion, not to mention bargaining with his or her fellow justices over its content. As an alternative strategy, the SAJ can assign the opinion to a justice with similar policy preferences. In this manner, the SAJ can ensure the opinion is written by an ideological ally without expending the effort required to write the opinion him- or herself.

However, assigning an ideological ally to write the majority opinion also comes with potential costs. First, even if the SAJ assigns the opinion in such a way, the selected opinion author may disagree with the SAJ on some policy points and work to assert his or her own influence over the opinion content. Second, even if the SAJ and the opinion author agree on preferred policy, the opinion author may shirk his or her responsibilities and devote little effort toward writing a high-quality opinion that clearly articulates that preferred policy. Finally, even if the opinion author initially agrees with the SAJ about the preferred policy outcome, the opinion author may change his or her mind about certain elements of the case and ultimately end up disagreeing with the SAJ on some points. Therefore, the SAJ should ideally try to find a justice less interested in exerting influence, more willing to devote effort toward writing the opinion, and less likely to change positions during the drafting and bargaining processes.

Opinion Assignment Hypotheses. Regardless of which justice assigns the majority opinion author, the psychoeconomic approach posits that justices' personality traits – both the assigner's traits and the potential assignees' traits – also affect the assignment of majority opinions. The assigners' traits should influence his or her assignment behavior just as they do any other type of behavior. However, because the assigner's traits do not vary within case, it is difficult to assess the direct relationship between these traits and assignment behavior. (It is possible to assess the interactive effect between the assigner's traits and contextual variables, as I do in the section regarding SAJ conscientiousness and ideological distance to the SAJ.) Therefore, I focus primarily on the influence of potential assignees' traits on the probability they are assigned. I expect assignee traits to influence assignment behavior based on the widely confirmed finding in personality psychology that individuals can accurately perceive each other's personality traits even after short interactions.[17] Because justices work closely together for years at a time, majority opinion assigners should be well aware of their colleagues' personality traits and, therefore, may use that knowledge to inform their assignment decisions.

Because different institutional considerations likely influence chief justices and SAJs, some of my hypotheses differ for chief assignments and SAJ assignments. Specifically, I propose the following hypotheses related to opinion assignments:

- More-extraverted justices are more likely to receive a chief assignment and less likely to receive an SAJ assignment because they tend to influence other justices and attract attention from judicial audiences.
- More-conscientious justices are more likely to receive an opinion assignment because they tend to expend effort and fulfill their judicial duty.
- The negative influence of the winning vote margin on receiving an opinion assignment is weaker for more-agreeable justices because securing a majority coalition undermines social harmony on the Court.

- More-neurotic justices are less likely to receive an opinion assignment because they tend to avoid potential criticism and express negativity toward other justices.
- The positive influence of prior issue experience on receiving a chief assignment is weaker for more-open justices because repeatedly authoring opinions on the same issues undermines intellectual engagement with different ideas. Additionally, more-open justices are less likely to receive an SAJ assignment because they tend to change their own views.
- The negative influence of a justice's ideological distance to the SAJ on receiving an SAJ assignment is stronger for more-conscientious SAJs because pursuing policy objectives violates their judicial duty.

Below I describe the empirical model I used to test these hypotheses. I then develop each hypothesis in more detail and report the results of the empirical tests.

The Opinion Assignment Models. In order to evaluate the role of personality traits in shaping the justices' opinion assignment behavior, I examine opinion assignments to the thirty-four justices serving during the 1946 through 2015 terms for whom SCIPEs are available.[18] The dependent variable is whether each justice in the majority coalition was assigned to write the majority opinion in each of the cases during this period (1 = assigned; 0 = not assigned).[19] Because unique institutional considerations likely influence assignment behavior by chief justices versus SAJs, I conduct separate analyses for each type of assignment.

The chief assignment model examines potential assignments to each justice in each of the 5,844 cases in which the chief assigned the majority opinion ($N = 41,598$). The model controls for several variables that capture potential influences on opinion assignment, including justice characteristics (the justices' ideological distance to the opinion assigner, the justices' issue experience, which is described in a following section, and indicators for chief justice and freshman justices), the winning vote margin, and the number of assignments each justice received from SAJs in that term (which the chief uses to promote assignment equity).[20] I also include the potential assignees' SCIPEs for the Big Five and the interaction terms described in later sections.

The SAJ assignment model examines potential assignments to each justice in each of the 1,093 cases in which the SAJ assigned the majority opinion ($N = 6,112$; the SAJ assignment model includes only thirty-two justices because Chief Justice Warren Earl Burger and Chief Justice John G. Roberts Jr. never served as associate justices and, therefore, could never be in the majority coalition when the SAJ assigned the majority opinion). The model controls for all of the variables in the chief assignment model except for the number of assignments each justice received from SAJs in that term. I also include the potential assignees' SCIPEs, the SAJ's SCIPEs, and the interaction term described in a later section. (See Appendix B for a full description of the chief assignment model and the SAJ assignment model.)

JUSTICE TRAITS AND OPINION ASSIGNMENTS

Figures 5.1(a) and (b) summarize the results of the opinion assignment models. The figures report the marginal effects of the justices' personality traits on the probability of receiving a majority opinion assignment from (a) the chief justice and (b) the SAJ, respectively, as well as the effects of all statistically significant control variables. As a point of reference, the average predicted probability of a justice receiving an opinion assignment is .14 when the chief justice assigns the opinion and .18 when the SAJ assigns the opinion. The probability of assignment varies depending on both institutional and ideological factors. For example, a justice receiving ten assignments from the SAJ in the same term is associated with a .04 decrease in the probability of that justice receiving an assignment from the chief.

As was the case with agenda setting, the magnitude of personality effects on majority opinion assignments rivals or exceeds that of several legal, institutional, and ideological influences on assignments. For example, the effects of a justice's extraversion (−.04), conscientious (+.06), neuroticism (−.03), and openness (−.02) on SAJ assignments are each comparable to or greater than the effect of the justice's ideological distance to the SAJ (−.03).[21] In other words, each of these individual personality traits explains as much variation in the justices' opinion assignments as their ideological preferences. Again, given the prominent role of ideology in explaining judicial behavior, this comparison is particularly noteworthy.

Extraversion and Opinion Assignments. When the chief justice assigns the majority opinion, one of his primary goals is to select a justice who will build consensus and unite the majority coalition. Accordingly, the chief should prefer assertive justices who are proficient at influencing their colleagues and, ultimately, persuading them to join the majority opinion. In contrast, chiefs should tend to avoid assigning the opinion to justices who are likely to have difficulty marshalling the Court, as Justice Murphy

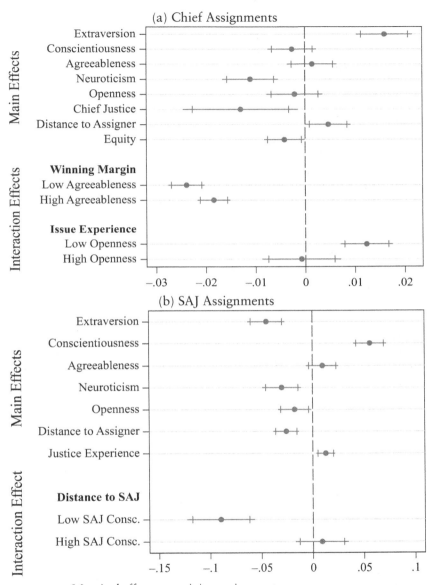

FIGURE 5.1 Marginal effects on opinion assignments

Note: Figure presents marginal effects of a one standard deviation increase in each continuous variable (and one-unit increase in each dichotomous variable) on the predicted probability of a justice receiving a majority opinion assignment from (a) the chief justice and (b) the SAJ with 95% confidence intervals. Predicted probabilities are based on multilevel logistic regression models with random intercepts for case. The full models are reported in Appendix B.

did in *Central Greyhound*. Moreover, because chiefs often prioritize the concerns of other justices, they should seek out justices who would enjoy the attention, social interaction, and potential influence inherent in writing the majority opinion and bargaining with other justices. Therefore, the chief justice should be more likely to assign the majority opinion to more extraverted justices (who value influence and attention).

Figure 5.1(a) illustrates the positive relationship between the justices' extraversion and their propensity to receive a majority opinion assignment from the chief. The probability of a justice receiving a chief assignment is .12 for less-extraverted justices and .15 for more-extraverted justices. Thus, despite the chiefs' general inclination towards equity, more-extraverted justices are 25 percent more likely to receive a chief assignment than less-extraverted justices, which presumably reflects the chief's preference for opinion authors who are more likely to unite the Court.

In contrast, SAJs tend to prioritize their own interests over institutional concerns. The same qualities that make extraverts skilled at uniting the Court (assertiveness, agency, and dominance) may also make them undesirable opinion authors in the eyes of the SAJ. Specifically, assertive opinion authors should be more likely to exert their own influence over the content of the majority opinion, possibly at the expense of the SAJ's preferences. In other words, if SAJs hope to maximize their own influence over opinion content, they should avoid assigning the opinion to justices who are likely to exert independent influence. Therefore, SAJs should be less likely to assign the majority opinion to more extraverted justices (who value influence).

Figure 5.1(b) illustrates the strong negative relationship between the justices' extraversion and their propensity to be assigned the majority opinion by the SAJ. The probability of a justice receiving an SAJ assignment is .22 for less-extraverted justices and .13 for more-extraverted justices. Thus, the former are 70 percent more likely to receive an SAJ assignment than the latter, which presumably reflects the SAJ's preference for authors who are less interested in influencing opinion content.

Conscientiousness and Opinion Assignments. On average, justices who are thorough, organized, and hardworking should be more likely to produce high-quality opinions that clearly and persuasively articulate the legal rules announced by the Court. Such clarity and persuasiveness in the majority opinion should reduce legal and academic criticism, mitigate the need for further litigation, and enhance the opinion's influence over lower-court outcomes. More-dutiful justices should also be less eager to pursue their own policy preferences at the expense of other justices in the majority coalition, which may smooth tensions on the Court and encourage consensus. Consequently, more-conscientious justices (who value industriousness and dutifulness) should be appealing candidates to author the Court's opinion for both chief justices and SAJs.

However, I find no evidence that justice conscientiousness is associated with opinion assignments from the chief justice (see Figure 5.1(a)).[22] A possible explanation for this null finding is that conscientious justices also possess several characteristics that make them undesirable opinion authors in the eyes of the chief. Conscientious justices tend to be thorough and detailed, so they may take longer to write opinions. Such delays would undermine one of the Court's most basic institutional goals: to keep up with its workload and produce opinions on a regular schedule. More-conscientious justices are also more likely to expend the effort necessary to find and highlight thorny complications (because they are industrious) and less likely to pressure other justices to abandon their own views for political expediency (because they are dutiful). Both of these characteristics may undermine their ability to form and maintain majority coalitions. Because chief justices have special interest in maintaining the Court's efficient productivity and uniting majority coalitions in order to enhance the Court's institutional legitimacy, assigning the opinion to more-conscientious justices may present both advantages and disadvantages. The lack of any relationship between conscientiousness and chief assignments suggests that the positives and negatives associated with conscientious opinion authors may balance out in the chief's mind.

In contrast, because SAJs tends to place less emphasis on these institutional goals, they may be willing to accept more delays and less unanimity in exchange for the thoroughness and clarity of opinions authored by more-conscientious justices. Consistent with that expectation, Figure 5.1(b) illustrates the strong positive relationship between justice conscientiousness and SAJ assignments. The probability of a justice receiving an SAJ assignment is .12 for less-conscientious justices and .22 for more-conscientious justices. Thus, the latter are nearly twice as likely as the former to receive an SAJ assignment, which presumably reflects the SAJ's preference for justices who will devote effort toward writing the opinion while adhering to their professional duties.

Agreeableness and Opinion Assignments. The relationship between agreeableness and opinion assignments is undoubtedly complicated. On the one hand, chiefs likely value social harmony and collegiality on the Court, and assigning the majority opinion to a justice that values these goals should tend to encourage cooperation, mutual respect, and a good working environment. On the other hand, the opinion author's most important task is to marshal a majority of the Court to support the Court's opinion, and this task may require activities that undermine social harmony, such as peer pressure, aggressive bargaining tactics, and interpersonal conflict. Therefore, I neither expect nor find any direct relationship between agreeableness and chief or SAJ assignments.

However, whether or not opinion assigners value social harmony may depend on the size of the majority coalition. In general, the odds of any one justice receiving the majority opinion is higher when the majority won by a narrow margin because there are fewer justices in the majority coalition. But in narrowly decided cases, the assigner is also unlikely to prioritize social harmony. Instead, the assigner may prefer a justice who is more willing to engage in aggressive negotiation tactics – even at the expense of collegiality – in order to secure a majority. In contrast, when the majority coalition is larger, the assigner can select a pleasant and collegial opinion author, confident in the knowledge that the majority coalition is secure. Therefore, the negative influence of the winning margin on opinion assignments should be stronger for more-agreeable justices (who value social harmony). Following Forrest Maltzman and Paul J. Wahlbeck, I calculate the winning margin by subtracting the number of votes needed to form a winning coalition (usually five) from the number of justices in the majority.[23] Thus, when all nine justices participate, the winning margin is zero in five-to-four decisions and four in unanimous decisions.

Figure 5.2 illustrates the relationship between the winning margin and the propensity of justices with different levels of agreeableness to receive chief assignments. The upper panel presents the predicted probability of justices receiving a chief assignment in cases with a winning margin of zero versus four. The lower panel presents the effect of the winning margin increasing by four on a justice's propensity to receive a chief assignment. For more-agreeable justices, the winning margin increasing by four is associated with a .07 decrease in the probability of a chief assignment (from .19 to .11). However, for less-agreeable justices, the effect of winning margin increasing by four is a .11 decrease (from .21 to .10). Stated another way, chiefs prefer to assign more-agreeable justices in cases with large winning majorities and disagreeable justices in cases with narrow margins of victory.[24] These results suggest that agreeable justices tend to promote social harmony, but this characteristic hinders their ability to marshal the Court.

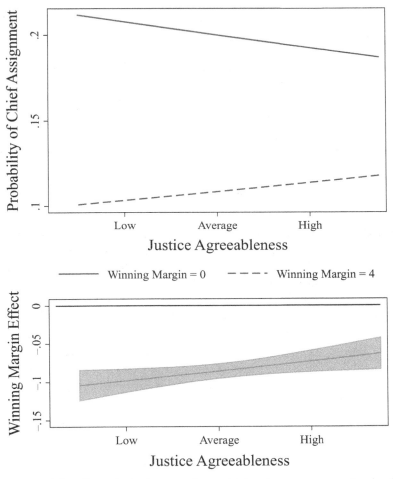

FIGURE 5.2 The effect of winning margin on chief assignments at varying levels of justice agreeableness

Note: The upper panel presents the predicted probability of a justice receiving a majority opinion assignment from the chief justice when the winning margin is zero versus four. The lower panel presents the marginal effects of the winning margin increasing by four with 95% confidence intervals. Predicted probabilities and marginal effects are based on a multilevel logistic regression model with random intercepts for case. The full model is reported in Appendix B.

I also test the interaction between justice agreeableness and the winning margin in the SAJ assignment model. However, I find no evidence for this conditional effect when SAJs assign the opinion.

Neuroticism and Opinion Assignments. Authoring the majority opinion can be a stressful task because it often involves substantial risks, such as criticism from other justices, lower-court judges, academics, the media, and the public. Therefore, justices who have difficulty handling these risks should prefer to avoid majority opinion assignments, and chief justices likely honor those preferences in order to maintain a good working environment. Moreover, the author of the majority opinion often repeatedly interacts with other justices in order to resolve any differences of opinion, and the other justices likely prefer to minimize interactions with more anxious, hostile, and negative colleagues. Accordingly, both chiefs and SAJs should avoid assigning opinions to justices who tend to express negativity. Therefore, both chief justices and SAJs should be less likely to assign the majority opinion to more-neurotic justices (who value loss avoidance and negativity expression).

Figure 5.1(a) illustrates the negative relationship between neuroticism and chief assignments. The probability of a justice receiving a chief assignment is .15 for less-neurotic justices and .13 for more-neurotic justices. Thus, less-neurotic justices are 13 percent less likely to receive a chief assignment than are more-neurotic justices, which presumably reflects the chief's preference for opinion authors who enjoy opinion assignments and are easier to work with.

Figure 5.1(b) illustrates the negative relationship between justice neuroticism and SAJ assignments. The probability of a justice receiving an SAJ assignment is .21 for less-neurotic justices and .15 for more-neurotic justices. Thus, the latter are almost one-third less likely to receive an SAJ assignment than are the former, which presumably reflects the SAJ's preference for opinion authors who are easier to work with and less volatile.

Openness and Opinion Assignments. Chief justices and SAJs likely have different views on the value of openness for opinion authors. If chiefs try to accommodate the preferences of other justices, they may consider their colleagues' preference for intellectual engagement when making opinion assignments. Justices who enjoy intellectually engaging with different ideas likely prefer greater variety in opinion assignments, but more assignments does not necessarily mean more variety. Accordingly, I neither expect nor find a direct relationship between openness and chief assignments (see Figure 5.1).

On average, chiefs encourage justices to specialize by repeatedly assigning them to write majority opinions on the same legal issues.[25] Such assignments may enhance the overall quality of the Court's opinions by encouraging justices to develop particular areas of expertise and then apply that expertise to new situations. Accordingly, chiefs should tend to assign opinions to justices with more experience writing on the legal issue before the Court. Following Maltzman and Wahlbeck, I assess issue experience by calculating the number of majority opinions each justice wrote on the same issue in prior terms.[26] As expected, a justice previously writing four majority opinions on the same issue as the current case is associated with a .012 increase in the probability of that justice receiving the opinion assignment from the chief.

However, the degree to which justices want to write opinions on the same legal issues likely varies across justices. Justices who value consistency and stability may especially enjoy thinking and writing about the same topics, or they may want to develop a reputation for expertise in certain areas. In contrast, justices who value intellectual engagement with different ideas and variety in their work should prefer to avoid repetitious assignments. And, as discussed above, chiefs often prioritize other justices' concerns in order to promote a good working environment. Therefore, the positive influence of issue experience on chief assignments should be weaker for more-open justices (who value intellectual engagement with different ideas and change).

Figure 5.3 illustrates the relationship between issue experience and the propensity of justices with different levels of openness to receive chief assignments. The upper panel presents the predicted probability of receiving a chief assignment for justices who previously wrote zero versus four majority opinions on the same issue. The lower panel presents this effect of issue experience on the probability of a chief assignment. For less-open justices, each prior majority opinion written by the justice on the same issue is associated with a .005 increase in the probability of a chief assignment. Thus, the probability of a justice who previously wrote four opinions on the same issue receiving a chief assignment is .02 greater than the probability for a justice who has never written a majority opinion on that issue; for justices who previously wrote eight opinions on the same issue, the probability of assignment increases by .04. However, for more-open justices, issue experience is not associated with chief assignments. In fact, at the highest levels of openness, issue experience may be negatively associated with chief assignments, suggesting that chiefs avoid

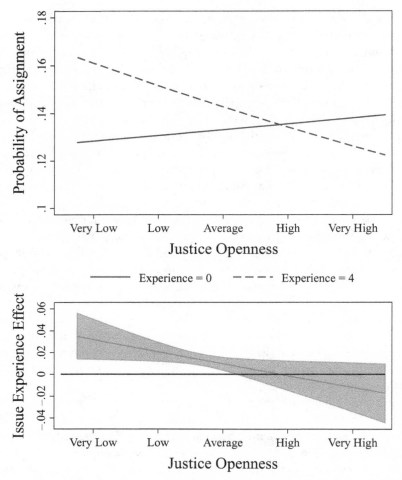

FIGURE 5.3 The effect of issue experience on chief assignments at varying levels of justice openness

Note: The upper panel presents the predicted probability of a justice receiving a majority opinion assignment from the chief justice for justices who previously wrote zero versus four majority opinions on the same issue in prior terms (issue experience). The lower panel presents the marginal effects of issue experience with 95% confidence intervals. Predicted probabilities and marginal effects are based on a multilevel logistic regression model with random intercepts for case. The full model is reported in Appendix B.

giving repetitious assignments to more-open justices, presumably because those justices value intellectual engagement with different ideas.

In contrast, for SAJs, the role of the justices' openness should be much simpler. Rather than emphasizing institutional concerns or the preferences of other justices, SAJs likely strive to assign the majority opinion in a manner that best serves their own interests. Consequently, SAJs should prefer to assign the opinion to justices who are less creative and more predictable in their thinking. Less-open justices are less likely to explore alternative polices, engage in (potentially persuasive) dialogue with their colleagues, change their preferences, or do something unexpected during the drafting and bargaining process. All of these qualities make less-open justices appealing candidates to SAJs in search of potential authors who will predictably write an opinion reflecting the SAJ's preferences. Therefore, the SAJ should be less likely to assign the majority opinion to more-open justices (who value intellectualism and change).

Figure 5.1(b) illustrates the negative relationship between justice openness and SAJ assignments. The probability of a justice receiving an SAJ assignment is .19 for less-open justices and .16 for more-open justices. Thus, more-open justices are about 15 percent less likely to receive an SAJ assignment than those who are less open, which presumably reflects the SAJ's preference for opinion authors who are more predictable and less likely to change their views.

SAJ Consciousness and SAJ Assignments. To this point, I have focused on the personality traits of those justices potentially receiving assignments from the chief justice or the SAJ. Because there are only four chief justices in the dataset, it is not possible to assess the influence of the chief's traits on assignment behavior. However, sixteen associate justices in the data assigned the opinion of the Court as the SAJ in at least one case, which facilitates an analysis of the SAJ's personality traits and their effects on assignments. Specifically, I examine the role of the SAJ's preference for dutifulness in shaping assignment behavior.

When making opinion assignments, chief justices usually prioritize the Court's institutional interests rather than their own policy preferences. In fact, chiefs tend to assign the opinion to ideologically distant justices, perhaps in an effort to preserve the majority coalition by satisfying the potential swing justice. SAJs are also expected to protect the Court's institutional interests; however, SAJs often prioritize their own policy preferences by assigning the majority opinion to an ideologically proximate justice (including assignments to themselves).[27] I assess the SAJ's ideological agreement with other justices using Segal–Cover ideology scores.[28] Segal–Cover scores are based on ideological descriptions of the justices in newspaper editorials after their nomination to the Court and before their confirmation. Justices who were frequently described as conservative in these editorials receive higher scores; those who were frequently described as liberal receive lower scores. Of critical importance, Segal–Cover scores are exogenous measures of the justices' ideological preferences because they are not based on the justices' merits votes.[29] I measure each justice's ideological distance to the SAJ by calculating the absolute difference between the Segal–Cover scores for each potential assignee and the SAJ. I then use this measure to test the influence of ideology on SAJ assignments.

As expected, SAJs do tend to assign majority opinions to their ideological allies. On average, increasing from low to high ideological distance to the SAJ (i.e., one standard deviation below to one standard deviation above the mean) is associated with a .06 decrease in the probability of that justice receiving the assignment (from .22 to .16). However, the SAJ's propensity to pursue his or her policy goals via opinion assignments should depend on the SAJ's personality. SAJs who value dutifulness should resist the temptation to pursue their own policy objectives and, consequently, refrain from assigning the majority opinion to their ideological allies. Therefore, the negative influence of a potential assignee's ideological distance to the SAJ on SAJ assignments should be weaker for more conscientious SAJs (who value dutifulness).

Figure 5.4 illustrates the relationship between a justice's ideological distance to the SAJ and the justice's propensity to receive an SAJ assignment at different levels of the SAJ's conscientiousness. The upper panel presents the predicted probability of a justice with low versus high ideological distance to the SAJ receiving an SAJ assignment. The lower panel presents the effect of distance to the SAJ on a justice's propensity to receive an SAJ assignment. For less-conscientious SAJs, increasing from low to high ideological distance to a potential assignee is associated with a .18 decrease in the probability of assigning the opinion to that justice (from .31 to .13). However, for more-conscientious justices, the effect of ideological distance to the SAJ is statistically indistinguishable from zero. In fact, the most-conscientious justices may actually tend to assign more ideologically distant justices, just as chief justices do.

In short, the influence of ideology on the SAJ's assignment behavior depends on the SAJ's conscientiousness. Less-conscientious SAJs appear to consider ideology when making majority opinion assignments despite legal norms discouraging such practices. In contrast, more conscientious SAJs (who value dutifulness) do not appear to favor their ideological allies with more assignments.

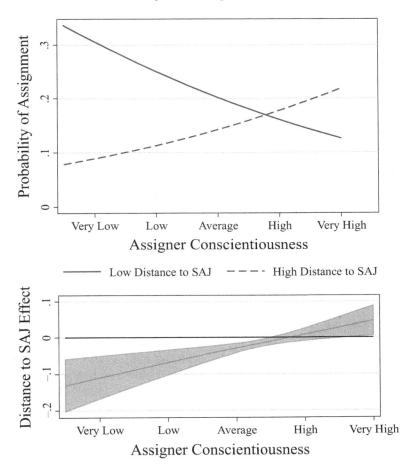

FIGURE 5.4 The effect of ideological distance to the SAJ on SAJ assignments at varying levels of SAJ conscientiousness

Note: The upper panel presents the predicted probability of a justice receiving a majority opinion assignment from the SAJ at low versus high levels of the justice's ideological distance to the SAJ (i.e., one standard deviation below versus above the mean). The lower panel presents the marginal effects of ideological distance to the SAJ with 95% confidence intervals. Predicted probabilities and marginal effects are based on a multilevel logistic regression model with random intercepts for case. The full model is reported in Appendix B.

PERSONALITY AND OPINION ASSIGNMENTS

To summarize, the justices' personality traits have a strong and direct association with the assignment of the majority opinion, but the influence of these traits varies depending on who assigns the opinion. When chief justices are in the majority and, therefore, control the assignment, they tend to prioritize the Court's institutional interests, such as an equitable distribution of assignments, unity in the majority coalition, and the preferences of other justices. These priorities prompt chiefs to select justices who are more extraverted and less neuritic (though, somewhat surprisingly, not justices who are more conscientious).

The justices' personality traits also condition the influence of other factors on whether the chief assigns them to write the majority opinion. In general, the probability of receiving a majority opinion assignment is lower when the winning vote margin is larger because there are more justices in the majority coalition to potentially receive the assignment. However, agreeableness conditions the influence of the winning margin on the probability of chief assignments: A narrow margin of victory has a smaller positive effect on assignments for more agreeable justices, presumably because these justices will have difficulty preserving the fragile majority coalition.

Additionally, chiefs tend to assign majority opinions to justices with more experience writing on the same legal issue. However, the effect of issue experience on assignments also varies among the justices: Chiefs only encourage specialization by less-open justices, suggesting that chiefs prefer the development of issue expertise so long as the justices enjoy repeated assignments on the same topic. However, chiefs appear to neglect this priority with regard to more-open justices who value intellectual engagement with different ideas.

Senior associate justices do not place as much emphasis on the Court's institutional interests when assigning the majority opinion. Instead, SAJs tend to prioritize their own interests by encouraging the production of high-quality opinions that will predictably reflect their own views of the case while minimizing negative interactions and the influence of other justices over opinion content. Consequently, SAJs tend to assign the majority opinion to justices who are less extraverted, more conscientious, less neurotic, and less open.

Finally, the SAJ's conscientiousness also conditions the influence of ideological considerations on SAJ assignments. On average, SAJs tend to assign the majority opinion to ideological allies in order to advance their own preferences. However, the SAJ's propensity to favor ideological allies depends on his or her own personality. Less-conscientious SAJs are highly prone to assign the opinion to ideologically proximate justices; in contrast, more-conscientious SAJs appear to prioritize their judicial duty by disregarding the ideology of potential assignees.

At the beginning of this chapter, I described Justice Murphy's failure to preserve the majority coalition in *Central Greyhound* as an example of a justice's personality traits influencing his effectiveness as an opinion author (specifically, Murphy's low extraversion made him less effective at marshalling the Court). The empirical findings in this chapter suggest that Murphy's failure (and the characteristics that prompted it) did not go unnoticed by his colleagues, nor were they likely to forget the incident when making opinion assignments in the future. Indeed, the justices' personality traits appear to strongly influence the opinion assignments they receive in several different ways. Accordingly, the justices' personalities may ultimately play a crucial role in determining which justice crafts the Court's majority opinion.

6

Intra-Court Bargaining

When Warren Earl Burger was appointed chief justice in 1969, he had big shoes to fill. Burger's predecessor, Earl Warren (the similarity in names was a coincidence), had earned a prominent reputation for leadership and integrity during his sixteen years on the bench. Dubbed "the super chief" by Justice William J. Brennan Jr., Warren's prestige extended back to the Court's unanimous ruling in *Brown v. Board of Education* during his first term.[1] Burger was eager to achieve a similar accomplishment early in his tenure. The new chief was known for vanity ("he placed a large cushion on his center seat on the bench, so that he would appear taller than his colleagues"),[2] and he cared a great deal about his public image (he was "deeply hurt by derogatory accounts about his performance" and "always sensitive to what he perceived to be slights to his office and to himself").[3] Accordingly, the new chief justice hoped to craft a landmark decision that would earn him the sort of clout and prestige that Warren had attained from *Brown*.

Burger saw his opportunity in another school desegregation case that reached the Court during his second term: *Swann v. Charlotte-Mecklenburg Board of Education*.[4] In the Spring of 1970, US District Court Judge James McMillan ordered total desegregation in each of the public schools in Charlotte, North Carolina, and the surrounding Mecklenburg County. McMillan's order demanded a "racial balance" in each school: Because the district was 71 percent white and 29 percent black, each school was required to strive for that ratio of students. Although McMillan admitted that "variations from the norm may be unavoidable," his drastic ruling ordered busing for thirteen thousand additional students, which often involved young students spending more than an hour on the bus each day.[5]

Burger felt McMillan's order went well beyond the desegregation ruling in *Brown*, which only required the end of separate schools for blacks and whites; instead, McMillan's ruling amounted to forced racial mixing – judicially mandated integration as opposed to desegregation. Such an order, in Burger's view, had no legal basis.[6] He believed the Supreme Court should set limits on how far district court judges could go in ordering desegregation, particularly with regard to busing.

Moreover, because the busing issue had become increasingly controversial in recent years, Burger wanted to issue a unanimous ruling. Unanimity was a tradition in segregation cases going back to *Brown*, and securing a unanimous decision would be a crucial test of his leadership on the Court.[7] To help promote unanimity, Burger proposed special rules for the Court's conference discussion in *Swann*: The justices would adopt an extra measure of confidentiality to encourage candor, and they would not take a preliminary vote to discourage entrenchment in divergent views.[8]

Though they took no formal vote, at the end of the conference, Justice William O. Douglas believed that the Court had split 7–2: Seven justices supported broad remedial powers for federal judges in desegregation cases (five favored McMillan's order itself); only two justices – Burger and Justice Hugo L. Black – firmly opposed the busing order. But Burger seized the initiative and claimed that there was no five-justice majority for any one approach. Therefore, the chief announced that he would assign himself as the majority opinion author and draft an opinion attempting to reconcile the justices' views.[9]

Burger's tactic frustrated Douglas. As the senior justice in the majority (at least by his own count), Douglas believed it was his privilege to assign the majority opinion.[10] Moreover, Burger's aggressive use of opinion assignments was not an uncommon strategy for the new chief. "Burger repeatedly irked his colleagues by changing his vote to remain in the majority ..."[11] Even Justice Harry A. Blackmun (who was best man at Burger's wedding) "had long thought Burger an uncontrollable, blustery braggart" who often attempted to "manipulate the Court."[12] But Burger was eager to assert himself and rally the Court behind a unanimous opinion that limited the power of federal judges to order busing. He knew "the important thing would be the wording."[13] So he took the opinion for himself.

On December 8, 1970, Burger circulated his first draft in *Swann*. The Court's reaction was not positive. Justice Potter Stewart considered it an "appalling effort" because it sharply criticized McMillan's order and seemed to limit lower courts' discretion in correcting constitutional wrongs;[14] he told his clerk the opinion was "disorganized and stupid."[15] Justice Brennan felt the chief had "insulted the intelligence of the conference" by trying to "frustrate the will of the majority."[16] Justices Douglas, Thurgood Marshall, and Byron R. White shared similar concerns.

In response, Stewart circulated a memorandum suggesting substantial changes to Burger's draft. On January 11, 1971, Burger circulated a second draft, supposedly addressing Stewart's concerns.[17] But the new draft was "a major disappointment to Stewart" and "incorporated little of the material in Stewart's memo."[18] Douglas, Brennan, and Marshall met with Stewart and urged him to make his memo a counter opinion that could rally their support along with Justice White's, and possibly Justices Blackmun and Harlan's. But Stewart insisted that his goal was to unite the Court: "He did not want to be the leader, or even a member, of any faction."[19] However, under pressure from the others, he agreed to negotiate with the chief. In the discussions with Stewart, Burger used Justice Black for leverage. Black had spurned the negotiation process and refused to sign an opinion that approved of busing to achieve racial balance; Burger insisted that he could not alter the opinion without losing Black. Nonetheless, Stewart insisted on revisions to the draft, and Justice Brennan circulated a memo urging specific changes to the opinion.

On March 4, Burger circulated a third draft. Stewart joined the chief's new draft, but the other justices were still not satisfied. On March 11, Justices Brennan and Harlan both circulated lengthy memos suggesting additional changes. On March 16, Burger responded by circulating a fourth "provisional" draft.[20] The same day, Douglas circulated a draft dissent, and Brennan later responded with still more suggestions. On March 22, Burger tried for a fifth time, explaining to his colleagues, "I have made substantial changes and now circulate what I trust is the final draft of the *Swann* opinion."[21] Justice Marshall called the fifth draft "mighty close," but he and Brennan both asked for more changes.[22]

Finally, the chief circulated a sixth draft on April 8. The final draft included greater remedial powers for district court judges – a victory for the liberal wing – but the opinion also allowed "a small number of one-race schools" and discouraged busing for younger school children.[23] Through his aggressive negotiating and multiple opinion drafts, Burger was able to push his preferences almost to the breaking point. The result was an opinion filled with internal inconsistencies: "There is a lot of conflicting language here," complained a judge from the Fifth Circuit. "It's almost as if there were two sets of views, laid side by side."[24] Regardless of the ambiguity, Burger had succeeded in pulling the conference together and bending the opinion toward his own preferences. Ironically, though, the new chief received little recognition for his efforts: A news article, citing inside sources, reported that the opinion had been pieced together by the other justices. Burger was furious.[25]

⌁

After a justice is assigned to write the opinion of the Court, that justice's clerks usually write the first draft of the Court's opinion based on instructions from the justice. The justice then revises the opinion and circulates the draft among members of the Court. Other justices can respond in a variety of ways. Some members of the majority simply indicate they will join the Court's opinion or offer minor suggestions. But some justices actively try to alter the opinion's content in substantial ways through persuasion or negotiation. Dissatisfied members of the majority usually respond to the opinion draft by sending a memorandum to the opinion author. They may even consider (or threaten) other options, such as writing a separate opinion or joining the dissenters. The opinion author must then decide how to respond.

This intra-Court bargaining process is critically important because the Court's opinion sets binding precedent for lower courts and future Supreme Court cases. The author of the Court's opinion sometimes makes substantial changes to the opinion draft in order to satisfy other justices and maintain a majority coalition. In some cases, members of the majority refuse to sign the majority opinion or (more rarely) actually change their vote as a result of the bargaining process. Even if the justices do not dissent, the Court's opinion does not set binding precedent unless it is joined by five justices. Therefore, the bargaining process has important implications for the future application of the law.

Justices also bargain over the content of separate opinions, especially dissenting opinions. Although these separate opinions do not set legal precedent, support for a separate opinion by multiple justices may reinforce the opinion's impact and garner more attention to the minority's view. However, just as members of the majority sometimes disagree over opinion content, members of minority factions must also negotiate over the content of their separate opinions.

Justices are rarely, if ever, truly required to circulate a memo, but they are also not limited in the number they can send. During the 1969 through

1985 terms, each justice circulated an average of 2.25 memos in each case, and the Court heard an average of 132 cases per term. Thus, each justice circulated about 300 memos each term. However, the justices vary widely in the number of memos they write. For example, during the 1969 term, Justice Marshall circulated only 160 memos; in contrast, during the 1971 term, Justice Douglas circulated more than 550 memos.

BARGAINING MEMOS

Justices circulate bargaining memos for a variety of reasons. First, and most obviously, the author of the Court's opinion must circulate an opinion draft in order to attract support from other justices. Majority opinion authors almost always circulate at least one draft opinion,[26] and they often circulate multiple drafts in order to build a majority coalition. On average, opinion authors circulate 2.83 opinion drafts in each case. However, opinion authors vary substantially in the number of subsequent drafts they circulate depending on various aspects of the justice and the case. For example, Justice Douglas circulated an average of 3.8 drafts when he was assigned to write the majority opinion. In contrast, Justice Blackman circulated an average of only 2.3 drafts as a majority opinion author.

Perhaps the most aggressive response a justice can offer to a majority opinion draft is to circulate a draft of a potential separate opinion (i.e., a concurring or dissenting opinion). Each justice circulates an average of .44 separate opinion drafts in each case. A justice may circulate a separate opinion draft for a variety of reasons. A justice may hope to intellectually engage with other justices by proposing alternative views of the case or to use a draft as a bargaining tactic in the hopes of altering the content of the majority opinion. In very rare circumstances, a justice may even try to supplant the majority opinion with the alternative draft. As such, separate opinion drafts often reflect an effort to influence the content of the majority opinion. Therefore, those justices who disagree with the majority opinion author and hope to exert influence over the opinion should be more likely to employ this tactic. Moreover, because drafting a separate opinion requires considerable time and energy, doing so is likely influenced by time pressures on the justices, such as the caseload and the number of days left in the term.

Justices may also respond to a majority opinion draft by making suggestions regarding the opinion's content. Such memos take several different forms, such as expressing general disagreement, suggesting specific changes, endorsing or disagreeing with another justice's suggestion, or stating conditions under which the justice will join the opinion, not join the opinion, or file a separate opinion. Although these memos vary substantially in form, they have several things in common: Opinion suggestions generally critique another justice's draft opinion without asserting an active leadership role or exposing the memo's author to potential criticism. On average, each justice circulates .24 opinion suggestions in each case. However, justices who are more likely to disagree with the opinion author likely circulate more of these memos. And, because writing opinion suggestions requires some effort, their circulation should also be influenced by time pressures.

Another common response to a draft majority opinion is a wait statement. A wait statement is a memo indicating that a justice is not yet ready to commit to a particular view because the justice is waiting to see a draft opinion, to hear other justices' views, to see developments in other cases, or to simply consider the matter further. On average, each justice circulates .08 wait statements in each case. Because wait statements inherently cause delay, they tend to frustrate other members of the Court. Yet, justices might circulate a wait statement for a variety of reasons, such as a desire to gain more information, consider strategic options, or buy time before making a decision. Therefore, the opinion author's ideological adversaries should also be more likely to engage in such tactics.

Finally, the most common, least effortful, and least risky response to an opinion draft is a join statement. Join statements express support for the content of an opinion draft by indicating that the justice sending the statement will join the opinion. On average, each justice circulates .92 join statements in each case. The vast majority of join statements express support for the majority opinion, which is especially important because majority opinions must be joined by at least five justices (the author and four others) to attain majority status and carry precedential value. Accordingly, the opinion author's ideological adversaries should be less likely to circulate join statements.

A variety of factors influence a justice's propensity to write bargaining memos, including justice characteristics, case characteristics, and time pressures. However, given the individual variation in justices' propensity to circulate memos, a justice's personality should also influence bargaining behavior.

Bargaining Hypotheses. The psychoeconomic approach posits that the justices' personality traits influence the circulation of bargaining memos.

Specifically, I propose the following hypotheses related to bargaining memos:

- More-extraverted justices circulate more majority opinion drafts, separate opinion drafts, and opinion suggestions because these memos influence other justices and attract attention from internal judicial audiences (i.e., clerks and other justices).
- More-conscientious justices circulate more separate opinion drafts and opinion suggestions because these memos require substantial effort and fulfill their judicial duty to express honest disagreement. Additionally, the influence of ideological preferences on circulating separate opinion drafts, opinion suggestions, wait statements, and join statements is weaker for more-conscientious justices because pursuing policy objectives violates their judicial duty.
- More-agreeable justices circulate fewer separate opinion drafts and wait statements, as well as more join statements, because separate opinion drafts and wait statements undermine social harmony on the Court, whereas join statements promote social harmony on the Court.
- More-neurotic justices circulate more join statements and wait statements, because wait statements and join statements avoid potential criticism. Additionally, more-neurotic justices circulate more opinion suggestions because opinion suggestions express negativity toward other justices.
- More-open justices circulate more majority opinion drafts, separate opinion drafts, and opinion suggestions because these memos reflect a willingness to intellectually engage with different ideas and change their own views. More-open justices also circulate fewer wait statements and join statements because these memos reflect an unwillingness to intellectually engage with different ideas and change one's own views.

Below I describe the empirical models I used to test these hypotheses. I then develop each hypothesis in more detail and report the findings of the empirical tests.

The Bargaining Models. In order to examine the role of personality traits in shaping the justices' behavior during the bargaining process, I employ data from the Burger Court Opinion Writing Database, which includes information on the 48,524 memoranda that were circulated by the thirteen justices who served on the Supreme Court during the 1969 through 1985 terms.[27] Specifically, I examine the number of majority opinion drafts, separate opinion drafts, opinion suggestions, wait statements, and join statements circulated by each justice in each

TABLE 6.1 *Bargaining statistics*

	Mean (1)	S.D.	Min	Max
Majority Opinion Drafts	2.83	1.31	0	9
Separate Opinion Drafts	0.44	1.04	0	12
Opinion Suggestions	0.24	0.60	0	13
Wait Statement	0.08	0.27	0	3
Join Statements	0.92	0.55	0	5
Observations	19,438			

Note: Table reports the mean, standard deviation, minimum, and maximum for the number of each type of bargaining memo circulated by each justice in each case. Majority opinion draft statistics are reported only for majority opinion authors; all other statistics are reported only for justices who did not author the majority opinion.

case.[28] Descriptive statistics are presented in Table 6.1. (See Appendix C for a full description of the bargaining models.)

First, I examine the number of majority opinion drafts circulated by the majority opinion author in each case during this time period ($N = 2,144$). Next, I examine the number of separate opinion drafts, opinion suggestions, wait statements, and join statements sent by any justice other than the majority opinion author in each case in four separate models ($N = 16,107$). Because the dependent variable in each model is the number of drafts sent by each justice in each case, I use regression models appropriate for count data.[29]

Each model includes several control variables that capture potential influences on memo circulation, including justice characteristics (indicators for the chief justice and freshman justices), case characteristics (the term-standardized number of amicus briefs filed, case complexity, the winning vote margin, and indicators for issue area), and time pressures (the Court's caseload, the number of days until the end of the term, and a time trend.)[30] Most importantly, the model includes the justices' SCIPEs for the Big Five (standardized within this sample of justices). Every model except the majority opinion drafts model also includes the ideological distance between each justice and the majority opinion author.

JUSTICE TRAITS AND BARGAINING MEMOS

Figures 6.1(a–e) summarize the results of the bargaining assignment models. The figures report the marginal effects of the justices' personality traits on the predicted number of each type of bargaining memo circulated by each justice as well as the effects of all statistically significant control variables. The models confirm most of my expectations regarding control variables, such as ideological distance to the opinion author and various time pressures. However, the magnitude of the personality effects rivals or exceeds that of ideological and institutional influences on bargaining behavior. For example, the effects of a justice's extraversion (+.08), conscientiousness (+.10), agreeableness (−.08), and openness (+.14) on circulating separate opinion drafts are each greater in magnitude than the effect of the justice's ideological distance to the majority opinion author (+.06). In other words, each of these personality traits explains more variation in the justices' bargaining behavior than do their ideological preferences.[31] Again, this comparison to ideology is particularly noteworthy given the prominence of ideological explanations for judicial behavior. **Extraversion and Bargaining Memos.** For the justice assigned to write the majority opinion, circulating majority opinion drafts is a valuable opportunity to marshal the Court's attention and emphasize the legal and policy issues of special concern to the opinion author. By circulating subsequent revised drafts, the majority opinion author may be able to press his or her views and secure a larger majority in support of the Court's ruling (as Burger did in *Swann*). The circulation of a draft opinion also tends to attract attention and prompt responses from other justices and encourage additional interactions regarding the content of the new draft. Those justices who place greater value on influencing and attracting attention from their fellow justices should be more likely to exploit this opportunity. Therefore, more extraverted majority opinion authors (who value influence and attention) should tend to circulate more opinion drafts.

Figure 6.1(a) illustrates the positive relationship between the justices' extraversion and the number of majority opinion drafts circulated in each case in which the justice was assigned to write the majority opinion. The average number of majority opinion drafts circulated in each case is 2.6 for less-extraverted opinion authors and 3.3 for more-extraverted authors. Therefore, more-extraverted majority opinion authors circulate about 25 percent more opinion drafts than less-extraverted authors, which presumably reflects their propensity to influence opinion content and attract attention from their colleagues.

For those justices who were not assigned to write the majority opinion, the most effective way to influence the Court's opinion and attract attention is to circulate a separate opinion draft. By drafting a separate opinion, a justice clearly signals that he or she has objections to the majority

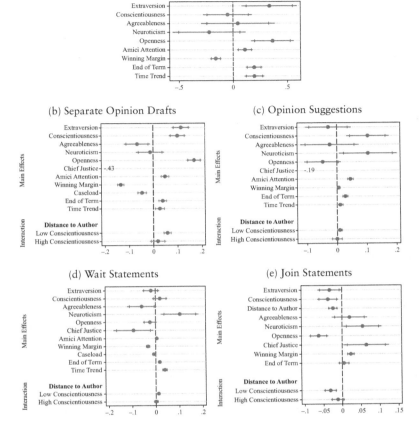

FIGURE 6.1 Marginal effects on bargaining memos

Note: Figure presents marginal effects of a one standard deviation increase in each continuous variable (and one-unit increase in each dichotomous variable) on the predicted number of (a) majority opinion drafts, (b) separate opinion drafts, (c) opinion suggestions, (d) wait statements, and (e) join statements with 95% confidence intervals. Predicted counts are based on a series of count models. The full models are reported in Appendix C.

opinion and may be willing to express those objections in public. Moreover, by circulating an opinion draft, the justice conveys important information about the probability of voicing such disagreement – specifically, that the justice has already devoted the time and energy necessary to think through the issues and write a separate opinion. In contrast, a memo merely suggesting the possibility of writing a separate opinion is undoubtedly a less credible and thus less persuasive threat. Separate opinion drafts also tend to attract attention from other justices, and the justices who write them sometimes take on a leadership role by organizing a faction of justices behind a particular view. Therefore, more-extraverted justices (who value influence and attention) should tend to circulate more separate opinion drafts.

Figure 6.1(b) illustrates the positive relationship between the justices' extraversion and the number of separate opinion drafts circulated in each case. The average number of separate opinion drafts circulated in each case is .38 for less-extraverted justices and .65 for more-extraverted justices. Therefore, the latter circulate 70 percent more separate opinion drafts than the former, which again presumably reflects their propensity to influence opinion content and attract attention from their colleagues.

As just described, opinion suggestions tend to be less credible threats than actually drafting a separate opinion and therefore involve fewer consequences for intra-Court negotiations. Thus, opinion suggestions tend to exert less influence and attract less attention than separate opinion drafts. Nonetheless, opinion suggestions are undoubtedly intended to influence other justices and usually attract the attention of the justices to whom they are directed. Therefore, more-extraverted justices (who value influence and attention) should also tend to circulate more opinion suggestions. However, as illustrated in Figure 6.1(c), I find no association between extraversion and opinion suggestions, indicating that separate opinion drafts represent a more preferable option for those who wish to exert influence and attract attention.

Wait statements may reflect a disinterest in influencing the Court's ruling or attracting attention, or they may reflect careful strategic planning in an effort to exert influence over other justices (and consequently attract a great deal of attention). Therefore, I neither expect nor find any relationship between extraversion and wait statements. Similarly, join statements may reflect a quick capitulation to an opinion author or an agreement to join an opinion after a series of aggressive negotiations. Therefore, I also neither expect nor find an association between extraversion and join statements.

Conscientiousness and Bargaining Memos. One might think that conscientious justices should tend to circulate more majority and separate opinion drafts. However, the circulation of majority versus separate opinion drafts is very different. Virtually every justice assigned to author the majority opinion must circulate at least one draft. Therefore, all variation in majority opinion drafts is driven by opinion authors circulating subsequent drafts. Conscientious justices should be more willing to exert the effort required to circulate multiple drafts; however, their careful, organized, and efficient natures should also improve the quality of their initial drafts and consequently minimize the need for subsequent drafts. That is, conscientious majority opinion authors should be more willing to circulate multiple drafts, but they should also have less need to do so, and these two inclinations should tend to cancel each other out. Accordingly, I neither expect nor find any association between conscientiousness and the circulation of multiple majority opinion drafts.

In contrast, separate opinion drafts are never mandatory. Therefore, even if more-conscientious justices do a perfect job on their initial draft (and thus have little need for subsequent drafts), they should still be more likely than less-conscientious justices to circulate an initial separate opinion draft. Specifically, researching and writing a separate opinion draft requires considerable effort, and expending such effort is completely optional (unlike writing an initial majority opinion draft). Additionally, circulating a separate opinion draft may prompt responses from other justices, and the draft author may feel compelled to expend additional time and energy reading the other justices' comments, writing memos in response to those comments, and revising the separate opinion. Moreover, justices who feel a professional duty to engage with their brethren by expressing honest disagreement may do so by circulating a separate opinion draft. Therefore, more-conscientious justices (who value industriousness and dutifulness) should tend to circulate more separate opinion drafts.

Figure 6.1(b) illustrates the positive relationship between justice conscientiousness and separate opinion drafts. The average number of separate opinion drafts circulated per case is .38 for less-conscientious justices and .58 for more-conscientious justices. Therefore, more-conscientious justices circulate about 50 percent more separate opinion drafts than less-conscientious justices, which presumably reflects their propensity to expend effort and fulfill their judicial duty to express honest disagreement.

Although a single justice usually drafts the Court's majority opinion, every justice has a professional obligation to ensure that the Court produces high-quality majority opinions. Therefore, every justice is expected to carefully research the legal issues at stake in each case, read the opinion drafts circulated by other justices (especially the majority opinion), and circulate memos expressing honest disagreement with suggestions to improve the other justices' drafts. Of course, fulfilling this professional duty requires substantial time and energy, and some justices may prefer to shirk these responsibilities rather than devote the required effort. Therefore, more-conscientious justices (who value industriousness and dutifulness) should tend to circulate more opinion suggestions.

Figure 6.1(c) illustrates the strong positive relationship between the justices' conscientiousness and the number of opinion suggestions they circulate in each case. The average number of opinion suggestions circulated per case is .16 for less-conscientious justices and .38 for more-conscientious justices. Therefore, more-conscientious justices circulate more than twice as many opinion suggestions as less-conscientious justices, presumably reflecting their willingness to exert the effort required to fulfill their judicial duty.

Wait statements may indicate that justices are devoting more effort to a case by gathering additional information and carefully considering their views, or they may indicate that justices are delaying their work rather than attending to their responsibilities in a timely fashion. Additionally, justices may feel a duty to carefully consider a case even if it means a delay, or they may feel a sense of duty to honestly express their views rather than wait for other justices. Therefore, I neither expect nor find any relationship between conscientiousness and wait statements.

In contrast to separate opinions and opinion suggestions, join statements are a much simpler and less effortful response to a draft opinion. They require no original thought or additional research, and they are very short and easy to write. And, in contrast to wait statements, join statements do not indicate that a justice is devoting effort toward a case or planing to do so in the future. Consequently, issuing a join statement is an ideal strategy for justices who want to avoid expending effort. Justices who care more about fulfilling their judicial duty by striving to improve other justices' opinions should be more willing to pay these costs in order to contribute to the Court's deliberate process. Therefore, more-conscientious justices (who value industriousness and dutifulness) should tend to circulate fewer join statements.

Figure 6.1(e) illustrates the negative relationship between the justices' conscientiousness and the number of join statements issued in each case. The average number of join statements circulated per case is .95 for less-conscientious justices and .88 for more-conscientious justices. Therefore, more-conscientious justices circulate almost 10 percent fewer join statements than less-conscientious justices, presumably reflecting their propensity to contribute to the Court's deliberations rather than simply joining an opinion.

Finally, most bargaining behavior is influenced by the justices' ideological preferences. Specifically, ideological distance between a justice and the majority opinion author is positively associated with separate opinion drafts, opinion suggestions, and wait statements, and it is negatively associated with join statements. However, the justices' judicial duty requires them to resist pursuing ideological policy objectives. Therefore, the influence of ideology on these behaviors should be weaker for more-conscientious justices (who value dutifulness).

To test this expectation, I include interaction terms between justice conscientiousness and the justice's ideological distance to the opinion author in each model (except, of course, for the majority opinion draft model, which includes only opinion authors). I assess the ideological distance to the author by calculating the absolute difference between the Segal–Cover ideology scores[32] for each justice and the majority opinion author. The interaction term is statistically significant and signed in the expected direction in the separate opinion drafts model and wait statements model. In the opinion suggestions model and the join statements model, the interaction terms are signed in the expected direction, but fall short of statistical significance ($p = .10$ and $p = .08$, one-tailed tests).

Figures 6.2(a–d) present the marginal effects of ideological distance to the opinion author on separate opinions, opinion suggestions, wait statements, and join statements at different levels of justice conscientiousness. As illustrated in the figures, the effects of ideology are always stronger for less- versus more-conscientious justices. However, even for less-conscientious justices, the effects of ideology on opinion suggestions and wait statements is substantively quite small. The effects of ideology on join statements are strong; however, that interaction fell short of statistical significance. Therefore, the only interaction that is both substantively and statistically significant is in the separate opinions model. For less-conscientious justices, an increase from low to high distance to the author is associated with a .11 increase in the probability of a separate opinion draft (from .29 to .40); for more-conscientious justices, the effect of justice disagreement is statistically indistinguishable from zero. Thus, it appears that only less-conscientious justices are influenced by their ideological preferences when circulating separate opinion drafts.

Agreeableness and Bargaining Memos. As mentioned above, one of the most aggressive possible responses to a majority opinion author is to circulate a separate opinion draft. Separate opinion drafts usually indicate some disagreement with the majority opinion, the willingness to express that disagreement among one's colleagues, and the potential willingness

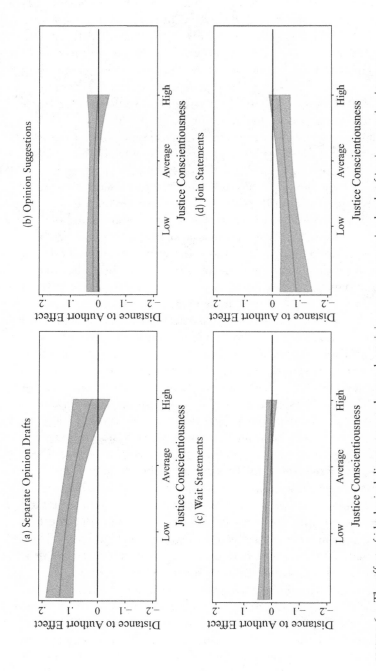

FIGURE 6.2 The effect of ideological distance to author on bargaining memos at varying levels of justice conscientiousness

Note: Figure presents marginal effects of a justice's ideological distance to the opinion author increasing from one standard deviation below the mean to one standard deviation above the mean on the predicted number of (a) separate opinion drafts, (b) opinion suggestions, (c) wait statements, and (d) join statements with 95% confidence intervals. Marginal effects are based on a series of count models. The full models are reported in Appendix C.

to express that disagreement publicly, all of which may disrupt social harmony on the Court. Moreover, the circulation of a separate opinion draft is sometimes an indication of a hardball negotiation tactic: The author of the draft is implicitly or explicitly threatening to go public with his or her objections if they are not addressed by the majority opinion author. Such a strategy may be an effective means of influencing the content of the majority opinion (indeed, that is one of the reasons why extraverted justices tend to circulate more separate opinion drafts); however, such threats likely incur substantial collegiality costs. Therefore, more-agreeable justices (who value social harmony) should tend to circulate fewer separate opinion drafts.

Figure 6.1(b) illustrates the negative relationship between justice agreeableness and separate opinion drafts. The average number of separate opinion drafts circulated per case is .52 for less-agreeable justices and .38 for more-agreeable justices. Therefore, more-agreeable justices circulate about 25 percent fewer separate opinion drafts than less-agreeable justices, presumably reflecting their propensity to avoid collegiality costs.

Wait statements also have the potential to disrupt social harmony by frustrating other members of the Court who are trying to understand their colleagues' preferences. Wait statements may indicate that a justice is engaged in strategic behavior or neglecting his or her duties, both of which may incur collegiality costs. And, even if the justice is motivated by a desire to carefully and sincerely consider the merits of a case, the wait statement may nonetheless delay the Court's decision process or undermine justices who are trying to anticipate their colleagues' behavior. Therefore, more-agreeable justices (who value social harmony) should tend to circulate fewer wait statements.

Figure 6.1(d) illustrates the negative relationship between justice agreeableness and wait statements. The average number of wait statements circulated per case is .21 for less-agreeable justices and .05 for more-agreeable justices. Therefore, more-agreeable justices tend to circulate about one-fourth as many wait statements as less-agreeable justices, presumably reflecting their desire to avoid the social costs associated with these memos.

Whereas aggressive bargaining and strategic delays likely frustrate other justices, simply joining an opinion should tend to please other justices and facilitate a good working relationship on the Court. Therefore, more-agreeable justices (who value social harmony) should tend to circulate more join statements. However, as illustrated in Figure 6.1(d), I find no evidence to support that expectation.

I do not expect the circulation of multiple majority opinion drafts or opinion suggestions to relate to either social harmony or altruism. Therefore, I neither expect nor find any relationship between agreeableness and these behaviors.

Neuroticism and Bargaining Memos. The content of the Court's opinions – particularly its majority opinion – is the Court's most important policy output. Consequently, justices care a great deal about opinion content, and they should be particularly concerned if the majority opinion contains language likely to attract criticism from judicial audiences. Justices who prefer to express negativity towards others should be more likely to criticize the content of the majority opinion, and, as described in earlier sections, the best mechanisms for doing so are separate opinion drafts and opinion suggestions. However, justices who worry about potential criticism should also try to express negativity in a manner that poses minimal risk to themselves personally. While circulating a separate opinion draft may prove a stronger tool to prompt changes in the majority opinion, it also exposes the justice to potential criticism from other justices (and external sources if the justice follows through and actually publishes the opinion). In contrast, by circulating opinion suggestions, justices can express negativity toward the majority opinion author (including threats to withhold support) without exposing themselves to potential criticism. Therefore, more-neurotic justices (who value loss avoidance and negativity expression) should tend to circulate more opinion suggestions (but not more separate opinion drafts).

As illustrated in Figure 6.1(c), and consistent with my expectations, I find no relationship between neuroticism and separate opinion drafts. However, I do find a strong positive relationship between justice neuroticism and opinion suggestions. The average number of opinion suggestions circulated per case is .14 for less-neurotic justices and .33 for more-neurotic justices. Therefore, more-neurotic justices circulate more than twice as many opinion suggestions as less-neurotic justices, presumably reflecting their propensity to express negativity toward others' opinions without exposing themselves to potential criticism.

Justices may also be able to avoid criticism by issuing wait statements. Wait statements usually help a justice acquire more information about the preferences and behaviors of the other justices, the legal issues at stake in a case, and the content of other opinions in the case without adopting a particular view. Justices can use this information to avoid several undesirable outcomes. For example, a justice may hope to avoid joining a separate opinion that has little support or staking out a position with which no other justices agree. A justice may also prefer to avoid the embarrassment of joining an opinion that is later revealed to suffer from substantial deficiencies. By waiting for more information, a justice can avoid these risks. Moreover, justices who intend to engage in strategic bargaining may prefer to minimize the risks associated with that bargaining. By collecting more information about others' preferences and choices, a justice can reduce the uncertainty inherent in the bargaining process. Therefore, more-neurotic justices (who value loss avoidance) should tend to circulate more wait statements.

Figure 6.1(d) illustrates the strong positive relationship between the justices' neuroticism and the number of wait statements they circulate in each case. Less-neurotic justices write an average of .02 wait statements per case; more-neurotic justices write an average of .25 wait statements per case. Therefore, only more-neurotic justices tend to circulate wait statements, presumably reflecting their desire to avoid the risks associated with staking out a position early in the bargaining process.

Perhaps the best way to avoid potential risks is to simply join another justices' opinion. Doing so mitigates the possibility of drawing criticism from other justices because any criticism will likely be directed at the opinion's author. And, even if there are problems with an opinion, joining the majority opinion is unlikely to be criticized by other justices because it is the expected default behavior. Therefore, more-neurotic justices (who value loss avoidance) should tend to circulate more join statements.

Figure 6.1(e) illustrates the positive relationship between the justices' neuroticism and the number of join statements they circulate in each case. Less-neurotic justices circulate .86 join statements per case, and more-neurotic justices circulate .97 join statements per case. Therefore, more-neurotic justices tend to circulate more than 10 percent more join statements than their less-neurotic colleagues, presumably because joining an opinion incurs little risk of criticism.

I do not expect the circulation of multiple majority opinion drafts to relate to either loss avoidance or negativity expression. Therefore, I neither expect nor find any relationship between neuroticism and majority opinion drafts.

Openness and Bargaining Memos. The intra-Court bargaining process is a valuable opportunity for justices to engage with one another over the substantive legal issues involved in a case. In the Court's conference discussion, justices are limited in their knowledge of the other justices' views and the amount of time they have to make arguments. However, the bargaining process provides justices with ample time to conduct legal research, consult with clerks, develop their arguments in written form, provide detailed citation to precedent and case facts, and make longer, more complicated points. Also, the justices are better informed about their fellow justices' positions, which party has majority support, who is writing the majority opinion, and the potential content of that opinion. Consequently, those justices who especially value such intellectual engagement should be more likely to exploit these opportunities. Moreover, circulating additional opinion drafts indicates an author's willingness to make (at least minor) changes and incorporate different ideas into the opinion. Therefore, more-open justices (who value intellectualism and change) should tend to circulate more majority opinion drafts, more separate opinion drafts, and more opinion suggestions.

Figures 6.1(a–c) illustrate the positive relationships between the opinion authors' openness and the number of (a) majority opinion drafts, (b) separate opinion drafts, and (c) opinion suggestions circulated in each case. The average number of majority opinion drafts circulated in each case is 2.5 for less-open opinion authors and 3.2 for more-open authors (30% increase). The average number of separate opinion drafts circulated per case is .29 for less-open justices and .62 for more-open justices (110% increase). However, contrary to my expectations, I find no association between openness and opinion suggestions.

In contrast to opinion drafts and suggestions, both wait statements and join statements effectively remove the justice who wrote them from the intellectual dialogue on the Court (at least temporarily). That is, wait statements and join statements neither critique other justices' ideas nor contribute original ideas. Moreover, these statements are unlikely to invite intellectual engagement with other justices. Justices who enjoy intellectual engagement with different ideas and who are open to changing their views should prefer to continue exchanging memos rather than issue one of these statements. Therefore, more-open justices (who value intellectualism and change) should tend to circulate fewer wait statements and join statements.

Figures 6.1(d) and (e) illustrate the negative relationship between justice openness and both wait and join statements. The average number of wait statements circulated per case is .12 for less-open justices and .07 for more-open justices (40% decrease). The average number of join statements circulated per case is 1.00 for less-open justices and .87 for more-open justices (13% decrease).

PERSONALITY TRAITS AND BARGAINING MEMOS

To summarize, the justices' personality traits are strongly associated with their behavior during the intra-Court bargaining process. In Chapter 5, I found that chief justices tend to assign more-extraverted justices to write the Court's majority opinion, presumably because extraverts are skilled leaders and enjoy exerting influence over other justices. Consistent with that view, more-extraverted opinion authors tend to circulate more majority opinion drafts, which should help them secure support from their colleagues and shape the opinion's content. When extraverts do not write the majority opinion, they aggressively assert their views and attempt to influence the majority opinion by circulating drafts of separate opinions (but, surprisingly, not more opinion suggestions).

More-conscientious justices are also more active during the bargaining process due to their willingness to expend effort and their sense of judicial duty. Those justices who are higher in conscientiousness are less likely to simply join other justices' opinions; instead, they tend to circulate more separate opinion drafts and opinion suggestions, reflecting a willingness to exert the effort required to participate in their professional duties. Similarly, more-open justices tend to actively participate in bargaining due to their desire to intellectually engage with other justices and potentially alter the content of their own or others' opinions. Thus, more-open justices tend to circulate more majority opinion drafts and separate opinion drafts, as well as fewer wait statements and join statements (but, surprisingly, not more opinion suggestions).

More-neurotic justices appear to participate in the bargaining process out of a desire to express dissatisfaction and minimize policy losses; however, their participation is tempered by their desire to avoid criticism. Thus, more-neurotic justices tend to circulate more opinion suggestions (but not more separate opinions, which might expose them to criticism), and they also circulate more wait statements and join statements. Similarly, more-agreeable justices limit their participation in bargaining activities, presumably to avoid collegiality costs. Therefore, they tend to circulate fewer separate opinion drafts and fewer wait statements (but, surprisingly, not more join statements).

At the beginning of this chapter, I described Chief Justice Burger's aggressive attempts to influence the opinion in *Swann* as an example of a justice's personality influencing his bargaining behavior (specifically, Burger's high extraversion prompted him to circulate numerous majority opinion drafts in order to assert influence over the opinion's content). The empirical findings in this chapter suggest that Burger's behavior was not rare. On the contrary, many of the justices' bargaining behaviors appear to be driven by their individual traits. Accordingly, justices' personalities may play a critical role in shaping the nature of the Court's bargaining process and, ultimately, the content of the Court's opinions.

7

Voting on the Merits

On May 17, 1954, Chief Justice Earl Warren announced the Supreme Court's unanimous decision in *Brown v. Board of Education*, declaring that "in the field of public education, 'separate but equal' has no place."[1] According to some legal experts, the Court's unanimity in *Brown* was "[s]econd in importance only to what the Supreme Court decided" that day.[2] For example, "[p]opular books and pamphlets supporting the [desegregation] decisions pointed to unanimity as evidence of the legitimacy of the rulings."[3] But unanimity in *Brown* was never a foregone conclusion. Just six months earlier, when the Court discussed the *Brown* case in conference, several justices still opposed a decision mandating desegregation. The clearest opposition came from Justice Stanley F. Reed, "who made it plain ... that his views remained what they had been – against closing up Jim Crow schools."[4]

What happened in the months between the conference discussion and the announcement of the Court's opinion? Why did Justice Reed change his mind and join the majority? Surprisingly, the explanation most commonly offered by historians, biographers, and legal scholars has little to do with constitutional law or politics. Justice Reed did not experience an ideological transformation, nor was he convinced by a legal argument. Instead, the most prominent accounts of Reed's evolution in *Brown* suggest that Chief Justice Warren persuaded him to change his vote through a steady dialogue that included frequent lunches between the would-be dissenter, the chief justice, and Warren's ally, Justice Harold H. Burton.[5] Eventually, Warren coaxed Reed into joining the majority by appealing to his sense of duty.

Justice Reed was a "conscientious, hard-working jurist, conservative by temperament and respectful of precedent."[6] He was known as an "incredibly methodical" and "prodigious worker, laboring often at night."[7] And Reed's "conscientious manner"[8] also included a strong sense of duty. As Justice Felix Frankfurter once put it, "Reed was a soldier and glad to do anything that the interest of the Court might require."[9]

Never was Reed's devotion to the Court more important than in *Brown*. "Because he was a Southerner, even a lone dissent by him would give a lot of people a lot of grist for making trouble."[10] Indeed, even with unanimity, the *Brown* decision provoked unprecedented backlash and violence in the South.[11] But Reed's dutifulness ultimately compelled him to bite his tongue: "For the good of the country, he put aside his own basis for dissent."[12] Were it not for Reed's strong sense of duty, unanimity in *Brown* might have been lost.

⤳

Every Supreme Court case involves a conflict between two parties: The state prosecutes an individual for violating a criminal law, a customer sues a corporation for making a faulty product, a divorced spouse sues for custody of the children, and so on. Accordingly, the most basic question justices must resolve in each case is which party wins and which party loses. That is, each justice must vote for either the petitioner (and reverse the decision of the lower court) or vote for the respondent (and affirm the lower court's decision). Occasionally, the justices determine that a case should be dismissed based on a procedural issue and do not reach the merits of the legal dispute. However, in most cases, the justices reach the substantive legal question and must decide which party should win based on the justices' interpretation of the law. This decision is called the vote on the merits.

In almost every case, the justices divide into a majority and (if there is disagreement) a minority on the merits vote.[13] Although justices cannot always anticipate each other's votes, several sources of information help them predict which party will ultimately prevail. Justices serve with one another for years at a time and resolve hundreds of cases together. As a result, they learn a great deal about each other's legal values, ideological preferences, and personal characteristics, and this information can help them predict each other's votes in specific cases. Additionally, the justices discuss the cert decision and hear each other ask questions during oral arguments, both of which may reveal their thinking about a case. They also hear each other share their views during the conference discussion near the time they cast an initial vote. Even after casting this initial vote, justices can always change their votes before the Court issues its final verdict. Consequently, justices can almost always choose whether to vote with the majority or dissent.

Disagreement on the merits vote was once relatively rare on the Supreme Court. Before the 1930s, the Court operated under a strong norm of consensus: Justices refrained from expressing public disagreement in all but the most extreme situations.[14] However, under the leadership of Chief Justice Harlan Fiske Stone, dissent became much more common on the Court, and justices now regularly express disagreement.[15] Since the 1946 term, an average of 1.6 justices have dissented in each case, and at least one justice has dissented in 62 percent of cases.

Although dissents do not alter a case's outcome, they nonetheless have important ramifications for the legal system. For example, when a justice dissents or threatens to dissent, the author of the majority opinion often feels compelled to respond; simply ignoring the dissenter's objection may invite criticism from politicians, the media, academics, or historians. In some situations, the threat of dissent may force concessions from majority opinion authors.[16] In other situations, it may prompt the majority opinion author to write a longer opinion justifying the majority's reasoning.[17] And, of course, repeated public disagreement may diminish collegiality among the justices.[18]

Moreover, dissenting opinions usually attack the majority's reasoning and create a permanent record of that criticism that can be read by lawyers and judges in the future. Accordingly, when justices dissent from a Supreme Court ruling, that ruling is more likely to be overruled in the future.[19] Dissents may also indirectly shape the content of future opinions.[20] More broadly, repeated disagreement between justices may subtly undermine public confidence in the Court: The more justices openly disagree, the more it appears that their decisions are based on personal preferences rather than neutral principles.[21]

DISSENT

The justices' merits votes are influenced by a variety of factors, including legal doctrine and precedent,[22] characteristics of the case, time pressures, and the anticipated behavior and reactions of the other justices.[23] Merits votes are also influenced by the justices' ideological policy preferences. In most cases, the merits vote can be categorized as supporting a liberal or conservative outcome. For example, liberal ideological preferences are generally associated with greater support for the rights of criminal defendants. Accordingly, votes in favor of criminal defendants are generally viewed as liberal votes. Following this logic, the creators of the Supreme Court Database developed a system for coding most Supreme Court rulings as either liberal or conservative. Cases involving criminal justice, civil rights, the First Amendment, due process, and privacy are coded as liberal if they are pro-defendant, pro-civil liberties or civil rights claimant, pro-child or juvenile, pro-indigent, etc. Cases involving unions and economic activity are coded as liberal if they are pro-union, pro-government, anti-business, anti-employer, etc. Rulings in favor of attorneys, judicial power, federal power, and the US government (in taxation cases) are also coded as liberal.[24] Of course, not every Supreme Court ruling can be categorized in terms of ideology; in cases involving interstate relations, private law, and miscellaneous issues, the ideological direction of the Court's decisions are not specifiable. Nonetheless, most votes can be categorized as liberal or conservative, and whether a justice casts a liberal or conservative vote is strongly influenced by that justice's ideological preferences.[25]

Supreme Court justices also tend to follow the public's ideological preferences when voting on the merits.[26] The relationship between the public's ideological mood and the justices' decision-making may be driven by a variety of factors. Justices may simply tend to share the public's preferences because the appointment process ensures that new justices hold popular views.[27] Or the justices' preferences may shift in response to the same social forces that shape the views of the general public.[28] Alternatively, the justices may strategically respond to changes in public opinion because they fear negative consequences from issuing unpopular rulings. For example, the justices may worry that the elected branches will enact a new law overriding one of their decisions,[29] sanction the Court or the justices (e.g., through Court-packing, jurisdiction stripping, or impeachment),[30] or refuse to implement the Court's rulings.[31] (Indeed, the Court also appears to respond to pressures from other political actors for similar reasons.)[32] The influence of public opinion on the justices tends to be weaker than that of their own preferences; nonetheless, the justices routinely issue decisions that are consistent with the public's ideological mood, especially in highly visible cases.[33]

Dissent Hypotheses. In addition to these traditional explanations, the psychoeconomic approach posits that the justices' personality traits also influence the vote on the merits. Specifically, I propose the following hypotheses related to dissent:

- More-extraverted justices are less likely to dissent because dissent reflects a failure to influence other justices. Additionally, the positive influence of popular opinion on dissent is stronger for more-extraverted justices, especially in cases that receive media attention, because casting popular votes in these cases attracts positive attention from judicial audiences.
- More-conscientious justices are more likely to dissent because dissent often requires substantial effort and fulfills their judicial duty to express honest disagreement. Additionally, the positive influence of ideological preferences on dissent is weaker for more-conscientious justices because pursuing policy objectives violates their judicial duty.
- The positive influence of other justices' votes on dissent is stronger for more-agreeable justices because voting with other justices promotes social harmony on the Court. Additionally, the negative influence of the Court issuing a liberal ruling on dissent is stronger for more-agreeable justices because liberal rulings promote the interests of disadvantaged members of society.
- More-neurotic justices are less likely to dissent because dissent exposes justices to potential criticism. Additionally, the negative influence of the Court ruling in favor of the US government on dissent is stronger for more-neurotic justices because supporting the US government avoids potential criticism.
- The positive influence of the Court altering one of its own precedents on dissent is weaker for more-open justices because altering precedent promotes legal change.

Below I describe the empirical model I used to test these hypotheses. I then develop each hypothesis in greater detail and report the findings of the empirical tests.

The Dissent Model. In order to evaluate the role of personality traits in shaping the justices' merits votes, I examine the justices' dissent behavior in each of the 6,222 cases decided during the 1951 through 2013 terms ($N = 49,001$).[34] The dependent variable in this analysis is the decision to cast a dissenting vote by each of the thirty-four justices serving during this period (1 = dissent; 0 = vote with majority).

The model controls for several variables potentially related to the justices' dissent behavior, including justice characteristics (each justice's ideological disagreement with the Court's ruling[35] and indicators for the chief justice and freshman justices), case characteristics (the term-standardized number of amicus briefs filed, case complexity, media attention, and indicators for the number of other dissenting justices, a ruling in favor of the federal government, an altered precedent, an invalidated statute, and issue area), time pressures (the Court's caseload, the number of days until the end of the term, and a time trend),[36] and the public's ideological disagreement with the Court's ruling. I also include the justices' SCIPEs for the Big Five, the majority opinion author's SCIPEs for the Big Five, and the interaction terms described below. (See Appendix D for a full description of the model.)

JUSTICE TRAITS AND DISSENT

Figure 7.1 summarizes the influence of the justices' personality traits and other factors on their dissent behavior. As a point of reference, the average predicted probability of a justice dissenting in a given case is .20, and this probability appears to be influenced by legal, strategic, and ideological factors. For example, the Court's invalidation of a federal statute as unconstitutional is associated with a .04 increase in the probability of dissent. And a one-standard-deviation increase in a justice's ideological disagreement with the majority decision is associated with a .08 increase in the probability of dissent. A few of the opinion author's traits reach conventional levels of statistical significance, but none of these effects are large enough to be substantively meaningful.[37]

Unlike the findings from prior chapters, the direct effects of personality on dissent are substantially smaller than the effects of some legal, institutional, and ideological influences on dissent. However, these personality effects are still quite substantial, especially when considered together. For example, the effects of a justice's extraversion (−.04), conscientiousness (+.04), and neuroticism (−.03) on dissent are each about half as strong as the effect of a justice's ideological disagreement with the majority decision (+.08).[38]

Extraversion and Dissent. As described in previous chapters, justices undoubtedly try to influence each other in order to shape the Court's rulings. However, some justices have greater desire and ability to influence their colleagues than others. Justices who are more influential on the Court should be more likely to find themselves in the majority for two reasons. First, they should be more likely to persuade other justices to adopt their own views and, consequently, help form a majority coalition. Second, if they cannot sway the Court's vote, they may join the majority as a strategic maneuver in order to influence the content of the majority opinion (recall Chief Justice Warren E. Burger's strategy in *Swann*). And,

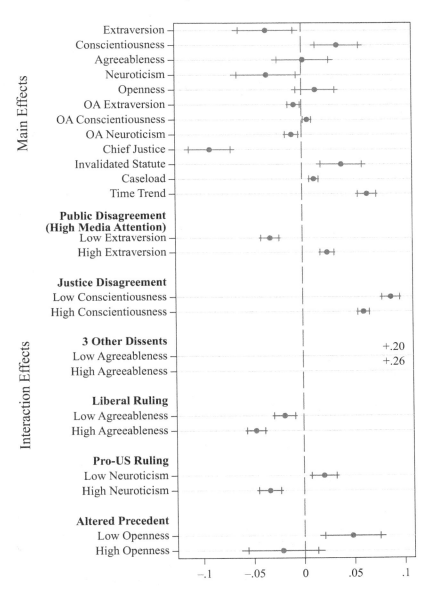

FIGURE 7.1 Marginal effects on dissent

Note: Figure presents marginal effects of a one standard deviation increase in each continuous variable (and one-unit increase in each dichotomous variable) on the predicted probability of dissent with 95% confidence intervals. Predicted probabilities are based on a multilevel logistic regression model with random intercepts for 34 justices. The full model is reported in Appendix D. OA = Opinion Author.

although more-extraverted justices seek attention and agency, they need not dissent in order to pursue these goals. Instead, more-extraverted justices can simultaneously exert influence by corralling a majority *and* attract attention by filing a concurring opinion (see Chapter 8). Thus, more-extraverted justices (who value influence) should be less likely to dissent.

Figure 7.1 illustrates the negative relationship between the justices' extraversion and their propensity to dissent. The probability of dissent is .24 for less-extraverted justices and .17 for more-extraverted justices. Thus, more-extraverted justices are about 30 percent less likely to dissent than less-extraverted justices, which presumably reflects their greater desire and ability to influence their colleagues.

Justices also generally desire attention from their peers, the media, and the public in order to attain prestige and celebrity.[39] Of course, "it would be difficult to develop influence, esteem, and prestige if their court or legal system did not enjoy a certain degree of respect," and "[c]ultivating and following public opinion are behaviors consistent with this end."[40] Thus, the justices often tend to make decisions that are consistent with the public's ideological mood in order to secure popular legitimacy and prestige.[41]

I assess public disagreement with the Court's rulings using James A. Stimson's Public Mood Indicator, which captures the public's shifting preferences along the standard liberal-conservative dimension over time.[42] Higher levels of the Stimson measure indicate more liberal public preferences. I code *public disagreement* as the Stimson measure if the majority supported a conservative outcome (i.e., a dissent would be a liberal vote). I code public disagreement as the inverted Stimson measure if the majority supported a liberal outcome (i.e., a dissent would be a conservative vote). Therefore, higher levels of public disagreement indicate that the Court issued a ruling that was inconsistent with the public's ideological preferences. Despite the common findings in the literature that justices follow public opinion,[43] I do not find an average association between public disagreement and dissent.

However, a justice's desire to follow popular preferences should depend on media attention to the case and the justice's interest in attracting attention and garnering popularity. I assess media attention using Tom S. Clark, Jeffrey R. Lax, and Douglas Rice's measure of latent case salience, which is based on predecision case coverage in three leading newspapers: the *New York Times*, the *Washington Post*, and the *Los Angeles Times*.[44] Justices who value public prestige should seek out such esteem by following popular preferences but only in cases that receive media attention (i.e., cases in which the public might actually hear about the justices' decisions). Those justices who do not value popular attention should be more willing to buck public opinion even in cases that attract media scrutiny. Therefore, public disagreement should primarily influence voting by more-extraverted justices (who value attention) in cases that receive media attention.

In most cases, public disagreement is not significantly associated with dissent regardless of a justice's extraversion; however, significant effects do emerge in cases that receive greater media attention. Figure 7.2 illustrates the relationship between public disagreement, justice extraversion, and dissent in cases that are one standard deviation above the mean in media attention. The upper panel presents the predicted probability of a justice dissenting in these cases with low versus high levels of public disagreement (i.e., one standard deviation below versus above the mean). The lower panel presents the effect of public disagreement on the probability of dissent in cases that receive high media attention. For more-extraverted justices, an increase from low to high public disagreement is associated with a .05 increase in the probability of dissent in these cases (from .15 to .20); for less-extraverted justices, public disagreement is actually associated with a decrease in the probability of dissent in these cases (from .29 to .22). Thus, the public's ideological preferences are positively associated with dissent behavior, but only for more-extraverted justices in cases that receive substantial attention from the media.

Conscientiousness and Dissent. Simply agreeing with the majority opinion requires relatively little effort. In contrast, learning enough about a case to develop a divergent viewpoint and expressing that viewpoint often requires considerable time and energy. Justices who are willing to expend the effort necessary to carefully evaluate the merits of a case and determine whether they disagree with the majority should be more likely to dissent. Moreover, justices often feel a judicial duty to express honest disagreement when their jurisprudential views diverge from their colleagues'. (Recall Justice John Paul Stevens's words: "There is a duty to explain your position if it isn't the same as the majority.")[45] Those justices who feel a greater sense of this duty should tend to dissent more frequently. (Recall from Chapter 2 that the norm of consensus on the Court collapsed in the 1940s.)[46] Therefore, more-conscientious justices (who value industriousness and dutifulness) should be more likely to dissent.

Figure 7.1 illustrates the positive relationship between justice conscientiousness and dissent. The probability of dissent is .17 for less-conscientious justices and .24 for more-conscientious justices. Thus,

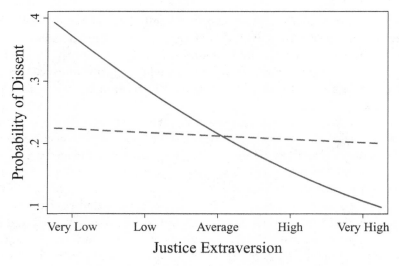

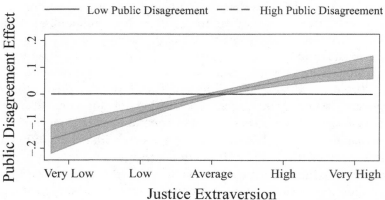

FIGURE 7.2 The effect of public disagreement on dissent at varying levels of justice extraversion in cases that receive high media attention

Note: The upper panel presents the predicted probability of a justice dissenting in cases with high media attention (i.e., one standard deviation above the mean) and low versus high levels of public disagreement (i.e., one standard deviation below versus above the mean). The lower panel presents the marginal effects of public disagreement in cases that receive high media attention with 95% confidence intervals. Predicted probabilities and marginal effects are based on a multilevel logistic regression model with random intercepts for 34 justices. The full model is reported in Appendix D.

more-conscientious justices are 40 percent more likely to dissent than less-conscientious justices, which presumably reflects their sense of obligation to explain disagreement with the majority and their willingness to expend the effort required to do so.

The justices' preference for dutifulness should also condition the influence of their policy preferences on voting. It is generally agreed that justices tend to make decisions that are consistent with their own policy preferences (e.g., liberal justices tend to support liberal outcomes).[47] Thus, justices should be more likely to dissent when they are ideologically inclined to disagree with the Court's ruling. I code justice disagreement with the Court's ruling as the justice's Segal–Cover score[48] if the Court issued a liberal ruling (recall that higher Segal–Cover scores indicate conservative preferences); I code justice disagreement as the justice's inverted Segal–Cover score if the Court issued a conservative ruling. Therefore, higher levels of justice disagreement indicate that the Court issued a ruling that was inconsistent with the justice's ideology. As expected, justices are much more likely to dissent in cases in which their ideology is inconsistent with the ideological direction of the Court's ruling. The probability of dissent for a justice with low versus high justice disagreement (i.e., one standard deviation below versus above the mean) is .13 versus .28, respectively.

The justices' professional duties require them to make impartial and unbiased decisions, and never is this obligation more important than when casting a vote on the merits. However, these "motivations of duty and professional responsibility ... sometimes pull against their policy preferences."[49] In other words, justices must often suppress their ideological preferences in order to conform to legal norms.[50] Consequently, justices must balance their desire to fulfill their professional duties against their desire to shirk those duties and pursue policy objectives. Those justices with a strong sense of judicial duty should resist the temptation to adopt their preferred policies; those who place less value on dutifulness should be more likely to do so. Therefore, more-conscientious justices (who value dutifulness) should be less likely to follow their own ideological preferences when voting on the merits.

Figure 7.3 illustrates the relationship between justice disagreement, justice conscientiousness, and dissent. The upper panel presents the predicted probability of a justice dissenting in cases with low versus high levels of justice disagreement. Consistent with my expectations, both lines slope upward as conscientiousness increases, indicating that, on average,

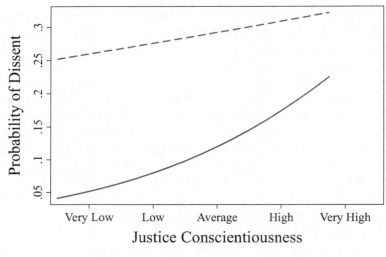

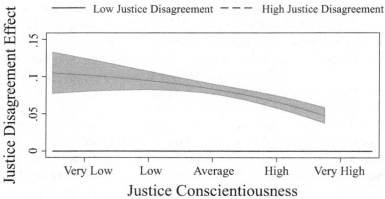

FIGURE 7.3 The effect of justice disagreement on dissent at varying levels of justice conscientiousness

Note: The upper panel presents the predicted probability of a justice dissenting with low versus high levels of justice disagreement (i.e., one standard deviation below versus above the mean). The lower panel presents the marginal effects of justice disagreement with 95% confidence intervals. Predicted probabilities and marginal effects are based on a multilevel logistic regression model with random intercepts for 34 justices. The full model is reported in Appendix D.

more-conscientious justices are more likely to dissent. The lower panel presents the effect of justice disagreement on the probability of dissent. For more-conscientious justices, an increase from low to high justice disagreement is associated with only a .12 increase in the probability of dissent (from .18 to .30); for less-conscientious justices, the same increase in justice disagreement is associated with a .19 increase in the probability of dissent (from .08 to .27). Thus, the influence of a justice's ideological preferences on dissent is almost 60 percent stronger for less-versus more-conscientious justices.[51]

Agreeableness and Dissent. Numerous studies of multimember courts have emphasized the "interdependent – i.e., strategic – nature of judicial decisions. On strategic accounts, in other words, judges do not make decisions in a vacuum, but rather take into account the preferences and likely actions of other relevant actors, including their colleagues."[52] Accordingly, as members of a multimember institution, Supreme Court justices often try to influence each other's decisions through logical persuasion, strategic bargaining, and social pressure.[53] More specifically, justices pressure one another to suppress dissent because dissents undermine the majority's interests.[54]

Dissents undermine majority interests in several ways. As noted above, majority opinion authors often feel an obligation to write longer opinions when a dissent is filed.[55] And the author of the majority opinion may feel especially compelled to write a longer opinion when multiple justices dissent. Thus, dissenting may impose time and effort costs on majority opinion authors. Additionally, when justices dissent from a Supreme Court decision, that decision is more likely to be overruled in the future.[56] Thus, dissenting may undermine the stability and longevity of the majority's decision. Finally, because the merits vote is the critical determination of a case, divergent views on the merits are likely to cause considerable social disharmony among the justices. As a result of these factors, justices who wish to dissent often incur collegiality costs for doing so. Therefore, more-agreeable justices (who value social harmony) should be less likely to dissent. However, as illustrated in Figure 7.1, I find no relationship between agreeableness and dissenting votes.

Alternatively, the collegiality costs associated with dissent may depend on the number of other justices who also dissent. When the Court is more evenly divided, it is less clear which side bears responsibility for disrupting the Court's harmony, and any collegiality costs associated with dissenting can be shared among the several dissenters. In contrast, when only one or two justices dissent, they alone must bear the costs of thwarting unanimity. Therefore, justices should be more likely to dissent when other justices do so. And, as expected, the probability of a justice dissenting alone is only .04, but the probability of dissenting when three others do so (the maximum possible) is .27.

Of course, the fact that justices tend to dissent when other justices do so does not necessarily mean that they are influencing each other's behavior. Justices may simply tend to agree on case outcomes irregardless of each other's views. Nonetheless, we may be able to infer that justices influence each other's dissent behavior if the association between a justice dissenting and other justices dissenting is stronger for some justices than for others. Specifically, if justices follow each other's dissent behavior out of a desire to avoid collegiality costs, then the influence of other dissents should depend on the degree to which the justice values social harmony. More-agreeable justices (who value social harmony) should have a stronger preference for avoiding collegiality costs and, therefore, be more susceptible to influence from their colleagues.[57]

Figure 7.4 illustrates the relationship between other justices' dissents, justice agreeableness, and dissent. The upper panel presents the predicted probability of a justice dissenting in cases with zero versus three other dissents. The lower panel presents the effect of three other dissents on the probability of dissent. For more-agreeable justices, three dissents by other justices (versus zero other dissents) is associated with a .26 increase in the probability of dissent (from .03 to .29); for less-agreeable justices, three other dissents is associated with only a .20 increase in the probability of dissent (from .05 to .25). Thus, the influence of other dissents on the probability of a justice dissenting is more than 20 percent stronger for more-versus less-agreeable justices.

The merits vote is also influenced by the justices' desire to help disadvantaged members of society. "One influential view of the Court ... is that it stands in some special way as a protection of minorities against tyranny by majorities"; consequently, justices often feel a desire to promote "norms of Right or Justice" against infringement by popular majorities.[58] In other words, some justices might prefer to use their position to promote the interests of disadvantaged members of society who tend to lose in the normal democratic process. In most cases, support for those who are disadvantaged will mean a liberal vote. In fact, in the Supreme Court Database, liberal votes are actually defined as votes that support disadvantaged groups, such as criminal defendants, racial minorities, and the indigent. (The database also codes any vote that is "pro-underdog" as a liberal vote, highlighting the definition of a liberal vote in this context as one that supports disadvantaged members of society.) Consistent with the notion that justices tend to help those who are less fortunate, the probability of a justice dissenting is .03 lower when the Court issues a liberal ruling even after controlling for the justices' ideological preferences.

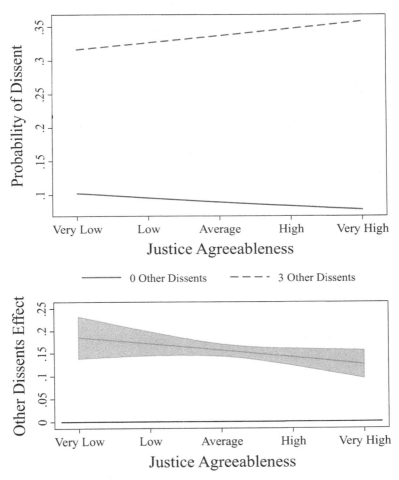

FIGURE 7.4 The effect of other dissents on dissent at varying levels of justice agreeableness

Note: The upper panel presents the predicted probability of a justice dissenting in cases with zero versus three other dissents. The lower panel presents the marginal effects of three other dissents with 95% confidence intervals. Predicted probabilities and marginal effects are based on a multilevel logistic regression model with random intercepts for 34 justices. The full model is reported in Appendix D.

However, the desire to help the less fortunate may vary across the justices, even after controlling for their ideological preferences. Those who are more compassionate, caring, and altruistic should feel a stronger desire to help disadvantaged members of society than those who are colder and less sympathetic. Therefore, when the Court issues a liberal

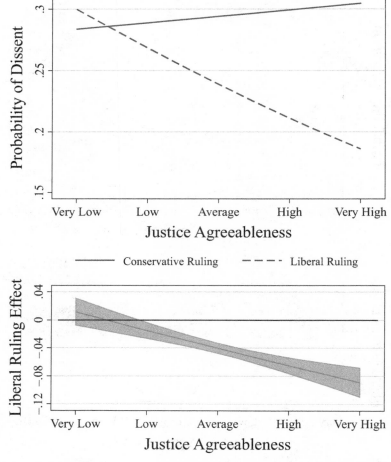

FIGURE 7.5 The effect of a liberal ruling on dissent at varying levels of justice agreeableness

Note: The upper panel presents the predicted probability of a justice dissenting in cases with a conservative versus liberal ruling. The lower panel presents the marginal effects of a liberal ruling with 95% confidence intervals. Predicted probabilities and marginal effects are based on a multilevel logistic regression model with random intercepts for 34 justices. The full model is reported in Appendix D.

ruling, more-agreeable justices (who value altruism) should be less likely to dissent than their less-agreeable colleagues.

Figure 7.5 presents the relationship between liberal rulings, justice agreeableness, and dissent. The upper panel presents the predicted probability of a justice dissenting in cases with a liberal versus conservative ruling. The lower panel presents the effect of a liberal ruling on the probability of dissent. For more-agreeable justices, a liberal ruling is associated with a .04 decrease in the probability of dissent (from .22 to .18); for less-agreeable justices, a liberal ruling is associated with only a .02 decrease in the probability of dissent (from .21 to .19). Thus, the influence of a liberal ruling on the probability of dissent is twice as strong for more-versus less-agreeable justices.

Neuroticism and Dissent. By definition, those justices who dissent separate themselves from their colleagues and stand apart by disagreeing with the prevailing view on the Court. Consequently, dissenters are more likely to attract criticism from the media, legal academics, and – perhaps most importantly – their fellow justices. Those justices who prefer to avoid such criticism should tend to refrain from dissenting and, instead, blend in with the majority. (Indeed, for many years, those justices who simply joined the majority without filing or joining a separate opinion were not mentioned by name in the Court's opinion.) Therefore, more-neurotic justices (who value loss avoidance) should be less likely to dissent in order to avoid potential criticism.

Figure 7.1 illustrates the negative relationship between justice neuroticism and dissent. The probability of dissent is .24 for less-neurotic justices and .17 for more-neurotic justices. Thus, more-neurotic justices are about 30 percent less likely to dissent than less-neurotic justices, which presumably reflects their desire to avoid criticism.

When casting their merits vote, justices also tend to support the US government, either as a party to the case or as an amicus.[59] Therefore, justices should be less likely to dissent when the Court rules in favor of the US government, i.e., when the federal government is the winning party or files an amicus brief supporting the winning party. Recall from Chapter 4 that the justices tend to follow the US government's recommendations due, in part, to separation of powers considerations (e.g., fear of nonimplementation, sanctions, and criticism), as well as special concern for the solicitor general's role as the "Tenth Justice" (and fear of the legal and institutional problems that may arise from disregarding the solicitor's recommendations).[60] Opposing the federal government may also provoke backlash from the elected branches of government. Indeed, Congress and the president possess a wide variety of tools with which to punish the Court for issuing undesirable rulings,[61] and the Court tends to refrain from invalidating federal statutes when Congress and the White House are controlled by ideologically distant officials.[62] Therefore, justices should be less likely to dissent when the Court issues a pro-federal ruling, in part, because defying the federal government may provoke criticism, sanctions, or other institutional problems. By the same logic, justices should be more likely to dissent when the Court rules against the US government. And, as expected, the probability of dissent is slightly lower when the Court rules in favor of the federal government and slightly higher when Court rules against it (both effects are about one percentage point).

However, the risks associated with opposing the federal government likely have different effects on different justices. Those justices who place greater value on avoiding criticism and negative consequences should tend to follow the government's recommendations and, consequently, vote in favor of decisions that support the US government; those justices who are willing to bear these risks should be more likely to oppose the federal government. Therefore, more-neurotic justices (who value loss avoidance) should be less likely to dissent when the Court rules in favor of the US government and more likely to dissent when the Court rules against it.

Figure 7.6 illustrates the relationship between a ruling in favor of the US government, justice neuroticism, and dissent. The upper panel presents the predicted probability of a justice dissenting in cases in which the Court did versus did not rule in favor of the US government. (Predicted probabilities of dissent in cases in which the Court ruled against are statistically indistinguishable from those in which the federal government was not involved.) The lower panel presents the effect of a pro-federal ruling on the probability of dissent. For more-neurotic justices, a pro-US government ruling is associated with a .04 decrease in the probability of dissent (from .18 to .14); for less-neurotic justices, pro-federal rulings are actually associated with a .02 increase in the probability of dissent (from .23 to .25). Thus, the Court ruling in favor of the US government only discourages dissent by more-neurotic justices, which suggests that only more-neurotic justices worry about defying the federal government.

However, I do not find a significant interaction between neuroticism and an anti-federal ruling. One possible explanation for this null finding is that, when the Court rules against the US government, the risks of criticism and reputational damage can be shared among the individual justices in the majority coalition, and these justices may be able to hide behind the Court's institutional legitimacy. If so, a concern for avoiding criticism may be less salient when the majority rules against the government.

Openness and Dissent. There is no clear reason why dissent might be associated with a preference for intellectualism or change. A dissenting vote does not necessarily represent engagement with different ideas (indeed, it may be the majority that has adopted new ideas), nor does

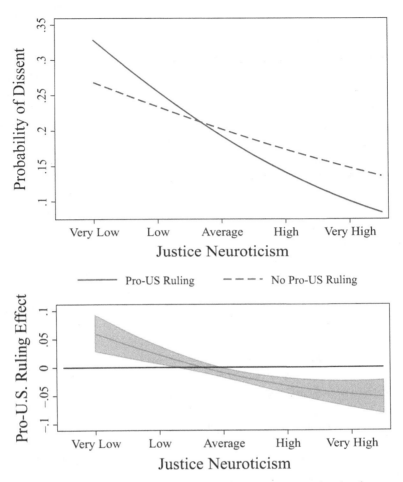

FIGURE 7.6 The effect of a pro-US ruling on dissent at varying levels of justice neuroticism

Note: The upper panel presents the predicted probability of a justice dissenting in cases with versus cases without a pro-US government ruling. The lower panel presents the marginal effects of a pro-US government ruling with 95% confidence intervals. Predicted probabilities and marginal effects are based on a multilevel logistic regression model with random intercepts for 34 justices. The full model is reported in Appendix D.

it imply legal or policy change. Indeed, intellectualism might prompt justices to explore new ideas that spur disagreement or it may prompt them to consider different views that facilitate compromise. Therefore, I neither expect nor find any relationship between openness and dissent.

Nonetheless, a dissenting vote may be closely related to a preference for change if the Court's ruling itself represents a substantial change to legal doctrine. The justices' merits votes are often influenced by a concern for stability, consistency, and predictability in the law. Indeed, one of the Court's most important legal norms is the principle of *stare decisis*: the expectation that justices will adhere to prior Court rulings and uphold precedent.[63] Accordingly, justices should be more likely to dissent when the Court violates this legal norm and overrules one of its own precedents. And, as expected, the probability of a justice dissenting increases by .02 when the Court overrules precedent.

However, some justices undoubtedly welcome legal change more than others; some may even actively pursue it. Often, the Court can bring about a desired change by distinguishing, limiting, or criticizing its prior rulings. But in some situations, the Court must formally alter one of its own precedents in order to reform legal doctrine. A justice's willingness to violate the norm of stare decisis and overturn precedent should depend on the degree to which he or she desires change. Those justices who greatly value change should be more willing to defy stare decisis than those who do not. Therefore, more-open justices (who value change) should be less likely to dissent when the Court alters precedent.

Figure 7.7 illustrates the relationship between the Court formally altering one of its own precedents, justice openness, and dissent. The upper panel presents the predicted probability of a justice dissenting in cases in which the Court did versus did not alter precedent. The lower panel presents the effect of an altered precedent on the probability of dissent. For less-open justices, an altered precedent is associated with a .03 increase in the probability of dissent (from .19 to .22); for more-open justices, the effect of an altered precedent on dissent is actually negative (though statistically insignificant). Thus, only less-open justices tend to dissent when the Court alters one of its own precedents. More-open justices may actually be less likely to dissent when the Court alters precedent, suggesting that they prefer to support legal change.

PERSONALITY AND THE MERITS VOTE

To summarize, the justices' personality traits are directly associated with their votes on the merits. Justices who are less extraverted, more conscientious, and less neurotic are more likely to dissent after controlling for numerous other influences on their voting behavior. These findings suggest that justices who value industriousness and dutifulness tend to

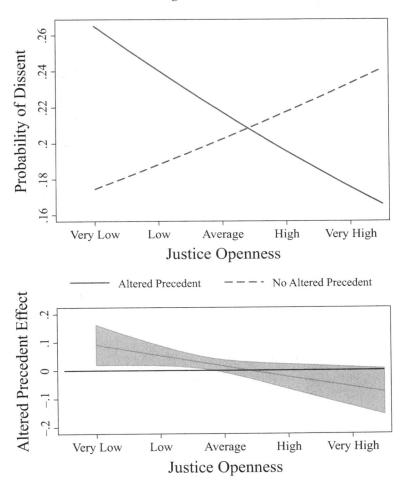

FIGURE 7.7 The effect of an altered precedent on dissent at varying levels of justice openness

Note: The upper panel presents the predicted probability of a justice dissenting in cases with versus cases without an altered precedent. The lower panel presents the marginal effects of an altered precedent with 95% confidence intervals. Predicted probabilities and marginal effects are based on a multilevel logistic regression model with random intercepts for 34 justices. The full model is reported in Appendix D.

dissent, while those who value influence and loss avoidance tend to find themselves in the majority coalition.

The justices' personality traits also condition the influence of other factors on the merits vote. In general, justices should be more likely to dissent when the Court issues a ruling that is inconsistent with the public's ideological preferences or the justice's own ideological preferences. However, the effect of these ideological factors both vary among the justices. Public disagreement appears to play a stronger role in merits voting by more-extraverted justices who value attracting attention from judicial audiences. More-conscientious justices are less likely to vote based on their own ideological preferences, presumably because they place greater value on dutifulness.

Additionally, the justices' agreeableness conditions the influence of other justices' behavior on their own votes. In general, justices are more likely to dissent when others do so. However, the influence of other justices' dissents appears to be much stronger for more-agreeable justices, suggesting that justices who value social harmony are more likely to follow each other's behavior in order to avoid collegiality costs. Agreeableness also appears to condition a justice's interest in helping disadvantaged members of society: Specifically, more-agreeable justices are less likely to dissent when the Court issues a liberal ruling.

The justices' personality traits also condition the influence of other case characteristics on their propensity to dissent. Justices should be less likely to dissent when the Court rules in favor of the federal government (in order to avoid criticism, sanctions, and institutional problems); however, this tendency only manifests among more-neurotic justices (who value loss aversion). Additionally, justices are generally more likely to dissent when the Court alters its own precedent (which changes legal doctrine). However, this tendency does not manifest among more-open justices (who value legal change).

At the beginning of this chapter, I described Justice Reed's decision to join the majority in *Brown* as an example of a justice's personality influencing his vote on the merits (specifically, Reed's conscientiousness prompted him to set aside his policy objectives out of a sense of judicial duty). The empirical findings in this chapter suggest that the importance of personality traits extend beyond that specific example. Indeed, the justices' traits appear to strongly influence their dissent behavior in a variety of ways. Accordingly, the justices' personalities may ultimately determine who wins and who loses at the US Supreme Court, and a complete understanding of the justices' decision-making (even regarding the influence of factors like ideology and public opinion) may require an understanding of the justices' traits.

8

Separate Opinions

George Chahsenah, a member of the Comanche Nation, died on October 11, 1963. His sole heir was an estranged, illegitimate daughter who, according to his will, had "shown no interest in" him. Therefore, Chahsenah bequeathed his entire estate to his niece and her three children, with whom he had lived for many years before his death. However, because his estate consisted of three Comanche allotments, US law required the secretary of the interior to approve the inheritance. Chahsenah's daughter challenged the will, arguing that her father had suffered from chronic alcoholism, cirrhosis of the liver, and diabetes, rendering him incompetent.

An examiner of inheritance for the Department of the Interior determined that the will was properly executed, witness statements showed that Chahsenah possessed testamentary capacity, and Chahsenah's failure to provide for his daughter was not unnatural since there had been no close relationship. However, the regional solicitor, acting for the secretary of the interior, set aside the examiner's action and ordered distribution to the daughter. Chahsenah's niece brought suit in the District Court, contending that the regional solicitor's action exceeded his authority. The District Court ruled for the niece, but the Court of Appeals reversed, holding that the secretary's action was unreviewable. On appeal, the US Supreme Court sided with the niece and reversed the secretary's action in *Tooahnippah v. Hickel*. After the Court's conference, Chief Justice Warren E. Burger assigned the majority opinion to himself.

Justice John Marshall Harlan II thought *Tooahnippah* was a "peewee" case – his term for insignificant matters that reached the High Court – but he disagreed with the secretary of the interior's "high-handed paternalism" and voted with the majority to reverse the court of appeals.[1] Harlan expected the chief justice to produce an opinion ordering the secretary to approve Chahsenah's will and distribute the inheritance to the niece, but he was disappointed with the first draft Burger circulated. Instead of fully resolving the case, Burger had restricted the opinion to the question of whether federal courts had the power to review the secretary's order. The chief did not reach the question of whether the secretary had properly exercised his authority and, instead, remanded the case back to the court of appeals to decide that issue. In Harlan's view, the chief's opinion was woefully inadequate. The "case might be a 'peewee,' but every case deserved as much time, effort, and explanation as it took to make the issues clear."[2]

Harlan's concerns in *Tooahnippah* were characteristic for him. As discussed in Chapter 4, Harlan was "the ultimate professional,"[3] and his conscientious nature made him industrious as well as dutiful. He was known for "well-thought-out" and "intellectually rewarding opinions," and, according to one law clerk, "[n]o amount of effort was too much to get the opinion just right – to make sure each sentence hit the mark and contained nothing inadvertent."[4] Harlan was also "the Court's most prolific writer. No matter how insignificant the disagreement or how minor the case, Harlan felt compelled to spell out his views for the sake of intellectual honesty."[5]

Harlan's conscientiousness was on full display in *Tooahnippah*. In response to Burger's draft, he wrote a memo urging the Court to address the real legal question and provide guidance to the lower courts. When Burger responded by tacking a single paragraph onto his opinion, Harlan conducted his own "careful review" of the "applicable statutes and legislative history," as well as "prior administrative decisions of the Interior Department."[6] He then circulated a separate opinion, concurring with the majority, but adding his own reasoning to explain the decision.

Burger was annoyed. He felt "concurrences detracted from the main opinion and were, in some cases, almost an insult to the author assigned for the majority."[7] So the chief revised his majority opinion a third time, borrowing much of Harlan's language in the hopes that Harlan would withdraw his concurrence. But Harlan was still not satisfied. The chief had left out most of Harlan's citations to prior cases and his thorough review of the legislative and administrative history. Harlan instructed his clerks to publish his concurrence despite the chief's efforts. In short, Harlan filed a concurring opinion because he "was determined to hold to his standard of meticulousness."[8]

⌒

After deciding how to vote, those justices not assigned to write the opinion of the Court must choose whether to file a separate opinion. Every justice has the option of filing a separate opinion in every case. Those who vote with the Court's majority can file a regular concurring opinion (which endorses the Court's opinion while offering additional reasoning or clarification) or an opinion concurring in the judgment (which supports the winning party without endorsing the majority's reasoning).[9] Those justices who dissent typically explain their reasoning by writing a dissenting opinion. However, no justice is required to file a separate opinion. Members of the majority usually join the opinion of the Court without comment, and dissenters often join another justice's dissenting opinion; occasionally, dissenters offer no explanation for their vote at all.[10]

"Separate opinions play a key role in shaping the law and determining the role of the Supreme Court in the broader polity."[11] Separate opinions may reduce the majority opinion's impact by highlighting flaws in its reasoning[12] or alter the opinion's perception among those responsible for its implementation.[13] Separate opinions may also provide clues about how future litigants might win majority support in a similar case.[14]

Nonetheless, justices – especially those in the majority coalition – typically refrain from filing separate opinions. More than a quarter of Supreme Court cases are decided unanimously without any separate opinions, and three or fewer justices file separate opinions in 95% of cases. In fact, the probability of a justice filing a concurring or dissenting opinion in any given case is only .17. Nonetheless, justices sometimes feel strongly compelled to write separately. In fact, in two cases since 1946, every justice on the Court filed a separate opinion explaining their views: *New York Times Co. v. United States* (the Pentagon Papers case) and *Furman v. Georgia* (invalidating the death penalty). Justices also vary a great deal in their propensity to write separate opinions: Earl Warren did so in only 4 percent of cases;[15] Justice Harlan did so in 28 percent of cases.

I focus my analysis of separate opinion filing on the decision by members of the majority coalition to file a concurring opinion. That is, I do not examine the decision by members of the minority coalition to file a dissenting opinion (rather than join another dissenter's opinion or dissent without explanation). I do so because the decision process for members of the minority coalition is complicated by several factors that make it difficult to empirically model. First, the decision to file a dissenting opinion is probably tied up with the decision to dissent in the first place in varied and complex ways. For example, dissenting justices have already invested enough effort into considering a case that they have decided to break with the majority (recall from Chapter 7 that more-conscientious justices are more likely to dissent). After devoting the time and energy necessary to dissent, drafting a dissenting opinion may require minimal additional effort. Indeed, such opinions can be relatively short, especially if other justices file longer dissenting opinions. Second, the decision to file a dissenting opinion is undoubtedly influenced by the number of other justices dissenting, whether those justices are dissenting for similar reasons, and – possibly – the personality traits of those other justices. Any accurate model would have to account for all of these interdependent factors. Nonetheless, I have run several exploratory models on the decision by members of the minority coalition to file a dissenting opinion. I find little evidence that justices' personality traits are associated with filing dissenting opinions with one exception: Neuroticism has a strong negative association with dissenters filing dissenting opinions. However, these exploratory models do not account for the theoretical complications I have described here. Therefore, these mostly null findings may be the result of inadequate modeling.

CONCURRING OPINIONS

Supreme Court justices file concurring opinions for a variety of reasons. First and foremost, concurrences usually reflect a justice's genuine disagreement or dissatisfaction with the majority opinion, and filing a concurrence fulfills the justice's professional duty to fully explain his or her reasoning. Accordingly, justices tend to file more concurrences in highly salient cases, complex cases, and cases in which the justice is ideologically divergent from the opinion author.[16] However, writing a concurrence requires time and energy; therefore, justices may write fewer concurrences later in a term or when the Court's caseload is heavier.[17] Additionally, writing a concurrence may expose a justice to criticism from peers, academics, or the public, or undermine the precedential value of the Court's opinion. Thus, freshmen justices and chief justices tend to write fewer concurrences, presumably due to these institutional concerns.[18]

Concurrence Hypotheses. The psychoeconomic approach posits that justices' personality traits also influence the decision to file a concurring opinion. Specifically, I propose the following hypotheses related to concurrences:

- More-extraverted justices are more likely to file a concurrence because concurrences influence other justices and attract attention from judicial audiences. Additionally, the positive influence of amici attention on concurrences is stronger for more-extraverted justices because writing concurrences in these cases attracts attention from judicial audiences.
- More-conscientious justices are more likely to file a concurrence because concurrences often require substantial effort and fulfill their judicial duty to express honest disagreement. Additionally, the positive influence of ideological preferences on filing a concurrence is weaker for more-conscientious justices because pursuing policy objectives violates their judicial duty.
- The influence of a liberal ruling on filing a concurrence is negative (positive) for more-(less-) agreeable justices because liberal rulings promote disadvantaged members of society.
- More-neurotic justices are less likely to file a concurrence because concurrences expose justices to potential criticism.

Below I describe the empirical model I used to test these hypotheses. I then develop each hypothesis in greater detail and report the findings of the empirical tests.

The Concurrence Model. In order to evaluate the role of personality traits in shaping justices' decisions to file concurrences, I replicate and extend research by Paul Wahlbeck, James Spriggs, and Forrest Maltzman[19] as well as work by Paul Collins.[20] To do so, I examine the justices' concurrence filing in each of the 7,473 cases during the 1946 through 2015 terms ($N = 39,793$).[21] The dependent variable in this analysis is the decision to file a concurring opinion by each of the 34 justices serving during this period (1 = concurring opinion; 0 = no concurring opinion; I exclude the justice assigned to author the opinion of the Court and those justices who dissented in each case).

The model controls for several variables that capture potential influences on concurrence filing, including justice characteristics (the ideological distance between each justice and the opinion author, as well as indicators for the chief justice and freshman justices), case

characteristics (case complexity, the winning vote margin, and indicators
for an invalidated statute and issue area), and time pressures (the Court's
caseload, days until the end of the term, and a time trend).[22] I also include
the justices' SCIPEs and the opinion authors' SCIPEs for the Big Five.
(See Appendix E for a full description of the model.)

JUSTICE TRAITS AND CONCURRENCES

Figure 8.1 summarizes the results of the concurrence model. The figure
reports the marginal effects of the justices' personality traits on the probability of filing a concurring opinion, as well as the effects of all statistically
significant control variables. As a point of reference, the average predicted
probability of a justice filing a concurrence is .10. The probability of a
concurrence is influenced by several legal, institutional, and ideological
factors. For example, the probability of a justice filing a concurrence is .02
lower in the justice's first year on the Court (the "freshman" effect) and
.03 higher when the Court invalidates the constitutionality of a federal
statute. Again, a few of the opinion author's traits reach conventional
levels of statistical significance, but none of these effects are large enough
to be substantively meaningful.[23]

As with most types of Supreme Court behavior, the magnitude of
personality effects on concurrence filing rivals or exceeds that of other
influences on this behavior. For example, the effects of a justice's conscientiousness (+.02), neuroticism (−.03), and openness (−.01) on filing
a concurrence are all comparable to the effect of a justice's ideological
distance to the opinion author (+.01).[24] In other words, each of these
personality traits explains as much variation in the justices' concurrence
filing as do their ideological preferences. Again, given the prominent role
of ideology in explaining Supreme Court behavior, this comparison is
particularly noteworthy.

Extraversion and Concurrences. As described in Chapter 6, circulating a
separate opinion draft is a good way for justices to influence and attract
attention from their colleagues. Similarly, proceeding to actually file and
publish a separate opinion is an ideal way for justices to attract attention from a broader audience, including lower court judges, legal academics, the media, and the public. Additionally, separate opinions may
also encourage lawyers and judges to view a particular legal issue differ-
ently in the future. For example, Justice Antonin Scalia once explained
that he wrote separate opinions with law students in mind because he
hoped to influence the next generation of lawyers.[25] Those justices who

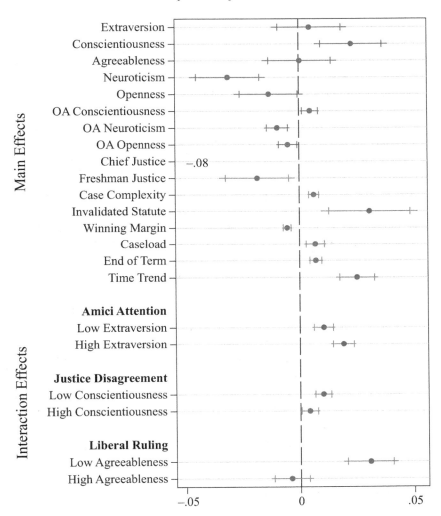

FIGURE 8.1 Marginal effects on filing a concurring opinion

Note: Figure presents marginal effects of a one standard deviation increase in each continuous variable (and one-unit increase in each dichotomous variable) on the predicted probability of a justice in the majority coalition filing a concurrence with 95% confidence intervals. Predicted probabilities are based on a multilevel logistic regression model with random intercepts for 34 justices. The full model is reported in Appendix E. OA = Opinion Author.

hope to attract attention from and potentially influence actors outside the Court should be more likely to exploit these opportunities. Therefore, more-extraverted justices (who value influence and attention) should be more likely to file a concurring opinion. However, as illustrated in Figure 8.1, I find no evidence that extraversion is directly associated with filing concurrences.

Filing separate opinions may be a useful way to influence and attract attention from external audiences; however, the efficacy of this tactic likely depends on the degree of attention the case in question is likely to receive. A strong signal that a case is likely to receive attention in the future is the amount of attention it has already received from amicus groups. Additionally, cases that attract substantial amici attention tend to be those with the most important legal and policy ramifications.[26] I measure the attention each case received from amicus groups by calculating the number of amicus briefs filed in each case, standardized within the term the case was filed. As expected, justices generally file more concurring opinions in cases in which outside groups file more amicus briefs. On average, the probability of a justice filing a concurrence in cases with low versus high amici attention (i.e., one standard deviation below versus above the mean) is .08 versus .11. Thus, the justices appear to pay some attention to these signals and on average seek out the opportunity to attract attention in these salient cases.

However, the effect of amicus briefs on concurrence filing should depend on the justices' extraversion. Justices who value the opportunity to attract attention from and potentially influence judicial audiences should be especially likely to file a concurrence when multiple parties have already expressed interest by filing amicus briefs. Thus, the influence of amici attention on filing a concurring opinion should be stronger for more-extraverted justices (who value influence and attention).

Figure 8.2 illustrates the relationship between amici attention and the propensity of justices at different levels of extraversion to file a concurrence. The upper panel presents the predicted probability of a justice filing a concurrence in cases with low versus high amici attention. The lower panel presents the effect of amici attention on the probability of a concurrence. For more-extraverted justices, an increase from less to more amici attention is associated with a .04 increase in the probability of a concurrence (from .08 to .12). For less-extraverted justices, the same increase in amici attention is associated with only a .02 increase in the probability of a concurrence (from .08 to .10). Thus, the influence of amici attention is twice as strong for more-versus less-extraverted justices.

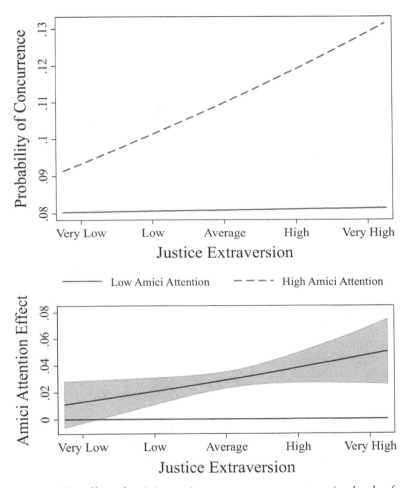

FIGURE 8.2 The effect of amici attention on concurrences at varying levels of extraversion

Note: The upper panel presents the predicted probability of a concurrence in cases with low versus high amici attention (i.e., one standard deviation below versus above the mean). The lower panel presents the marginal effects of amici attention with 95% confidence intervals. Predicted probabilities and marginal effects are based on a multilevel logistic regression model with random intercepts for 34 justices. The full model is reported in Appendix E.

Conscientiousness and Concurrences. Researching, drafting, and revising opinions is difficult and time-consuming work. Those justices who are willing to devote the time and energy necessary to complete these tasks (especially when doing so is neither necessary nor expected) should tend to file more concurrences. Moreover, the decision to file a concurrence is often motivated by a justice's sense of professional responsibility. (Recall Justice John Paul Stevens' view that "[t]here is a duty to explain your position if it isn't the same as the majority.")[27] Those justices who feel a greater sense of judicial duty to express any disagreement with the majority should also tend to file more concurrences. Therefore, more-conscientious justices (who value industriousness and dutifulness) should be more likely to file a concurrence.

Figure 8.1 illustrates the positive relationship between the justices' conscientiousness and their propensity to file a concurring opinion. The probability of a concurrence is .07 for less-conscientious justices and .12 for more-conscientious justices. Thus, more-conscientious justices are 70 percent more likely to file a concurrence than less-conscientious justices, which presumably reflects their sense of obligation to explain disagreement with the majority and their willingness to invest the effort required to do so.

The justices' preference for dutifulness should also condition the influence of their policy preferences on filing concurrences. As described in an earlier section, concurring opinions often express some disagreement with the majority opinion. Therefore, justices who are ideologically inclined to disagree with the majority ruling should be more likely to file a concurrence. (I measure a justice's disagreement with the ideological direction of the majority ruling in the same manner described in Chapter 7.) As expected, increasing from low to high justice disagreement (i.e., one standard deviation below to one standard deviation above the mean) is associated with a .01 increase in the probability of filing a concurrence (from .09 to .10). However, just as a justice's professional duty has restrained ideological biases in other contexts, dutiful justices should also resist the temptation to let their personal policy objectives affect whether they file a concurring opinion. Therefore, the influence of ideological preferences should be weaker for more conscientious justices (who value dutifulness).

Figure 8.3 illustrates the relationship between justice disagreement and the propensity of justices at different levels of conscientiousness to file a concurrence. The upper panel presents the predicted probability of a justice filing a concurrence in cases with low versus high justice disagreement. The lower panel presents the effect of justice disagreement on the probability of a concurrence. For less-conscientious justices, an increase from low to high justice disagreement is associated with a .02 increase in the probability of a concurrence (from .07 to .09). For

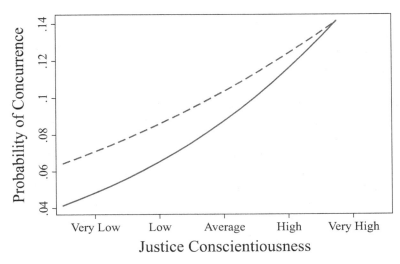

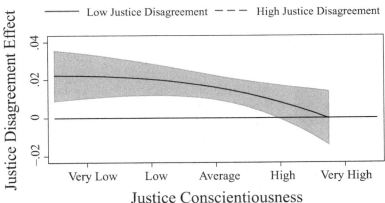

FIGURE 8.3 The effect of justice disagreement on concurrences at varying levels of conscientiousness

Note: The upper panel presents the predicted probability of a concurrence with low versus high levels of justice disagreement (i.e., one standard deviation below versus above the mean). The lower panel presents the marginal effects of justice disagreement with 95% confidence intervals. Predicted probabilities and marginal effects are based on a multilevel logistic regression model with random intercepts for 34 justices. The full model is reported in Appendix E.

more-conscientious justices, the same increase in justice disagreement is not associated with filing a concurrence.[28] Therefore, a justice's ideological disagreement with the Court's ruling only encourages concurrence filing by less-conscientious justices.

Agreeableness and Concurrences. Concurring opinions usually express some disagreement with the majority opinion author and in some cases undermine the majority opinion's persuasive force (or even, in the case of special concurrences, its precedential value). Both of these dynamics suggest that filing concurring opinions tends to undermine social harmony on the Court. Therefore, more-agreeable justices (who value social harmony) should be less likely to file a concurring opinion, just as I expected them to be less likely to dissent. However, once again, I fail to find evidence supporting this expectation. (In Chapter 9, I discuss my inability to confirm several of my expectations regarding agreeableness and the potential implications of these null findings.)

Like the merits vote, filing concurring opinions should also be influenced by the justices' desire to help disadvantaged members of society. Recall from Chapter 7 that Supreme Court justices generally tend to promote the interests of the disadvantaged, which means, on average, they are less likely to dissent when the Court issues a liberal ruling. However, even after dividing into majority and dissenting coalitions, some members of the majority may continue to have reservations about the ruling, depending on the ideological direction of the decision. As described above, filing a concurrence is often a reflection of disagreement or dissatisfaction with the majority opinion; therefore, filing a concurrence is a useful mechanism for expressing those reservations. Members of the majority coalition who value altruism should be less likely to express reservations when the Court issues a liberal ruling (so as to not undermine a decision that supports disadvantaged members of society). In contrast, those justices with less interest in helping the disadvantaged should be more likely to file a concurrence when the Court issues a liberal ruling (because they are prone toward undermining such rulings). Therefore, when the Court issues a liberal ruling, more agreeable justices in the majority coalition should be less likely to file a concurrence. When the Court issues a conservative ruling, the reverse should be true.

Figure 8.4 presents the relationship between liberal rulings, justice agreeableness, and concurrences. The upper panel presents the predicted probability of a justice filing a concurrence in cases with a conservative versus liberal ruling. The lower panel presents the effect of a liberal ruling on the probability of dissent. For less-agreeable justices, a liberal ruling is associated with a .03 increase in the probability of a concurrence (from .08 to .11). Thus, consistent with my expectations, less-agreeable justices are more prone to filing a concurring opinion when the Court supports the interests of disadvantaged members of society. Additionally,

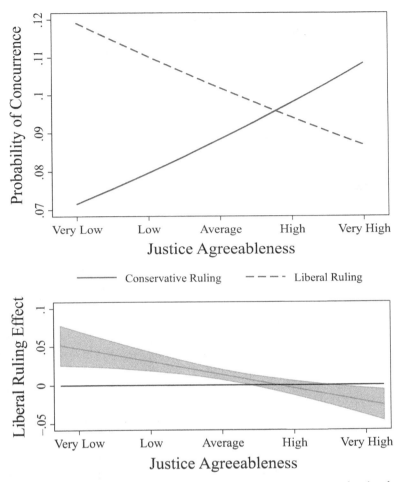

FIGURE 8.4 The effect of a liberal ruling on concurrences at varying levels of agreeableness

Note: The upper panel presents the predicted probability of a concurrence in cases with a conservative versus liberal ruling. The lower panel presents the marginal effects of a liberal ruling with 95% confidence intervals. Predicted probabilities and marginal effects are based on a multilevel logistic regression model with random intercepts for 34 justices. The full model is reported in Appendix E.

extremely-agreeable justices (those two standard deviations above the mean) are more prone to filing a concurrence when the Court opposes the interests of the disadvantaged.

Neuroticism and Concurrences. Filing a concurring opinion inherently involves the risk of attracting criticism from peers, academics, the media, and the public.[29] Justices who are less willing to accept these risks in exchange for potential benefits should be less likely to expose themselves to potential criticism by writing separately. Therefore, more-neurotic justices (who value loss avoidance) should be less likely to file a concurrence.

Figure 8.1 illustrates the negative relationship between the justices' neuroticism and their propensity to file a concurring opinion. The probability of a concurrence is .13 for less-neurotic justices and .07 for more-neurotic justices. Thus, more-neurotic justices are about 50 percent less likely to file a concurrence than less-neurotic justices, which presumably reflects their propensity to avoid exposing themselves to potential criticism.

Openness and Concurrences. The relationship between openness and concurrence filing is likely complicated. A preference for intellectualism and creativity might prompt a justice to write more concurrences as an outlet for engaging with other justices and sharing different ideas. Indeed, recall from Chapter 6 that more-open justices tend to circulate more separate opinion drafts. Yet, merely circulating a separate draft is one thing; actually publishing it is quite another. Filing a concurrence often reflects an intellectual divide on the Court that could not be reconciled through intra-Court bargaining. The ability to compromise in such a constructive manner also depends on the justices' willingness to intellectually engage with one another and consider different ideas. Recall also from Chapter 6 that more-open justices tend to send more majority opinion drafts, likely for two reasons: They prefer to engage in intellectual debate and they are open to changing their own and each other's minds. Justices who are deeply engaged in intra-Court bargaining should be more likely to resolve their differences with the majority opinion author and ultimately withdraw any separate opinion. Therefore, I neither expect nor find any relationship between openness and concurrences. (As illustrated in Figure 8.1, openness is negatively associated with concurring opinions; however, this finding does not reach conventional levels of statistical significance. Therefore, the data do not support any firm conclusions.)

PERSONALITY TRAITS AND SEPARATE OPINIONS

To summarize, the justices' personality traits are strongly associated with the decision to file a concurring opinion. Justices who are more conscientious and less neurotic are more likely to file a concurrence, even after controlling for numerous other influences on their opinion filing. These findings suggest that justices who value industriousness and dutifulness tend to file more concurring opinions, while those who value loss avoidance tend to file fewer concurrences.

The justices' personality traits also condition the influence of other factors on filing concurring opinions. In general, justices are more likely to file a concurrence when a case receives attention from amici and when justices ideologically disagree with the Court's ruling. However, as in other stages of the Court's decision-making, both of these effects depend on the justices' personality traits. The influence of amici attention is stronger for more-extraverted justices, presumably because they prefer to attract attention from judicial audiences. And the influence of a justice's ideological preferences is weaker for more-conscientious justices, presumably because they feel a stronger sense of judicial duty. Additionally, the justices' agreeableness conditions their reactions to the ideological direction of the Court's ruling. Only less-agreeable justices are more likely to file a concurrence when the Court issues a liberal ruling, presumably because they are more willing to express disagreement when the Court tries to help disadvantaged members of society. Similarly, extremely agreeable justices are more likely to file a concurrence when the Court issues a conservative ruling.

At the beginning of this chapter, I described Justice Harlan's decision to write separately in *Tooahnippah* as an example of a justice's personality influencing his opinion filing behavior (specifically, Harlan's conscientiousness prompted him to file a concurring opinion). The empirical findings suggest that Harlan's behavior is not uncommon. Indeed, justices' personality traits appear to strongly influence their decision to file concurring opinions in a variety of ways. Accordingly, the justices' personalities may ultimately determine whether the Court speaks with one voice or fractures into several separate opinions.

9

Behind the Black Robes

For the last century, the study of the US Supreme Court has consistently focused on a few tried-and-true explanations for the justices' behavior: the content of the law and legal norms, the ideological and partisan consequences of justices' decisions, and the institutional context in which justices operate. Surprisingly, though, few studies of justices' choices have focused on the justices themselves. To the extent that scholars have examined justices' individual characteristics, they tend to reduce these characteristics to one-dimensional policy preferences. Indeed, an apt metaphor for the predominant view of Supreme Court justices is their official "class photo": a group of nine justices, arrayed from left to right, concealed beneath identical black robes.

In contrast, this book has adopted a very different approach to studying Supreme Court justices – an approach centered around *who they are* and *what they want*. In short, I have argued that justices pursue a variety of goals, well beyond the bare desire to influence policy or follow the law. As such, I join several scholars who have recently argued that justices pursue multiple objectives, such as prestige, effort aversion, and collegiality.[1] However, in contrast to these studies, I emphasize the justices' individual differences. In other words, prior studies have suggested that justices pursue multiple goals, but they have generally neglected the possibility that different justices want different things. Instead, I argue that justices possess distinct personality traits and, consequently, vary considerably in the value they attach to different goals.

PERSONALITY TRAITS ACROSS THE DECISION PROCESS

Throughout this book, I have found that the justices' personality traits shape their priorities when making decisions and, therefore, influence their behavior at each stage of the decision-making process, including agenda setting, the assignment of the majority opinion, intra-Court bargaining, the merits vote, and the decision to file a separate opinion. At each stage, the justices' decisions appear to fit the behavior one would expect based on their personality traits. And each of these individual outcomes is important in its own right; indeed, volumes have been written on each of the decisions I have examined. However, when taking a broad view of the relationship between traits and behavior across decision contexts, personality emerges as a remarkably powerful force in shaping the justices' choices – far more powerful than any one association between a particular trait and a particular behavior might suggest. Below I summarize the findings related to each Big Five trait across each stage of the Court's decision-making process. In particular, I emphasize the strategic advantages and disadvantages associated with each trait.

Extraversion. More-extraverted justices value influence and attention, and these goal preferences manifest across decision contexts. Their active and assertive nature makes them particularly influential: They are less likely to dissent on average and, despite circulating more separate opinions, they do not actually file more separate opinions – suggesting they use the threat of a separate opinion to influence majority opinion content. Chief justices tend to prefer more-extraverted justices when assigning the opinion of the Court, and, when assigned to write the majority opinion, more-extraverted justices tend to circulate more opinion drafts, presumably in an effort to influence their colleagues. These justices also seek out attention from judicial audiences by voting to grant cert and filing concurring opinions in cases that receive attention from amicus groups. However, their preference for influence and attention also has costs: For example, senior associate justices tend to assign fewer majority opinions to extraverts (possibly in an attempt to limit their influence), and the desire for attention makes extraverts more beholden to popular pressures, especially in cases that receive media attention.

Conscientiousness. Conscientious justices value industriousness and dutifulness, and these goal preferences prompt them to put more care and effort into their professional responsibilities across contexts. During the bargaining process, these justices contribute heavily to the Court's dialogue by circulating more separate opinion drafts and opinion suggestions (as well as fewer join statements). Their strict adherence to judicial duty prompts conscientious justices to cast fewer votes to grant cert and resist the temptation to pursue their ideological policy objectives when assigning the majority opinion, circulating bargaining memos, casting the merits vote, and filing concurring opinions. Senior associate justices also tend to reward conscientious justices by favoring them for majority opinion assignments. Yet, despite the admirable qualities associated with these justices, their dutiful and industrious nature also yields problematic qualities. Most importantly, they tend to undermine consensus on the Court by expressing honest disagreement through dissent and separate opinions.

Agreeableness. Agreeable justices prioritize social harmony on the Court and altruism for disadvantaged members of society. These justices are more likely to provide the critical fourth grant vote when three other justices vote to grant cert, and they are more likely to dissent when other justices do so. They also circulate fewer separate opinion drafts and wait statements, presumably to avoid frustrating their colleagues. However, their amiable natures also makes them poor candidates to receive the opinion assignment from the chief justice in narrowly decided cases. Finally, their concern for other people extends beyond the other justices. As a result, more-agreeable justices tend to cast more liberal votes – that is, votes that support the interests of disadvantaged members of society, such as criminals, civil rights claimants, and the indigent. When less-agreeable justices find themselves in a liberal majority, they tend to file more concurring opinions, presumably to express reservations about these decisions.

Neuroticism. Neurotic justices avoid losses and express negativity. Their loss avoidance prompts theses justices to withdraw from judicial activities: More-neurotic justices vote to hear fewer cases, avoid opinion assignments (from the chief and the senior associate justice), and circulate more wait statements and join statements during the bargaining process. More-neurotic justices also try to avoid criticism from their colleagues, legal academics, the media, and the public by casting grant votes when the federal government supports cert, dissenting less frequently (especially when the Court rules in favor of the federal government), and filing fewer concurring opinions. Their volatility also prompts them to express negativity more often when they can do so with little risk. This tendency prompts them to circulate more opinion suggestions and makes them less desirable candidates to write the majority opinion.

Openness. Open justices value intellectualism and change throughout the Court's decision-making process. Their flexibility and philosophical orientation prompts them to actively engage in the Court's decisions: They circulate more majority opinion drafts and separate opinion drafts, and they circulate fewer wait statements and join statements. More-open justices also place greater value on change in legal doctrine, prompting them to dissent less frequently when the Court alters one of its own precedents. And their desire for change prompts chief justices to give them opinion assignments on a variety of issues (rather than repeated assignments on the same issue, as most justices tend to receive). Their interests in intellectualism and change both make open justices more likely to reach agreements with others (their intellectualism leads them to engage with others' ideas; their interest in change leads them to revise their own ideas). As a result, they are less likely to file concurring opinions. However, their willingness to change their views and compromise also makes them poor choices for opinion assignments from senior associate justices (who prefer to assign more predictable justices).

Problems with Agreeableness? For most of the Big Five traits, I found all or nearly all of the associations that I expected to emerge between the justices' traits and their behavior. However, my analyses failed to uncover several potential associations related to agreeableness. Given that agreeable justices value social harmony, I expected agreeableness to be associated with circulating more join statements, dissenting less frequently, and filing fewer concurring opinions. I also expected justice agreeableness to condition the influence of the winning margin on opinion assignments from the senior associate justice. However, I found no evidence to support these four hypotheses. (In contrast, I found evidence supporting all but four of my hypotheses related to all of the other Big Five traits combined.[2] Additionally, the relationship between cert votes and openness fell just short of statistical significance in Chapter 4.) These null findings suggest one of two possibilities.

First, the textual analysis process used to generate SCIPEs may have had difficulty detecting agreeableness from the justices' opinions – either due to peculiarities of legal language or the justices' deliberate efforts to conceal this trait. Indeed, recall that agreeableness was the only Big Five trait for which I found inconsistent evidence in the face validity tests (specifically with regard to Justice Harold H. Burton). Nonetheless, several aspects of my findings cast doubt on this conclusion. The SCIPEs for agreeableness were supported by descriptions for five of the six most extreme justices on this trait. Moreover, I found several associations between agreeableness and the justices' behavior that comport with my theoretical expectations. Indeed, the finding that more-agreeable justices are more influenced by the behavior of other justices was particularly convincing given that it manifested in the agenda-setting, opinion assignment, and merits vote stages. Accordingly, this evidence suggests it is premature to discount the agreeableness measure based on a few null findings.

Alternatively, these null findings may simply indicate that concern for social harmony plays a diminished role on the modern US Supreme Court. As described in Chapter 2, a strong norm of consensus once existed on the High Court, which discouraged dissent and separate opinions; but this norm collapsed in the 1940s, and dissent rates on the Court have remained high ever since.[3] In contrast, norms of consensus and collegiality continue to play a strong role in the US Courts of Appeals.[4] Therefore, agreeableness may play a more important role on other courts with stronger professional norms related to collegiality and consensus building.

PERSONALITY AND POLITICAL BEHAVIOR

This book is intended to be only the first – and hopefully far from the last – word on the systematic study of personality traits shaping behavior on the US Supreme Court. My findings suggest that personality traits play a critical and seriously understudied role in shaping judicial behavior, and my approach fundamentally challenges the preeminent approaches in the literature. Contrary to social-psychological approaches (which portray judicial choices as responses to stimuli), my account incorporates the more realistic conception of judges as rational actors striving to maximize their utility over a set of goals. And, contrary to economic/rational choice approaches (which generally assume that judges hold uniform preferences for those goals), my account recognizes an obvious truth of human thought and behavior: Different people want different things. As such, the psychoeconomic approach offers a rich and, most importantly, realistic account of how judges make decisions, which highlights the importance of individual differences – beyond ideological differences – in shaping judicial outcomes.

Yet, for as many questions as this theoretical and empirical approach answers, it raises many more. Do a justice's traits have interactive effects on his or her behavior? For example, are justices who are both less extraverted and less neurotic even less likely to dissent than these separate traits would independently suggest? What about justices who are low in one trait but high in the other? Do the effects simply average out, or does the influence of one trait tend to trump the other? And do the personality traits of different justices interact with one other? For example, do justices who are more conscientious tend to join each other's opinions because they appreciate each other's professionalism and effort? Researchers may even explore the role of a Court's aggregate personality in shaping outcomes: Just as we speak of the "liberal Warren Court" or the "conservative Rehnquist Court," perhaps we should refer to the "unconscientious Burger Court" (a description that is supported by the data). Future research should explore these and other questions related to the myriad of ways that personality traits may influence judicial behavior.

Perhaps the most promising avenue for future research is the study of personality traits in the lower courts. Such studies offer several valuable advantages. First, the study of personality on the US Supreme Court is inherently limited by the small number of judges that have served in this elite institution. The comparatively large number of judges on the US Courts of Appeals, state courts of last resort, and the numerous lower courts in the American judicial system would provide considerably greater variation in personality traits (which may be especially valuable for studies of interactions between judges). Moreover, several (but not all) US Courts of Appeals randomly assign judges to panels, and prior studies have used this feature to test panel effects on these courts – that is, the effect of assigning judges with a particular party identification or demographic characteristic on the behavior of other judges on the panel.[5] The same design could be utilized to test the effects of assigning judges with certain personality traits on the other judges' behavior. For example, judges may tend to write longer opinions when other members of the panel are more conscientious (and, presumably, monitoring the opinion's quality). Lastly, the institutional rules and norms surrounding the Supreme Court, especially their lack of accountability to a higher court and their lack of incentives for promotion, may facilitate the influence of personality traits, but this possibility remains untested. Are Supreme Court justices especially prone to indulge the impulses inherent in their personalities? Or are these tendencies difficult to suppress, regardless of a judge's incentives? If so, the influence of personality may be ubiquitous across courts.

Finally, the psychoeconomic approach need not be limited to the judicial context. On the contrary, this approach could be applied to the study of both the mass public and elites in a variety of institutions. Indeed, comparable work has recently been produced on the role of personality traits in shaping congressional behavior.[6] In much the same way, personality traits may offer considerable leverage for theorizing about individuals' goals (and measuring their preferences for those goals) across numerous institutional domains. In short, the study of political behavior by countless actors may be greatly enhanced by accounting for *who they are* and *what they want.*

Appendix A Agenda-Setting Analysis

Table A.1 reports the results of the agenda setting model. The data consist of cert votes by 12 justices in a random sample of 358 paid nondeath penalty petitions coming out of a federal court of appeals that made the US Supreme Court's discuss list during the 1986 through 1993 terms.[1] The data and the control variables were derived from Black and Owens' study of Supreme Court agenda setting.[2] The dependent variable is each justice's cert vote in each case (1 = grant; 0 = deny; N = 3,002). Because the dependent variable is dichotomous and cert votes by the same justice may be interdependent, I employ a multilevel logistic regression model with random intercepts for justice. The model includes the justices' SCIPEs for the Big Five (*Extraversion*, *Conscientiousness*, *Agreeableness*, *Neuroticism*, and *Openness*), as well as the following control variables and interaction terms:

- The number of amicus curie briefs filed in each case before cert was granted, standardized within the term the case was filed (*Amici Attention*), as well as an interaction term between this variable and *Extraversion*.
- Dichotomous indicators for the number of grant votes cast by other justices, as well as interaction terms between each indicator and *Agreeableness*. I use dichotomous indicators rather than a continuous variable to account for potential nonlinear effects.
- A dichotomous indicator taking on the value one if the United States asked for review either as petitioner or through participation as amicus curiae and zero otherwise (*US Supports Petition*), as well as an interaction term between this variable and *Neuroticism*.

TABLE A.1 *Agenda-setting model*

	Coefficient	S.E.	p-Value
Extraversion	0.10	0.35	0.77
Amici Attention	0.08	0.05	0.11
Extraversion × Amici Attention	0.11	0.06	0.05
Conscientiousness	−0.70	0.25	0.00
Agreeableness	−0.14	0.45	0.76
1 Other Grant Vote	2.19	0.29	0.00
2 Other Grant Votes	2.78	0.29	0.00
3 Other Grant Votes	3.56	0.29	0.00
4 Other Grant Votes	2.60	0.30	0.00
5 Other Grant Votes	4.55	0.33	0.00
6 Other Grant Votes	4.43	0.34	0.00
7 Other Grant Votes	4.58	0.36	0.00
8 Other Grant Votes	6.66	0.61	0.00
Agreeableness × 1 Other Grant Vote	0.67	0.26	0.01
Agreeableness × 2 Other Grant Votes	0.73	0.26	0.01
Agreeableness × 3 Other Grant Votes	0.79	0.26	0.00
Agreeableness × 4 Other Grant Votes	0.70	0.28	0.01
Agreeableness × 5 Other Grant Votes	0.98	0.33	0.00
Agreeableness × 6 Other Grant Votes	1.00	0.34	0.00
Agreeableness × 7 Other Grant Votes	0.75	0.37	0.04
Agreeableness × 8 Other Grant Votes	1.99	0.75	0.01
Neuroticism	−0.82	0.44	0.06
US Supports Petition	0.57	0.17	0.00
US Opposes Petition	0.04	0.15	0.79
Neuroticism × US Supports Petition	0.43	0.22	0.05
Neuroticism × US Opposes Petition	0.16	0.19	0.39
Openness	0.30	0.21	0.14
Chief Justice	0.13	0.54	0.80
Freshman Justice	−0.14	0.21	0.52
Ideological Preference	0.57	0.12	0.00
Alleged Conflict	0.10	0.17	0.54
Weak Conflict	0.14	0.14	0.34
Strong Conflict	0.68	0.15	0.00
Intermediate Reversal	0.18	0.11	0.12
Intermediate Dissent	0.13	0.13	0.32
Intermediate Strike	0.86	0.28	0.00
Intermediate En Banc	−0.02	0.24	0.94
Intermediate Unpublished	−0.20	0.27	0.47
U.S. Law Week Article	0.11	0.12	0.37
Constant	−4.89	0.36	0.00
Bayesian Information Criterion	2,627.36		
Log Likelihood	−1,149.54		
Number of Observations	3,002		

Note: Table reports the results of a multilevel logistic regression model of votes to grant cert by Supreme Court justices with random intercepts for justice.

- A dichotomous indicator taking on the value one if the United States is the respondent or filed an amicus brief opposing review and zero otherwise (*US Opposes Petition*), as well as an interaction term between this variable and *Neuroticism*.
- A dichotomous indicator taking on the value one for the chief justice and zero otherwise (*Chief Justice*).
- A dichotomous indicator taking on the value one for justices in their first term on the Court and zero otherwise (*Freshman Justice*).
- A dichotomous indicator taking on the value one if the justice is ideologically closer to the predicted policy location of the Supreme Court's decision on the merits than to the status quo policy and zero otherwise (*Ideological Preference*). This variable is based on the Judicial Common Space scores[3] for the median justice on the Supreme Court and the median judge on the federal circuit panel (i.e., the intermediate court) that heard the case. See Black and Owens for more details.[4]
- A dichotomous indicator taking on the value one if the petitioner alleged the presence of inter-circuit conflict and zero otherwise (*Alleged Conflict*).
- A dichotomous indicator taking on the value one if a clerk noted the presence of inter-circuit conflict but indicated that it was shallow or unworthy of attention and zero otherwise (*Weak Conflict*).
- A dichotomous indicator taking on the value one if a clerk indicated the presence of real inter-circuit conflict and zero otherwise (*Strong Conflict*).
- A dichotomous indicator taking on the value one if the intermediate court reversed the decision of the court below it (usually a trial court) and zero otherwise (*Intermediate Reversal*).
- A dichotomous indicator taking on the value one if a judge in the intermediate court filed a dissenting opinion and zero otherwise (*Intermediate Dissent*).
- A dichotomous indicator taking on the value one if the intermediate court invalidated a federal statute as unconstitutional and zero otherwise (*Intermediate Strike*).
- A dichotomous indicator taking on the value one if the intermediate court made an en banc decision and zero otherwise (*Intermediate En Banc*).
- A dichotomous indicator taking on the value one if the intermediate court's opinion was not published in the relevant federal or state reporter and zero otherwise (*Intermediate Unpublished*).

- A dichotomous indicator taking on the value one if the intermediate court's opinion was summarized in an article published by the legal periodical *U.S. Law Week* and zero otherwise (*U.S. Law Week* Article).

An attentive reader will notice that the coefficient for *Neuroticism* reported in Table A.1 falls just short of conventional levels of statistical significance using a two-tailed test. However, given that there is no theoretical reason to think neuroticism would be associated with more grant votes, a one-tailed *t*-test is appropriate for evaluating this relationship.

Appendix B Opinion Assignment Analysis

Table B.1 reports the results of the opinion assignment models. The data consist of majority opinion assignments to 34 justices during the 1946 through 2015 terms.[1] Unless noted otherwise, the data were obtained from the Supreme Court Database.[2] The dependent variable indicates whether each justice was assigned to write the majority opinion in each case (1 = assigned; 0 = not assigned). I conduct two separate analyses: one for the 5,844 cases in which the chief justice assigned the majority opinion ($N = 41,598$) and one for the 1,093 cases in which the senior associate justice (SAJ) assigned the majority opinion ($N = 6,112$). Modeling opinion assignments is especially complex because "the likelihood that a chief will assign the opinion to one justice is dependent on the probability that the chief justice will assign it to another member of the majority."[3] Because my models include an interaction term with an assignment specific variable (winning margin), I follow Maltzman and Wahlbeck by utilizing a random effects estimator for case. Therefore, I employ multilevel logistic regression models with random intercepts for case. However, my results are also robust to including random intercepts for justice. Both models include the justices' SCIPEs for the Big Five (*Extraversion, Conscientiousness, Agreeableness, Neuroticism* and *Openness*), as well as the following control variables:

- The *Winning Margin*, which was calculated by subtracting the number of votes needed to form a winning coalition from the number of justices voting with the assignor (e.g., when all nine justices participate, the winning margin is zero if the majority has five justices and four if the

TABLE B.1 *Opinion assignment models*

	(a) Chief Assignment Model			(b) SAJ Assignment Model		
	Coefficient	S.E.	p-value	Coefficient	S.E.	p-Value
Extraversion	0.14*	0.02	0.00	−0.32*	0.07	0.00
Conscientiousness	−0.02	0.02	0.30	0.40*	0.06	0.00
Agreeableness	−0.05	0.03	0.15	0.08	0.07	0.24
Winning Margin	−0.18*	0.01	0.00	−0.20*	0.03	0.00
Agreeableness × Winning Margin	0.03*	0.01	0.02	−0.01	0.04	0.79
Neuroticism	−0.09*	0.02	0.00	−0.21*	0.07	0.00
Openness	0.02	0.03	0.41	−0.12*	0.06	0.03
Issue Experience	0.02*	0.01	0.00	0.04*	0.01	0.01
Openness × Issue Experience	−0.02*	0.01	0.03			
SAJ Extraversion				0.16	0.11	0.12
SAJ Conscientiousness				−0.14*	0.07	0.05
Distance to Assigner				−0.25*	0.04	0.00
SAJ Conscientiousness × Distance to SAJ				0.32*	0.09	0.00
SAJ Agreeableness				0.04	0.10	0.67
SAJ Neuroticism				0.25*	0.12	0.03
SAJ Openness				0.10	0.10	0.32
Freshman Justice	0.06	0.07	0.41	−0.27	0.21	0.22
Equity	−0.03*	0.01	0.04			
Chief Justice	−0.11*	0.05	0.03			
Distance to Assigner	0.14*	0.07	0.04			
Constant	−1.43*	0.04	0.00	−1.34*	0.08	0.00
Bayesian Information Criterion	33,061.76			5,683.43		
Log Likelihood	−16,451.11			−2,763.26		
Number of Observations	41,598			6,112		

Note: Table reports the results of multilevel logistic regression models of majority opinion assignments by the (a) chief justice and (b) senior associate justice with random intercepts for case.

decision is unanimous), as well as an interaction term between *Winning Margin* and *Agreeableness*.[4]

- The number of majority opinions written by each justice on the same legal issue in prior terms (*Issue Experience*).
- A dichotomous indicator taking on the value one for justices in their first term on the Court and zero otherwise (*Freshman Justice*).
- The absolute difference in Segal–Cover ideology scores[5] between each justice and the majority opinion assigner, whether the chief justice or the SAJ (*Distance to Assigner*).

The chief assignment model also includes the following control variables and interaction terms:

- A dichotomous indicator taking on the value one for the chief justice and zero otherwise (*Chief Justice*).
- The number of assignments each justice received from SAJs in that term (*Equity*).
- An interaction term between *Issue Experience* and *Openness*.

The SAJ assignment model also includes the following control variables and interaction terms:

- The SAJ's SCIPEs for the Big Five (*SAJ Extraversion, SAJ Conscientiousness, SAJ Agreeableness, SAJ Neuroticism,* and *SAJ Openness*).
- An interaction term between *Distance to SAJ* and *SAJ Conscientiousness*.

Appendix C Intra-Court Bargaining Analysis

Tables C.1–C.5 report the results of the intra-Court bargaining models. The data consist of 48,524 memoranda circulated between the 13 justices who served on the US Supreme Court during the 1969 through 1985 terms. The data were derived from the Burger Court Opinion Writing Database.[1] I conducted separate analyses for the following types of memoranda: majority opinion drafts, separate opinion drafts, opinion suggestions, wait statements, and join statements. The first model, examining majority opinion drafts, includes only the justice in each case who wrote the opinion of the Court ($N = 2,136$). The other models include every justice in each case who did not write the opinion of the Court ($N = 16,086$). The dependent variables are the number of each memo type sent by each justice in each case; therefore, I used regression models appropriate for count data. To examine majority opinion drafts and wait statements, I employed a multilevel Poisson model with random intercepts for justice, which assumes a Poisson distribution and accounts for potential interdependence between justices. However, a likelihood-ratio test indicated overdispersion (suggesting that the Poisson regression model is inappropriate) for separate opinion drafts and opinion suggestions; therefore, I employed a negative binomial regression model for these dependent variables. Additionally, a likelihood-ratio test indicated that I cannot reject the null hypothesis that the multilevel model is not an improvement over the standard model for separate opinion drafts and join statements; therefore, I excluded the random intercepts for justice in these models. All of the models include the justices' SCIPEs for the Big Five (*Extraversion*, *Conscientiousness*, *Agreeableness*, *Neuroticism*, and *Openness*), as well as the following control variables:

TABLE C.1 *Majority opinion drafts model*

	Coefficient	S.E.	p-Value
Extraversion	0.12	0.05	0.01
Conscientiousness	−0.02	0.04	0.67
Agreeableness	0.02	0.06	0.80
Neuroticism	−0.08	0.06	0.20
Openness	0.13	0.04	0.00
Chief Justice	0.02	0.10	0.88
Freshman Justice	−0.01	0.09	0.88
Amici Attention	0.04	0.01	0.00
Case Complexity	0.03	0.02	0.10
Winning Margin	−0.06	0.01	0.00
Caseload	−0.21	0.17	0.22
End of Term	0.15	0.03	0.00
Time Trend	0.01	0.00	0.00
Civil Rights	−0.07	0.04	0.06
First Amendment	0.04	0.05	0.42
Due Process	−0.02	0.06	0.74
Privacy	0.10	0.09	0.28
Attorneys	−0.07	0.11	0.54
Unions	−0.21	0.07	0.00
Economic Activity	−0.12	0.04	0.00
Judicial Power	−0.05	0.05	0.33
Federalism	−0.16	0.08	0.04
Federal Taxation	−0.16	0.08	0.05
Constant	1.40	0.85	0.10
Bayesian Information Criterion	7,357.57		
Log Likelihood	−3,582.95		
Number of Observations	2,136		

Note: Table reports the results of a multilevel Poisson model of majority opinion drafts circulated by Supreme Court justices with random intercepts for justice.

- A dichotomous indicator taking on the value one for the chief justice and zero otherwise (*Chief Justice*).
- A dichotomous indicator taking on the value one for justices in their first term on the Court and zero otherwise (*Freshman Justice*).
- The number of amicus curie briefs filed in each case, standardized within the term the case was filed (*Amici Attention*).

TABLE C.2 *Separate opinion drafts model*

	Coefficient	S.E.	*p*-Value
Extraversion	0.27	0.04	0.00
Conscientiousness	0.26	0.04	0.00
Distance to Author	0.08	0.02	0.00
Conscientiousness × Distance to Author	−0.07	0.02	0.00
Agreeableness	−0.15	0.06	0.01
Neuroticism	−0.03	0.07	0.69
Openness	0.38	0.03	0.00
Chief Justice	−0.94	0.09	0.00
Freshman Justice	−0.10	0.13	0.45
Amici Attention	0.11	0.02	0.00
Case Complexity	0.06	0.03	0.05
Winning Margin	−0.30	0.01	0.00
Caseload	−1.45	0.28	0.00
End of Term	0.19	0.05	0.00
Time Trend	0.01	0.01	0.02
Civil Rights	−0.27	0.06	0.00
First Amendment	0.15	0.08	0.06
Due Process	−0.20	0.09	0.04
Privacy	−0.02	0.15	0.91
Attorneys	−0.35	0.17	0.04
Unions	−0.38	0.11	0.00
Economic Activity	−0.53	0.07	0.00
Judicial Power	−0.29	0.08	0.00
Federalism	−0.52	0.12	0.00
Federal Taxation	−0.68	0.14	0.00
Constant	6.04	1.38	0.00
Bayesian Information Criterion	25,638.11		
Log Likelihood	−12,688.30		
Number of Observations	16,086		

Note: Table reports the results of a negative binomial regression model of separate opinion drafts circulated by Supreme Court justices.

- The score that resulted from a factor analysis of the number of legal issues raised and the number of legal provisions at issue in the case (*Case Complexity*).[2]
- The *Winning Margin*, which was calculated by subtracting the number of votes needed to form a winning coalition from the number of justices

TABLE C.3 *Opinion suggestions model*

	Coefficient	S.E.	*p*-Value
Extraversion	−0.13	0.16	0.43
Conscientiousness	0.46	0.14	0.00
Distance to Author	0.03	0.02	0.07
Conscientiousness × Distance to Author	−0.03	0.02	0.19
Agreeableness	−0.09	0.21	0.67
Neuroticism	0.44	0.19	0.03
Openness	−0.20	0.13	0.12
Chief Justice	−0.81	0.38	0.03
Freshman Justice	−0.07	0.12	0.56
Amici Attention	0.19	0.02	0.00
Case Complexity	0.07	0.03	0.01
Winning Margin	0.02	0.01	0.06
Caseload	−0.22	0.28	0.42
End of Term	0.26	0.04	0.00
Time Trend	0.01	0.00	0.07
Civil Rights	−0.27	0.06	0.00
First Amendment	−0.13	0.08	0.09
Due Process	−0.15	0.08	0.08
Privacy	0.01	0.12	0.92
Attorneys	−0.02	0.15	0.89
Unions	−0.38	0.10	0.00
Economic Activity	−0.38	0.06	0.00
Judicial Power	−0.22	0.07	0.00
Federalism	−0.67	0.12	0.00
Federal Taxation	−1.03	0.16	0.00
Constant	−1.67	1.37	0.22
Bayesian Information Criterion	19,020.95		
Log Likelihood	−9,374.87		
Number of Observations	16,086		

Note: Table reports the results of a multilevel negative binomial regression model of opinion suggestions circulated by Supreme Court justices with random intercepts for justice.

voting with the assignor (e.g., when all nine justices participate, the winning margin is zero if the majority has five justices and four if the decision is unanimous).[3]

- The log number of cases the Court heard in that term (*Caseload*).
- The log number of days between the oral arguments and the end of the term (*End of Term*).

TABLE C.4 *Wait statements model*

	Coefficient	S.E.	p-Value
Extraversion	−0.24	0.21	0.27
Conscientiousness	0.28	0.20	0.15
Distance to Author	0.08	0.03	0.00
Conscientiousness × Distance to Author	−0.08	0.03	0.00
Agreeableness	−0.71	0.36	0.05
Neuroticism	1.26	0.42	0.00
Openness	−0.30	0.17	0.08
Chief Justice	−1.15	0.49	0.02
Freshman Justice	0.21	0.18	0.25
Amici Attention	0.05	0.03	0.03
Case Complexity	−0.02	0.04	0.64
Winning Margin	−0.40	0.02	0.00
Caseload	−1.16	0.44	0.01
End of Term	0.44	0.07	0.00
Time Trend	0.10	0.01	0.00
Civil Rights	0.07	0.08	0.38
First Amendment	−0.03	0.11	0.81
Due Process	−0.17	0.14	0.22
Privacy	0.02	0.20	0.93
Attorneys	0.10	0.20	0.64
Unions	−0.03	0.14	0.83
Economic Activity	−0.06	0.09	0.51
Judicial Power	−0.06	0.12	0.63
Federalism	0.06	0.15	0.69
Federal Taxation	0.09	0.18	0.61
Constant	0.37	2.19	0.87
Bayesian Information Criterion	8,430.22		
Log Likelihood	−4,084.35		
Number of Observations	16,086		

Note: Table reports the results of a multilevel Poisson model of wait statements circulated by Supreme Court justices with random intercepts for justice.

- A linear *Time Trend*.
- Dichotomous indicators for the issue area.

All of the models except the majority opinion model also include the following control variable:

- The absolute difference in Segal–Cover ideology scores[4] between each justice and the majority opinion author (*Distance to Author*).

TABLE C.5 *Join statements model*

	Coefficient	S.E.	p-Value
Extraversion	−0.04	0.02	0.04
Conscientiousness	−0.05	0.02	0.00
Distance to Author	−0.02	0.01	0.00
Conscientiousness × Distance to Author	0.01	0.01	0.17
Agreeableness	0.02	0.03	0.41
Neuroticism	0.06	0.03	0.04
Openness	−0.07	0.01	0.00
Chief Justice	0.07	0.03	0.04
Freshman Justice	−0.01	0.05	0.87
Amici Attention	0.00	0.01	0.81
Case Complexity	−0.01	0.01	0.32
Winning Margin	0.03	0.01	0.00
Caseload	−0.19	0.11	0.09
End of Term	0.01	0.02	0.55
Time Trend	−0.00	0.00	0.70
Civil Rights	0.01	0.03	0.83
First Amendment	−0.04	0.04	0.22
Due Process	0.03	0.04	0.36
Privacy	−0.02	0.06	0.79
Attorneys	0.02	0.07	0.78
Unions	0.04	0.04	0.39
Economic Activity	0.04	0.03	0.09
Judicial Power	0.07	0.03	0.03
Federalism	0.10	0.05	0.03
Federal Taxation	0.03	0.05	0.54
Constant	0.72	0.56	0.20
Bayesian Information Criterion	34,508.90		
Log Likelihood	−17,128.53		
Number of Observations	16,086		

Note: Table reports the results of a Poisson model of join statements circulated by Supreme Court justices.

An attentive reader will notice that the coefficient for *openness* reported in Table C.4 falls short of conventional levels of statistical significance. However, given that there is no theoretical reason to think openness would be associated with more wait statements, a one-tailed *t*-test is appropriate for evaluating this relationship.

Appendix D Voting on the Merits Analysis

Table D.1 reports the results of the dissent model. The data consist of votes on the merits by 34 justices in 6,222 cases during the 1951 through 2013 terms. Unless noted otherwise, the data were obtained from the Supreme Court Database.[1] The dependent variable is each justice's vote on the merits in each case (1 = dissent, 0 = vote with majority; N = 49,001). Because the dependent variable is dichotomous and dissents by the same justice may be interdependent, I employ a multilevel logistic regression model with random intercepts for justice. The model includes the justices' SCIPEs for the Big Five (*Extraversion, Conscientiousness, Agreeableness, Neuroticism,* and *Openness*), the SCIPEs for the majority opinion author (*OA Extraversion, OA Conscientiousness, OA Agreeableness, OA Neuroticism,* and *OA Openness*), and the following control variables and interaction terms:

- The public's ideological disagreement with the direction of the Court's ruling (*Public Disagreement*), measured as the Stimson Public Mood[2] if the Court issued a conservative ruling and the inverted Stimson Public Mood if the Court issued a liberal ruling.
- The Clark, Lax, and Rice measure of latent case salience, which is based on pre-decision case coverage in three leading newspapers: the *New York Times,* the *Washington Post,* and the *Los Angeles Times,*[3] as well as a three-way interaction term between this variable, *Public Disagreement,* and *Extraversion* (and the constituent two-way interactions).
- Each justice's ideological disagreement with the direction of the Court's ruling (*Justice Disagreement*), measured as the justice's Segal–Cover ideology score[4] if the Court issued a liberal ruling and the inverted

TABLE D.I *Dissent model*

	Coefficient	S.E.	p-Value
Extraversion	−0.283*	0.135	0.04
Public Disagreement	−0.013	0.013	0.33
Media Attention	0.105*	0.014	0.00
Extraversion × Public Disagreement	0.165*	0.024	0.00
Extraversion × Media Attention	−0.023	0.022	0.30
Public Disagreement × Media Attention	0.005	0.012	0.66
Extraversion × Public Disagreement × Media Attention	0.056*	0.023	0.01
Conscientiousness	0.316*	0.106	0.00
Justice Disagreement	0.629*	0.014	0.00
Conscientiousness × Justice Disagreement	−0.197*	0.015	0.00
Agreeableness	−0.168	0.140	0.23
1 Other Dissent	2.380*	0.052	0.00
2 Other Dissents	2.902*	0.049	0.00
3 Other Dissents	2.432*	0.048	0.00
Agreeableness × 1 Other Dissent	0.211*	0.069	0.00
Agreeableness × 2 Other Dissents	0.164*	0.065	0.01
Agreeableness × 3 Other Dissents	0.346*	0.063	0.00
Liberal Ruling	−0.274*	0.029	0.00
Agreeableness × Liberal Ruling	−0.117*	0.035	0.00
Neuroticism	−0.223	0.146	0.13
Pro-US Ruling	−0.084*	0.032	0.01
Anti-US Ruling	0.105*	0.039	0.01
Neuroticism × Pro-US Ruling	−0.229*	0.047	0.00
Neuroticism × Anti-US Ruling	0.027	0.057	0.64
Openness	0.118	0.096	0.22
Altered Precedent	0.111	0.081	0.17
Openness × Altered Precedent	−0.270*	0.126	0.03
OA Extraversion	−0.062*	0.030	0.04
OA Agreeableness	0.016	0.024	0.52
OA Conscientiousness	0.046*	0.020	0.02
OA Neuroticism	−0.079*	0.033	0.02
OA Openness	−0.035	0.022	0.11
Chief Justice	−0.741*	0.101	0.00
Freshman Justice	−0.035	0.072	0.62
Amici Attention	0.002	0.014	0.86
Case Complexity	0.025	0.018	0.17
Invalidated Statute	0.310*	0.101	0.00
Caseload	0.371*	0.087	0.00
End of Term	−0.001	0.027	0.96
Time Trend	0.029*	0.002	0.00
Civil Rights	−0.073	0.040	0.07
First Amendment	0.020	0.051	0.70
Due Process	−0.041	0.068	0.54
Privacy	−0.152	0.110	0.17
Attorneys	0.041	0.119	0.73
Unions	−0.097	0.068	0.15
Economic Activity	−0.099*	0.040	0.01
Judicial Power	−0.217*	0.051	0.00
Federalism	−0.209*	0.066	0.00
Constant	−6.044*	0.474	0.00
Bayesian Information Criterion	38,239.97		
Log Likelihood	−18,844.59		
Number of Observations	49,001		

Note: Table reports the results of a multilevel logistic regression model of dissent by Supreme Court justices with random intercepts for 34 justices. OA = Opinion Author.

Segal–Cover score if the Court issued a conservative ruling, as well as an interaction term between this variable and *Conscientiousness*.

- Dichotomous indicators taking on the value one for cases with *1 Other Dissent, 2 Other Dissents,* and *3 Other Dissents* (zero otherwise), as well as interaction terms between each of these indicators and *Agreeableness*.
- A dichotomous indicator taking on the value one if the Court issued a liberal ruling and zero otherwise (*Liberal Ruling*), as well as an interaction term between this variable and *Agreeableness*.
- A dichotomous indicator taking on the value one if the Court ruled in favor of the federal government and zero otherwise (*Pro-US Ruling*), as well as an interaction term between this variable and *Neuroticism*.
- A dichotomous indicator taking on the value one if the Court ruled against the federal government and zero otherwise (*Anti-US Ruling*), as well as an interaction term between this variable and *Neuroticism*.
- A dichotomous indicator taking on the value one if the Court altered one of its own precedents and zero otherwise (*Altered Precedent*), as well as an interaction term between this variable and *Openness*.
- A dichotomous indicator taking on the value one for the chief justice and zero otherwise (*Chief Justice*).
- A dichotomous indicator taking on the value one for justices in their first term on the Court and zero otherwise (*Freshman Justice*).
- The number of amicus curie briefs filed in each case, standardized within the term the case was filed (*Amici Attention*).
- The score that resulted from a factor analysis of the number of legal issues raised and the number of legal provisions at issue in the case (*Case Complexity*).[5]
- A dichotomous indicator taking on the value one if the Court invalidated a federal statute and zero otherwise (*Invalidated Statute*).
- The log number of cases the Court heard in that term (*Caseload*).
- The log number of days between the oral arguments and the end of the term (*End of Term*).
- A linear *Time Trend*.
- Dichotomous indicators for the issue area.

Appendix E Separate Opinion Analysis

Table E.1 reports the results of the concurrence model. The data for the concurrence model consist of decisions by 34 justices in 7,473 cases during the 1946 through 2015 terms. The dependent variable is each justice's decision to file a concurring opinion (1 = concurring opinion; 0 = no concurring opinion; N = 39,793). Unless noted otherwise, the data were derived from the Supreme Court Database.[1] Because the dependent variable is dichotomous and separate opinions by the same justice may be interdependent, I employ a multilevel logistic regression model with random intercepts for justice. The model includes the justices' SCIPEs for the Big Five (*Extraversion, Conscientiousness, Agreeableness, Neuroticism,* and *Openness*), the SCIPEs for the majority opinion author (*OA Extraversion, OA Conscientiousness, OA Agreeableness, OA Neuroticism,* and *OA Openness*), and the following control variables:

- The number of amicus curie briefs filed in each case, standardized within the term the case was filed (*Amici Attention*), as well as an interaction term between this variable and *Extraversion*.
- Each justice's ideological disagreement with the direction of the Court's ruling (*Justice Disagreement*), measured as the justice's Segal–Cover ideology score[2] if the Court issued a liberal ruling and the inverted Segal–Cover score if the Court issued a conservative ruling, as well as an interaction term between this variable and *Conscientiousness*.
- A dichotomous indicator for cases in which the Court issued a liberal ruling (*Liberal Ruling*), as well as an interaction term between this variable and *Agreeableness*.

TABLE E.1 *Concurrence model*

	Coefficient	S.E.	p-Value
Extraversion	0.06	0.10	0.58
Amici Attention	0.18*	0.02	0.00
Extraversion × Amici Attention	0.04	0.02	0.06
Conscientiousness	0.27*	0.10	0.01
Justice Disagreement	0.10*	0.02	0.00
Conscientiousness × Justice Disagreement	−0.06*	0.02	0.00
Agreeableness	0.12	0.11	0.26
Liberal Ruling	0.13*	0.04	0.00
Agreeableness × Liberal Ruling	−0.21*	0.05	0.00
Neuroticism	−0.38*	0.10	0.00
Openness	−0.16	0.09	0.08
OA Extraversion	−0.03	0.04	0.36
OA Conscientiousness	0.06*	0.03	0.02
OA Agreeableness	−0.01	0.03	0.83
OA Neuroticism	−0.12*	0.03	0.00
OA Openness	−0.07*	0.03	0.02
Chief Justice	−1.02*	0.18	0.00
Freshman Justice	−0.22*	0.10	0.03
Case Complexity	0.13*	0.02	0.00
Invalidated Statute	0.36*	0.13	0.01
Winning Margin	−0.07*	0.01	0.00
Caseload	0.33*	0.11	0.00
End of Term	0.18*	0.04	0.00
Time Trend	0.02*	0.00	0.00
Civil Rights	−0.27*	0.05	0.00
First Amendment	0.36*	0.06	0.00
Due Process	−0.25*	0.09	0.01
Privacy	0.17	0.12	0.15
Attorneys	−0.28	0.16	0.08
Unions	−0.69*	0.10	0.00
Economic Activity	−0.66*	0.06	0.00
Judicial Power	−0.43*	0.07	0.00
Federalism	−0.77*	0.10	0.00
Miscellaneous	−0.05	0.53	0.92
Constant	−5.03*	0.60	0.00
Log Likelihood	23,562.12		
Bayesian Information Criterion	−11,590.41		
Number of Observations	39,793		

Note: Table reports the results of a multilevel logistic regression model of concurring opinions filed by Supreme Court justices with random intercepts for justice. OA = Opinion Author.

- A dichotomous indicator taking on the value one for the chief justice and zero otherwise (*Chief Justice*).
- A dichotomous indicator taking on the value one for justices in their first term on the Court and zero otherwise (*Freshman Justice*).
- The score that resulted from a factor analysis of the number of legal issues raised and the number of legal provisions at issue in the case (*Case Complexity*).[3]
- A dichotomous indicator for cases in which the Court invalidated a federal statute (*Invalidated Statute*).
- The *Winning Margin*, which was calculated by subtracting the number of votes needed to form a winning coalition from the number of justices voting with the assignor (e.g., when all nine justices participate, the winning margin is zero if the majority has five justices and four if the decision is unanimous).[4]
- The log number of cases the Court heard in that term (*Caseload*).
- The log number of days between the oral arguments and the end of the term (*End of Term*).
- A linear *Time Trend*.
- Dichotomous indicators for the issue area.

Notes

1 Who They Are and What They Want

1 *Griswold v. Connecticut*. 381 U.S. 479. 1965.
2 Ibid.
3 *Tileston v. Ullman*. 318 U.S. 44. 1943.
4 *Poe v. Ulman*. 367 U.S. 497. 1961.
5 *Griswold v. Connecticut*, pp. 483–484.
6 Newman, Roger K. *Hugo Black: A Biography*. 2nd ed. New York: Fordham University Press, 1994, p. 235; Domnarski, William. *The Great Justices: 1941–54*. Ann Arbor: University of Michigan Press, 2004, p. 102; Rosen, Jeffrey. *The Supreme Court: The Personalities and Rivalries That Defined America*. New York: Times Books, 2007, p. 157.
7 Ibid., p. 178
8 Calculated based on data from the Supreme Court Database. Spaeth, Harold J. et al. *Supreme Court Database, Version 2016 Release 01*. http:// supremecourtdatabase.org. 2016. Black and Douglas voted together in 2,051 of the 2,595 cases in which they both cast a vote (79%). Compared to other notable duos on the Court, that rate of agreement is somewhat low. For example, Justices Brennan and Marshall voted together in 93% of cases (2,757 out of 2,969). Justices Scalia and Thomas voted together in 91% of cases (1,666 out of 1,838). However, the Douglas–Black rate of agreement is still very high compared to most pairings, especially pairings who served together for long periods of time. For example, consider the two justices who also served with Justice Douglas for long periods: Justices Brennan and Stewart. Their rates of agreement with Douglas were 39% and 61%, respectively.
9 Garrow, David J. *Liberty and Sexuality: The Right to Privacy and the Making of Roe v. Wade*. Berkeley: University of California Press, 1994, p. 241.
10 Ibid., p. 241.
11 Rosen, *The Supreme Court*, pp. 143–144.
12 Garrow. *Liberty and Sexuality*, p. 247.

13 *Griswold v. Connecticut*, p. 484.
14 Ibid., p. 507.
15 Newman, *Hugo Black*, p. 537.
16 Ibid.
17 Ibid.
18 Newman. *Hugo Black*, p. 12.
19 Rosen. *The Supreme Court*, p. 149.
20 Ibid.
21 Newman, *Hugo Black*, p. 8.
22 Rosen, *The Supreme Court*, p. 150.
23 Ibid.
24 Ibid.
25 Newman, *Hugo Black*, p. 20.
26 Rosen, *The Supreme Court*, p. 151.
27 Newman, *Hugo Black*, p. 93.
28 Rosen, *The Supreme Court*, p. 151.
29 Newman, *Hugo Black*, p. 200.
30 Rosen, *The Supreme Court*, p. 154.
31 Ibid., pp. 159, 167.
32 Ibid., pp. 159–160.
33 Newman, *Hugo Black*, p. 570.
34 Rosen, *The Supreme Court*, p. 155.
35 Ibid.
36 Ibid., p. 156.
37 Ibid., p. 147.
38 Ibid., p. 144.
39 Ibid., pp. 159, 163, 183.
40 Ibid., p. 167.
41 Garrow, *Liberty and Sexuality*, p. 246.
42 Rosen, *The Supreme Court*, p. 159.
43 Ibid.
44 Ibid., p. 187.
45 See Edwards, Harry T. and Livermore, Michael A. "The Pitfalls of Empirical Studies That Attempt to Understand the Factors Affecting Appellate Decisionmaking." *Duke Law Journal* 58.8 (2009), pp. 1895–1989.
46 *Confirmation Hearing on the Nomination of John G. Roberts, Jr. to Be Chief Justice of the United States*. Washington, DC: Committee on the Judiciary, U.S. Senate, 2005.
47 *Federalist* 78.
48 See Epstein, Lee and Segal, Jeffrey A. "Measuring Issue Salience." *American Journal of Political Science* 44.1 (2000), pp. 66–83, p. 630.
49 See, e.g., Scherer, Nancy. "Blacks on the Bench." *Political Research Quarterly* 119.4 (2004), pp. 655–672; Boyd, Christina L., Epstein, Lee, and Martin, Andrew D. "Untangling the Causal Effects of Sex on Judging." *American Journal of Political Science* 54.2 (2010), pp. 389–411.
50 Tate, C. Neal. "Personal Attribute Models of the Voting Behavior of U.S. Supreme Court Justices: Liberalism in Civil Liberties and Economics

Decisions, 1946–1978." *American Political Science Review* 75.2 (1981), pp. 355–367; Ulmer, S. Sidney. "Dissent Behavior and the Social Background of Supreme Court Justices." *Journal of Politics* 32.3 (1970), pp. 580–598; Ulmer, S. Sidney. "Social Background as an Indicator to the Votes of Supreme Court Justices in Criminal Cases: 1947–1956 Terms." *American Journal of Political Science* 17.3 (1973), pp. 622–630.

51 Becker, Theodore L. "A Survey Study of Hawaiian Judges: The Effect on Decisions of Judicial Role Variations." *American Political Science Review* 60.3 (1966), pp. 677–680; Gibson, James L. "Judges' Role Orientations, Attitudes, and Decisions: An Interactive Model." *American Political Science Reivew* 72.3 (1978), pp. 911–924; James, Dorothy B. "Role Theory and the Supreme Court." *Journal of Politics* 30.1 (1968), pp. 160–186.

52 Pritchett, C. Herman. *The Roosevelt Court: A Study in Judicial Politics and Values, 1937–1947*. New York: Macmillan Press, 1948; Schubert, Glendon. "The 1960 Term of the Supreme Court: A Psychological Analysis." *American Political Science Review* 56.1 (1962), pp. 90–107.

53 Grossman, Joel B. and Tanenhaus, Joseph, ed. *Frontiers of Judicial Research*. New York: Wiley, 1969, pp. 10–11.

54 Glynn, Adam N. and Sen, Maya. "Identifying Judicial Empathy: Does Having Daughters Cause Judges to Rule for Women's Issues?" *American Journal of Political Science* 59.1 (2015), pp. 37–54.

55 Baum, Lawrence. *The Puzzle of Judicial Behavior*. Ann Arbor: University of Michigan Press, 1997, p. 40.

56 Segal, Jeffrey A. and Spaeth, Harold J. *The Supreme Court and the Attitudinal Model Revisited*. New York: Cambridge University Press, 2002, p. 86.

57 See, e.g., Edwards and Livermore, "The Pitfalls of Empirical Studies That Attempt to Understand the Factors Affecting Appellate Decisionmaking."

58 See, e.g., Pritchett, *The Roosevelt Court*; Segal and Spaeth, *The Supreme Court and the Attitudinal Model Revisited*; Landes, William M. and Posner, Richard A. "Legal Precedent: A Theoretical and Empirical Analysis." *Journal of Law and Economics* 14.2 (1976), pp. 249–307.

59 See, e.g., Smith, Rogers M. "Symposium: The Supreme Court and the Attitudinal Model." *Law & Courts* 4 (1994), pp. 8–9.

60 See Epstein, Lee, Landes, William M., and Posner, Richard A. *The Behavior of Federal Judges: A Theoretical & Empirical Study of Rational Choice*. Cambridge, MA: Harvard University Press, 2013, p. 103.

61 Segal and Spaeth, *The Supreme Court and the Attitudinal Model Revisited*.

62 Haines, Charles Grove. "General Observations on the Effects of Personal, Political, and Economic Influences in the Decision of Judges." *Illinois Law Review* 17 (1922), pp. 96–116; Frank, Jerome. *Law and the Modern Mind*. New York: Coward McCann, 1930.

63 Atkins, Burton, Alpert, Lenore, and Ziller, Robert. "Personality Theory and Judging: A Proposed Theory of Self Esteem and Judicial Policy-Making." *Law & Policy* 2.2 (1980), pp. 189–220; Gibson, James L. "Personality and Elite Political Behavior: The Influence of Self Esteem on Judicial Decision Making." *Journal of Politics* 43.1 (1981), pp. 104–125; Lasswell, Harold D. "The Structure and Function of Communication in Society." *The*

Communication of Ideas: A Series of Addresses. Ed. by Bryson, Lyman. New York: Harper & Row, 1948.

64 McGuire, Kevin T. "Birth Order, Preferences, and Norms on the U.S. Supreme Court." *Law & Society Review* 49.4 (2015), pp. 945–972.

65 Danelski, David J. "The Influence of the Chief Justice in the Decisional Process." *Courts, Judges, and Politics: An Introduction to the Judicial Process.* Ed. by Murphy, Walter F. and Pritchett, C. Herman. 6th ed. New York: Random House, 1961; Walker, Thomas G., Epstein, Lee, and Dixon, William J. "On the Mysterious Demise of Consensual Norms in the United States Supreme Court." *Journal of Politics* 50.2 (1988), pp. 361–389.

66 Gibson, James L. "From Simplicity to Complexity: The Development of Theory in the Study of Judicial Behavior." *Political Behavior* 5.1 (1983), pp. 7–49, p. 26.

67 Collins Paul M., Jr. "The Contributions of Psychology to Law and Courts Research." *Law & Courts* 22.3 (2012), pp. 5–11.

68 See Epstein, Lee and Jacobi, Tonja. "The Strategic Analysis of Judicial Decisions." *Annual Review of Law and Social Science* 6 (2010), pp. 341–358.

69 Baum, *The Puzzle of Judicial Behavior*; Epstein, Lee and Knight, Jack. "Reconsidering Judicial Preferences." *Annual Review of Political Science* 16 (2013), pp. 11–31; Posner, Richard A. "What Do Judges and Justices Maximize? (The Same Thing Everyone Else Does)." *Supreme Court Economic Review* 3 (1993), pp. 1–41.

70 Almlund, Mathilde et al. "Personality Psychology and Economics." *Handbook of the Economics of Education.* Ed. by Hanushek, Eric A., Machin, Stephen, and Woessmann, Ludger. Amsterdam: North Holland, 2011.

2 Goals and Personality

1 Baum, *The Puzzle of Judicial Behavior*; Epstein, Landes, and Posner, *The Behavior of Federal Judges*; Posner, "What Do Judges and Justices Maximize? (The Same Thing Everyone Else Does)."

2 Gulati, Mitu and McCauliff, C.M.A. "On 'Not' Making Law." *Law and Contemporary Problems* 61.3 (1998), pp. 157–227, p. 188; Macey, Jonathan R. "Judicial Preferences, Public Choice, and the Rules of Procedure." *Journal of Legal Studies* 23.S1 (1994), pp. 627–646, p. 630.

3 Cass, Ronald A. "Judging: Norms and Incentives of Retrospective Decision-Making." *Boston University Law Review* 75 (1994), pp. 941–996, p. 944. For example, Epstein, Landes, and Posner posit that judges' votes depend on their willingness to dissent, but they assume that willingness to dissent is the same for all judges. Epstein, Lee, Landes, William M., and Posner, Richard A. "Why (and When) Judges Dissent: A Theoretical and Empirical Analysis." *Journal of Legal Analysis* 3.1 (2011), pp. 101–137.

4 Gulati and McCauliff, "On 'Not' Making Law," pp. 172–173.

5 Macey, "Judicial Preferences, Public Choice, and the Rules of Procedure," p. 630.

6 Rohde, David W. and Spaeth, Harold J. *Supreme Court Decision Making.* San Francisco: W.H. Freeman, 1976; Segal and Spaeth, *The Supreme Court*

and the Attitudinal Model Revisited; Epstein, Lee and Knight, Jack. *The Choices Justices Make*. Washington, DC: CQ Press, 1998.

7 Gerber, Alan S. et al. "The Big Five Personality Traits in the Political Arena." *Annual Review of Political Science* 14 (2011), pp. 256–287, p. 266.

8 John, Oliver P. "The 'Big Five' Factor Taxonomy: Dimensions of Personality in the Natural Language and in Questionnaires." *Handbook of Personality: Theory and Research*. Ed. by Pervin, Lawrence A. New York: Guilford Press, 1990, pp. 66–100.

9 John, Oliver P., Naumann, Laura P., and Soto, Christopher J. "Paradigm Shift to the Integrative Big-Five Trait Taxonomy: History, Measurement, and Conceptual Issues." *Handbook of Personality: Theory and Research*. Ed. by John, Oliver P., Robins, Richard W., and Pervin, Lawrence A. New York: Guilford Press, 2008, pp. 114–158.

10 Bouchard, Thomas J. "The Genetics of Personality." *The Handbook of Psychiatric Genetics*. Ed. by Blum, Kenneth and Noble, Ernest P. Boca Raton, FL: CRC Press, 1997, pp. 273–296.

11 Caspi, Avshalom, Roberts, Brent W., and Shiner, Rebecca L. "Personality Development: Stability and Change." *Annual Review of Psychology* 56 (2005), pp. 453–484, see pp. 466–467.

12 Roberts, Brent W. et al. "The Power of Personality: The Comparative Validity of Personality Traits, Socioeconomic Status, and Cognitive Ability for Predicting Important Life Outcomes." *Perspectives on Psychological Science* 2.4 (2007), pp. 313–345.

13 John, Naumann, and Soto, "Paradigm Shift to the Integrative Big-Five Trait Taxonomy"; Ramey, Adam J., Klingler, Jonathan D., and Hollibaugh, Gary E. Jr. *More Than a Feeling: Personality, Polarization, and the Transformation of the U.S. Congress*. Chicago: University of Chicago Press, 2017, p. 22.

14 Gerber et al., "The Big Five Personality Traits in the Political Arena."

15 Alford, John R., Funk, Carolyn L., and Hibbing, John R. "Are Political Orientations Genetically Transmitted?" *American Political Science Review* 99.2 (2005), pp. 153–167; Gerber, Alan S. et al. "Personality and Political Attitudes: Relationships across Issue Domains and Political Contexts." *American Political Science Review* 104.1 (2010), pp. 111–133; Gerber et al., "The Big Five Personality Traits in the Political Arena"; Mondak, Jeffery J. et al. "Personality and Civic Engagement: An Integrative Framework for the Study of Trait Effects on Political Behavior." *American Political Science Review* 104.1 (2010), pp. 85–110; Mondak, Jeffery J. *Personality and the Foundations of Political Behavior*. Cambridge: Cambridge University Press, 2010; Mondak, Jeffery J. and Halperin, Karen D. "A Framework for the Study of Personality and Political Behaviour." *British Journal of Political Science* 38.2 (2008), pp. 335–362.

16 Dietrich, Bryce J. et al. "Personality and Legislative Politics: The Big Five Trait Dimensions among U.S. State Legislators." *Political Psychology* 33.2 (2012), pp. 195–210; Ramey, Klingler, and Hollibaugh, Jr. *More than a Feeling*.

17 E.g., Rosen, *The Supreme Court*; Hirsch, H. N. *The Enigma of Felix Frank-furter*. New York: Basic Books, 1981.

18 McCrae, Robert R. and John, Oliver P. "An Introduction to the Five-Factor Model and Its Applications." *Journal of Personality* 60.2 (1992), pp. 175–215, see p. 175.

19 Gerber et al., "The Big Five Personality Traits in the Political Arena," p. 266.

20 Almlund et al. adopt a similar interpretation of personality traits: "Since personality psychologists define traits as 'relatively' stable, person-specific determinants of behavior, preferences are the natural counterpart of these traits in economics." Almlund, et al. "Personality Psychology and Economics." p. 65 Consistent with this view, personality traits have been found to moderate how individuals weigh costs and benefits as they make political decisions. Gerber, Alan S. et al. "Big Five Personality Traits and Responses to Persuasive Appeals: Results from Voter Turnout Experiments." *Political Behavior* 35.4 (2013), pp. 687–728.

21 McCrae and John, "An Introduction to the Five-Factor Model and Its Applications."

22 See ibid.

23 McCrae, Robert R. and Costa Paul T., Jr. "Toward a New Generation of Personality Theories: Theoretical Contexts for the Five-Factor Model." *The Five-Factor Model of Personality: Theoretical Perspectives*. Ed. by Wiggins, Jerry S. New York: Guilford Press, 1996, pp. 51–87. See also John, Naumann, and Soto, "Paradigm Shift to the Integrative Big Five Trait Taxonomy; McCrae, Robert R. and Costa, Paul T., Jr. "The Five-Factor Theory of Personality." *Handbook of Personality: Theory and Research*. Ed. by John, Oliver P., Robins, Richard W., and Pervin, Lawrence A. New York: Guilford, 2008.

24 One notable exception is Epstein et al., who propose a utility function structured around the hours in a day (i.e., satisfaction from one's job, external professional activities, and leisure activities). Epstein, Landes, and Posner, *The Behavior of Federal Judges*, p. 48. However, they also include components unrelated to time (e.g., salary), and they do not develop a detailed theory of why judges derive satisfaction from certain aspects of these activities (e.g., why a judge derives job satisfaction from collegiality).

25 McCrae and Costa Jr., "The Five-Factor Theory of Personality," pp. 164, 170.

26 Almlund, et al. "Personality Psychology and Economics." I argue that goal preferences can be incorporated into economic choice models like any other preference parameter. The integration of psychological theories into choice models is increasingly popular in political science, especially among proponents of behavioral economics. See, e.g., Wilson, Rick K. "The Contribution of Behavioral Economics to Political Science." *Annual Review of Political Science* 14 (2011), pp. 201–223. However, "many studies in behavioral economics attempt to establish inconsistency in behavior across situations, in violation of standard assumptions of stable preferences used in mainstream economics." Almlund, et al. "Personality Psychology and Economics." p. 14. In contrast, I follow studies of personality psychology, biology, and

neuroscience, which establish that stable and heritable personality traits influence individual behavior. See Almlund, et al. "Personality Psychology and Economics."

27 Borghans, Lex et al. "The Economics and Psychology of Personality Traits." *Journal of Human Resources* 43.4 (2008), pp. 972–1059.

28 John, Naumann, and Soto, "Paradigm Shift to the Integrative Big-Five Trait Taxonomy," p. 138.

29 De Young, Colin G., Quilty, Lena C., and Peterson, Jordan B. "Between Facets and Domains: 10 Aspects of the Big Five." *Journal of Personality and Social Psychology* 93.5 (2007), pp. 880–896, p. 881. Depue, Richard A. and Collins, Paul F. "Neurobiology of the Structure of Personality: Dopamine, Facilitation of Incentive Motivation, and Extraversion." *Behavioral and Brain Sciences* 22.3 (1999), pp. 491–517, p. 492. Hogan, Robert and Hogan, Joyce. *Hogan Personality Inventory Manual.* Tulsa, OK: Hogan Assessment Systems, 2007, p. 9.

30 See Epstein, Landes, and Posner, *The Behavior of Federal Judges*, p. 103.

31 Epstein and Knight, *The Choices Justices Make*.

32 Baum, Lawrence. *Judges and Their Audiences: A Perspective on Judicial Behavior.* Princeton, NJ: Princeton University Press, 2006.

33 Atkins, Alpert, and Ziller, "Personality Theory and Judging," p. 196.

34 Maslow, A.H. "A Theory of Human Motivation." *Psychological Review* 50.4 (1943), pp. 370–396; McClelland, David C. *Human Motivation.* New York: Cambridge University Press, 1987.

35 Alpert, Lenore, Atkins, Burton M., and Ziller, Robert C. "Becoming a Judge: The Transition from Advocate to Arbiter." *Judicature* 62 (1979), pp. 325–336, p. 331.

36 Ibid.

37 Georgakopoulos, Nicholas L. "Discretion in the Career and Recognition Judiciary." *University of Chicago Law School Roundtable* 7 (2000), pp. 205–225; Miceli, Thomas J. and Cosgel, Metin M. "Reputation and Judicial Decision-making." *Journal of Economic Behavior & Organization* 23.1 (1994), pp. 31–51; Schauer, Frederick. "Incentives, Reputation, and the Inglorious Determinants of Judicial Behavior." *University of Cincinnati Law Review* 68 (2000), pp. 615–636; Baum. *Judges and Their Audiences.*

38 Epstein and Knight, "Reconsidering Judicial Preferences," p. 21.

39 Greenhouse, Linda. "David H. Souter: Justice Unbound." *New York Times,* (2 May 2009).

40 John, Naumann, and Soto, "Paradigm Shift to the Integrative Big-Five Trait Taxonomy," p. 138.

41 DeYoung, Quilty, and Peterson, "Between Facets and Domains," p. 881. Hogan and Hogan, *Hogan Personality Inventory Manual*, p. 9. Moon, Henry. "The Two Faces of Conscientiousness: Duty and Achievement Striving in Escalation of Commitment Decisions." *Journal of Applied Psychology* 86.3 (2001), pp. 533–540, p. 535.

42 Macey, "Judicial Preferences, Public Choice, and the Rules of Procedure"; Posner, "What Do Judges and Justices Maximize? (The Same Thing Everyone Else Does)"; Epstein and Knight, "Reconsidering Judicial Preferences."

43 Georgakopoulos, "Discretion in the Career and Recognition Judiciary"; Miceli and Cosgel, "Reputation and Judicial Decision-making"; Schauer, "Incentives, Reputation, and the Inglorious Determinants of Judicial Behavior"; Baum, *Judges and Their Audiences*.

44 Epstein, Landes, and Posner assume "the large size and quality of staff relative to the number of Justices and the Court's light caseload in recent years imply that a Justice's leisure activities and nonjudicial work activities are not significantly constrained by his or her judicial duties" (*The Behavior of Federal Judges*, p. 103). In contrast, I empirically test whether some justices minimize their job-related effort.

45 Segal and Spaeth, *The Supreme Court and the Attitudinal Model Revisited*; Hansford, Thomas G. and Spriggs, James F. *The Politics of Precedent on the U.S. Supreme Court*. Princeton, NJ: Princeton University Press, 2006; Bartels, Brandon L. "The Constraining Capacity of Legal Doctrine on the U.S. Supreme Court." *American Political Science Review* 103.3 (2009), pp. 474–495.

46 Segal and Spaeth, *The Supreme Court and the Attitudinal Model Revisited*; Pritchett, C. Herman. "Divisions of Opinion among Justices of the U.S. Supreme Court, 1939–1941." *American Political Science Review* 35.5 (1941), pp. 890–898.

47 Keck, Thomas M. "Party, Policy, or Duty: Why Does the Supreme Court Invalidate Federal Statutes?" *American Political Science Review* 101.2 (2007), pp. 321–338; Bartels, "The Constraining Capacity of Legal Doctrine on the U.S. Supreme Court"; Bailey, Michael A. and Maltzman, Forrest. "Does Legal Doctrine Matter? Unpacking Law and Policy Preferences on the U.S. Supreme Court." *American Political Science Review* 102.3 (2008), pp. 369–384.

48 Gibson, "From Simplicity to Complexity," pp. 9, 17.

49 Bailey and Maltzman, "Does Legal Doctrine Matter?"; Bailey, Michael A. and Maltzman, Forrest. *The Constrained Court: Law, Politics, and the Decisions Justices Make*. Princeton, NJ: Princeton University Press, 2011.

50 Edwards, Harry T. "The Effects of Collegiality on Judicial Decision Making." *University of Pennsylvania Law Review* 151.5 (2003), pp. 1639–1690; Edwards and Livermore, "The Pitfalls of Empirical Studies That Attempt to Understand the Factors Affecting Appellate Decisionmaking."

51 Epstein, Landes, and Posner, "Why (and When) Judges Dissent."

52 Epstein, Lee, Segal, Jeffrey A., and Spaeth, Harold J. "The Norm of Consensus on the U.S. Supreme Court." *American Journal of Political Science* 45.2 (2001), pp. 362–377.

53 Danelski, David J. "The Influence of the Chief Justice in the Decisional Process." *Courts, Judges, and Politics: An Introduction to the Judicial Process*. Ed. by Murphy, Walter M. et al. 6th ed. New York: McGraw-Hill, 2005; Haynie, Stacia L. "Leadership and Consensus on the U.S. Supreme Court." *Journal of Politics* 54.4 (1992), pp. 1158–1169; Caldeira, Gregory A. and Zorn, Christopher J.W. "Of Time and Consensual Norms in the Supreme Court." *American Journal of Political Science* 42.3 (1998), pp. 874–902;

Walker, Epstein, and Dixon, "On the Mysterious Demise of Consensual Norms in the United States Supreme Court."

54 Liptak, Adam. *The End of an Era, for Court and Nation. New York Times,* (9 April 2010).

55 Justice John Marshall Harlan, II, was named after his grandfather, the first Justice John Marshall Harlan.

56 Woodward, Bob and Armstrong, Scott. *The Brethren: Inside the Supreme Court.* New York: Simon & Schuster Press, 1979, p. 59.

57 Maltzman, Forrest James, Spriggs II, James F., and Wahlbeck, Paul J. *Crafting Law on the Supreme Court: The Collegial Game.* New York: Cambridge University Press, 2000; Liptak, Adam. *Justices Are Long on Words but Short on Guidance. New York Times,* (17 November 2010); Owens, Ryan J. and Wedeking, Justin. "Justices and Legal Clarity: Analyzing the Complexity of U.S. Supreme Court Opinions." *Law & Society Review* 45.4 (2011), pp. 1027–1061.

58 John, Naumann, and Soto, "Paradigm Shift to the Integrative Big-Five Trait Taxonomy," p. 138.

59 DeYoung, Quilty, and Peterson, "Between Facets and Domains," p. 881. Hogan and Hogan, *Hogan Personality Inventory Manual,* p. 9. McCrae and John, "An Introduction to the Five-Factor Model and Its Applications," p. 196.

60 Edwards, "The Effects of Collegiality on Judicial Decision Making"; Wald, Patricia M. "Some Thoughts on Judging as Gleaned from One Hundred Years of the *Harvard Law Review* and Other Great Books." *Harvard Law Review* 100.4 (1987), pp. 887–908; Epstein, Landes, and Posner, *The Behavior of Federal Judges.*

61 John, Naumann, and Soto, "Paradigm Shift to the Integrative Big-Five Trait Taxonomy," p. 138.

62 Hogan and Hogan, *Hogan Personality Inventory Manual,* p. 9.

63 DeYoung, Quilty, and Peterson, "Between Facets and Domains," p. 881.

64 McCrae and John, "An Introduction to the Five-Factor Model and Its Applications," p. 195.

65 Tversky, Amos and Kahneman, Daniel. "Loss Aversion in Riskless Choice." *Quarterly Journal of Economics* 106.4 (1991), pp. 1039–1061.

66 Ibid.; Montier, James. *Behavioural Investing: A Practitioners Guide to Behavioural Finance.* Chichester: John Wiley & Sons Ltd., 2007.

67 Kahneman, D. and Tversky, A. "Prospect Theory: An Analysis of Decision under Risk." *Econometrica* 47.2 (1979), pp. 263–291.

68 Brown, John R. "Hail to the Chief: Hutcheson, the Judge." *Texas Law Review* 38 (1959), pp. 140–146, p. 145.

69 Bainbridge, Stephen M. and Gulati, G. Mitu. "How Do Judges Maximize? (The Same Way Everyone Else Does–Boundedly): Rules of Thumb in Securities Fraud Opinions." *Emory Law Journal* 51 (2002), pp. 83–151; Gulati and McCauliff, "On 'Not' Making Law"; Georgakopoulos, "Discretion in the Career and Recognition Judiciary"; Miceli and Cosgel, "Reputation and Judicial Decision-making"; Schauer, "Incentives, Reputation, and the

Inglorious Determinants of Judicial Behavior"; Baum, *Judges and Their Audiences*.

70 See, e.g., Pennebaker, James W. and Beall, Sandra Klihr. "Confronting a Traumatic Event: Toward an Understanding of Inhibition and Disease." *Journal of Abnormal Psychology* 95.3 (1986), pp. 274–281.

71 Hogan and Hogan, *Hogan Personality Inventory Manual*, p. 9.

72 DeYoung, Quilty, and Peterson, "Between Facets and Domains"; McCrae and John, "An Introduction to the Five-Factor Model and Its Applications."

73 See, e.g., Bainbridge and Gulati, "How Do Judges Maximize? (The Same Way Everyone Else Does–Boundedly)"; Macey, "Judicial Preferences, Public Choice, and the Rules of Procedure."

74 Rule 10, *Rules of the Supreme Court of the United States*, 2013. Available at https://www.supremecourt.gov/ctrules/2013RulesoftheCourt.pdf.

75 Edwards and Livermore, "The Pitfalls of Empirical Studies That Attempt to Understand the Factors Affecting Appellate Decisionmaking."

76 McCrae and Costa, "Toward a New Generation of Personality Theories."

77 Almlund et al., "Personality Psychology and Economics," p. 65.

78 Big Five aspects and characteristics were derived from DeYoung, Quilty, and Peterson, "Between Facets and Domains," pp. 880–896, pp. 887–888; Hogan and Hogan, *Hogan Personality Inventory Manual*, p. 9; and John, Naumann, and Soto, "Paradigm Shift to the Integrative Big Five Trait Taxonomy," pp. 114–158, p. 126.

79 Segal and Spaeth, *The Supreme Court and the Attitudinal Model Revisited*; Epstein and Knight, *The Choices Justices Make*; Epstein, Landes, and Posner, *The Behavior of Federal Judges*; Brisbin, Richard A. "Slaying the Dragon: Segal, Spaeth, and the Function of Law in Supreme Court Decision Making." *American Journal of Political Science* 40.4 (1996), pp. 1004–1017; Smith, "Symposium: The Supreme Court and the Attitudinal Model."

3 Measuring Justice Personality

1 Gerber et al. "The Big Five Personality Traits in the Political Arena," pp. 256–287, p. 267; internal quotation marks omitted. For examples of commonly used personality surveys, see Gosling, Samuel D., Rentfrow, P. Jason, and Swann, William B., Jr. "A Very Brief Measure of the Big-Five Personality Domains." *Journal of Research in Personality* 37.2 (2003), pp. 504–528; John, Oliver P., Donahue, E.M., and Kentle, R.L. *The Big Five Inventory– Versions 4a and 54*. Berkeley: University of California Berkley, Berkeley Institute of Personality and Social Research, 1991; Saucier, Gerard. "Mini-Markers: A Brief Version of Goldberg's Unipolar Big-Five Markers." *Journal of Personality Assessment* 63.3 (1994), pp. 506–516.

2 See Paulhus, Delroy L. "Two-Component Models of Socially Desirable Responding." *Journal of Personality and Social Psychology* 46.3 (1984), pp. 598–609.

3 Hall, Matthew E.K. et al. "Attributes Beyond Attitudes: Measuring Personality Traits on the U.S. Supreme Court. 2016." Available at: https://ssrn.com/abstract=3018156.

4 Tausczik, Yla R. and Pennebaker, James W. "The Psychological Meaning of Words: LIWC and Computerized Text Analysis Methods." *Journal of Langauge and Social Psychology* 29.1 (2010), pp. 24–54.

5 Mairesse, Francois et al. "Using Linguistic Cues for the Automatic Recognition of Personality in Conversation and Text." *Journal of Artificial Intelligence Research* 30 (2007), pp. 457–500; Pennebaker, James W. and King, Laura L. "Linguistic Styles: Language Use as an Individual Difference." *Journal of Personality and Social Psychology* 77.6 (1999), pp. 1296–1312.

6 The Oyez Project has made considerable progress identifying speakers in pre-2004 oral arguments and generating transcripts of those arguments using a combination of hand coding and computerized voice recognition. However, after an extensive exploration of this data, I concluded that these transcripts would not be appropriate for my purposes. First, and most obviously, these transcripts are not available before the Court started recording oral arguments in 1955. Second, these transcripts only confirm that prior to the mid-1970s (and some degree, prior to Justice Scalia's confirmation in 1986), justices rarely spoke during oral arguments. For example, the vast majority of Chief Justice Warren's comments in these transcripts are simple phrases repeated frequently, such as "Let's break for lunch." Third, in earlier terms, the recordings had difficulty picking up several justices who were seated farther away from the microphones. Considering these factors together, I believe the challenges involved in relying on these transcripts outweigh those of relying on the justices' written opinions.

7 See, e.g., Owens, Ryan J. and Wedeking, Justin. "Predicting Drift on Politically Insulated Institutions: A Study of Ideological Drift on the United States Supreme Court." *Journal of Politics* 74.2 (2012), pp. 487–500.

8 For example, Owens and Wedeking use the language in US Supreme Court opinions to estimate the clarity of those opinions and then estimate a "complexity score" for each justice. Owens and Wedeking, "Justices and Legal Clarity."

9 Rehnquist, William H. *The Supreme Court: How It Was, How It Is*. New York: Morrow, 1987, p. 74.

10 Wahlbeck, Paul J., Spriggs II, James F., and Sigelman, Lee. "Ghostwriters on the Court? A Stylistic Analysis of U.S. Supreme Court Opinion Drafts." *American Politics Research* 30.2 (2002), pp. 166–192.

11 Ibid., p. 179. The authors call this finding "especially pertinent."

12 Hall et al. "Attributes Beyond Attitudes."

13 Caspi, Roberts, and Shiner, "Personality Development," pp. 466–467. See also Roberts, Brent W. and DelVecchio, Wendy F. "The Rank-Order Consistency of Personality Traits from Childhood to Old Age: A Quantitative Review of Longitudinal Studies." *Psychological Bulletin* 126.1 (2000), pp. 3–25; Fraley, R. Chris and Roberts, Brent W. "Patterns of Continuity: A Dynamic Model for Conceptualizing the Stability of Individual Differences in Psychological Constructs Across the Life Course." *Psychological Review* 112.1 (2005), pp. 60–74.

14 Opinions of the Court and judgments of the Court.

15 Maltzman, Spriggs, and Wahlbeck, *Crafting Law on the Supreme Court.*

16 Wahlbeck, Spriggs, and Sigelman, "Ghostwriters on the Court?" p. 179.
17 Posner, Richard A. *The Federal Courts: Challenge and Reform.* Cambridge, MA: Harvard University Press, 1996, p. 351.
18 Opinions dissenting, dissenting in part, or concurring in part and dissenting in part.
19 A regular concurrence is a separate opinion filed by a justice who joins the opinion of the Court. A special concurrence is a separate opinion filed by a justice who votes with the majority but does not join the opinion of the Court (i.e., an opinion concurring in the judgment).
20 Coffin, Frank M. *On Appeal: Courts, Lawyering, and Judging.* New York: Norton, 1994, p. 227.
21 Owens and Wedeking, "Predicting Drift on Politically Insulated Institutions."
22 The quantity of opinion language is also affected by the justice's length of service. The use of more language may slightly enhance the precision of the scores; however, the Personality Recognizer was developed using comparatively short writing samples. Therefore, for most justices, the program has ample language with which to generate precise estimates. See Hall et al., "Attributes Beyond Attitudes." for more details.
23 Pennebaker and King, "Linguistic Styles."
24 Ramey, Klinger, and Hollibaugh, Jr. "More than a Feeling."
25 We generate static personality estimates for each justice based on the well-established finding in the personality literature that traits are highly stable after the age of 30 and extremely stable after the age of 50. Caspi, Roberts, and Shiner, "Personality Development," pp. 466–467. Roberts and DelVecchio, "The Rank-Order Consistency of Personality Traits from Childhood to Old Age." Fraley and Roberts, "Patterns of Continuity." We have also generated dynamic personality estimates based on each justices' concurrences in each term in order to explore the possibility that these traits vary over time. A visual inspection of the justices' dynamic trait estimates suggests strong stability over time. We also have conducted 34 Harris–Tzavalis tests for unit roots on these dynamic scores (treating each justice as a separate panel with their year on the Court as the time variable and the type of Big Five trait as the panel variable). These tests indicate that we can reject the null hypothesis that the panels contain unit roots for 32 of the 34 justices. (The two exceptions are Justices Whittaker and Kagan, for which we have the smallest sample sizes.) In other words, the tests strongly suggest that SCIPEs are generated through a stationary process (i.e., the mean, variance, and autocorrelation process do not vary over time). Also notice that Ramey et al.'s jackknife approach is also not truly dynamic. Ramey, Klinger, and Hollibaugh, Jr. *More Than a Feeling.* Jackknife estimates for Supreme Court justices yield very similar results to those presented here.)
26 Mairesse et al., "Using Linguistic Cues for the Automatic Recognition of Personality in Conversation and Text." Java code for the Personality Recognizer is found at http://people.csail.mit.edu/francois/research/personality/recognizer.html The program performs both the LIWC and MRCPD processing as well as the fitting of the machine-learning models. While these

steps can be performed separately, the program provides a useful wrapper for performing all steps.

27 Lowe, Will and Benoit, Kenneth. *Estimating Uncertainty in Quantitative Text Analysis*. Available at www.kenbenoit.net/pdfs/Midwest_2011_Lowe_Benoit.pdf. 2011.

28 See Hall et al., "Attributes Beyond Attitudes."

29 None of my empirical findings are dependent on this methodological choice.

30 American Educational Research Association American Psychological Association, National Council on Measurement in Education, Educational, Joint Committee on Standards for, and Testing, Psychological. *Standards for Educational and Psychological Testing*. Washington, DC: American Educational Research Association, 2014; Rubenzer, Steven J. and Faschingbauer, Thomas R. "Assessing the U.S. Presidents Using the Revised NEO Personality Inventory." *Assessment* 7.4 (2000), pp. 403–420.

31 Notice that the common spelling "extroversion" differs from the spelling used by psychologists ("extraversion").

32 Lithwick, Dahlia. "Her Honor." *New York Magazine* (27 Nov. 2011).

33 Tushnet, Mark. *In the Balance: Law and Politics on the Roberts Court*. New York: W.W. Norton, 2013, p. 86.

34 Farago, Jason. "Of the People: Sonia Sotomayor's Amazing Rise." *National Public Radio* (14 Jan. 2013). Available at: www.npr.org/2013/01/14/169157494/of-the-people-sonia-sotomayor-s-amazing-rise. Note that Sotomayor was described as the most extraverted justice on the Court before Kagan's appointment.

35 Toobin, Jeffrey. *The Oath: The Obama White House and The Supreme Court*. New York: Anchor, 2012, p. 58.

36 Peppers, Todd and Ward, Artemus. *In Chambers: Stories of Supreme Court Law Clerks and Their Justices*. Charlottesville: University of Virginia Press, 2012, p. 400.

37 Toobin. *The Oath*, p. 77.

38 Ibid., p. 278.

39 Carmon, Iran and Knizhnik, Shana. *Notorious RBG: The Life and Times of Ruth Bader Ginsburg*. New York: Dey Street Books, 2015, pp. 5–8.

40 Taylor, Jessica. "Ginsburg Apologizes for 'Ill-Advised' Trump Comments." *National Public Radio* (14 July 2016). Available at: www.npr.org/2016/07/14/486012897/ginsburg-apologies-for-ill-advised-trump-comments.

41 Berry, Mary Frances. *Stability, Security, and Continuity: Mr. Justice Burton and Decision-Making in the Supreme Court*. Westport, CT: Greenwood Press, 1978, p. vii.

42 Ferren, John M. *Salt of the Earth, Conscience of the Court: The Story of Justice Wiley Rutledge*. Chapel Hill, NC: The University of North Carolina Press, 2004, p. 344.

43 Ibid.

44 Peppers and Ward. *In Chambers*, p. 239.

45 "Frank Murphy." *Encyclopedia of World Biography*, 2004. Available at: www.encyclopedia.com/doc/1G2-3404704655.html.

46 Morice, Jane. "Former Jones Day Colleague Remembers Scalia as Conscientious Lawyer with 'Twinkle in his Eye.'" *Cleveland Plain Dealer*, (13 Feb. 2016).

47 Rossum, Ralph A. *Antonin Scalia's Jurisprudence: Text and Tradition*. Lawrence: University Press of Kansas, 2006.

48 Toobin, *The Oath*, p. 67.

49 Peppers and Ward, *In Chambers*, pp. 398–399.

50 Bailey and Maltzman, *The Constrained Court*, p. 12.

51 Toobin, *The Oath*, p. 173.

52 Ibid., pp. 9, 15.

53 Lamb, Brian, Swain, Susan, and Farkas, Mark, eds. *The Supreme Court: A C-SPAN Book Featuring the Justices in Their Own Words*. Philadelphia: PublicAffairs, 2010, p. 291.

54 Ibid., pp. 181, 286.

55 Epps, Garrett. *American Justice 2014: Nine Clashing Visions on the Supreme Court*. Philadelphia: University of Pennsylvania Press, 2014, p. 112.

56 Ibid., p. 165.

57 Starks, Glenn L. and Brooks, F. Erik. *Thurgood Marshall: A Biography*. Santa Barbara, CA: Greenwood, 2012, p. 7.

58 Woodward and Armstrong. *The Brethren*, p. 197.

59 Cushman, Claire. *The Supreme Court Justices: Illustrated Biographies, 1789–1995*. Washington, DC: CQ Press, 1995, p. 480.

60 Maveety, Nancy. *Justice Sandra Day O'Connor: Strategist on the Supreme Court*. Lanham, MD: Rowman & Littlefield Publishers, 1996, p. 19.

61 Lamb, Swain, and Farkas, *The Supreme Court*, p. 241.

62 Ibid., p. 237.

63 Gronlund, Mimi Clark. *Supreme Court Justice Tom C. Clark: A Life of Service*. Austin: University of Texas Press, 2010.

64 Ibid., pp. 8, 256.

65 Green, Charles, Schneider, Karen, and Otto, Mary. "Feminist and Family Person, With Friends on Left and Right." *Philidelphia Inquirer*, (15 June 1993).

66 Peppers and Ward, *In Chambers*, p. 399.

67 Toobin, Jeffrey. *The Nine: Inside the Secret World of the Supreme Court*. New York: Anchor, 2007, p. 244.

68 Ibid., pp. 280, 335.

69 Tushnet, *In the Balance: Law and Politics on the Roberts Court*, p. xi.

70 Toobin, Jeffrey. "No More Mr. Nice Guy: The Supreme Courts Stealth Hard-Liner." New Yorker (25 May 2009).

71 Davies, A. Powell. "Memorial for Justice Wiley Blount Rutledge." *American Bar Association Journal* 35.12 (1949), pp. 1008–1009.

72 Rostow, Eugene V. "Judge Louis H. Pollak." *University of Pennsylvania Law Review* 127.2 (1978), pp. 304–305.

73 Ferren. *Salt of the Earth, Conscience of the Court*, p. 419.

74 Ibid., pp. 341–342.

75 "Harold H. Burton Is Dead at 76." *New York Times* (29 Oct. 1964).

76 Kluger, Richard. *Simple Justice: The History of Brown v. Board of Education and Black America's Struggle for Equality*. New York: Vintage Books, 2004, pp. 248, 587.

77 Ibid., p. 242.

78 Ibid., p. 600.

79 "Harold H. Burton Is Dead at 76."

80 Murphy, Bruce Allen. *Fortas: The Rise and Ruin of a Supreme Court Justice*. New York: William Morrow & Co., 1988, p. 35.

81 Cushman. *The Supreme Court Justices*, p. 480.

82 Peppers and Ward, *In Chambers*, p. 316.

83 Woodward and Armstrong, *The Brethren*, p. 59.

84 Weinberg, Zoe Y. "Elena Kagan's Management Style Amped Up Pressure at Harvard Law School." *Crimson* (14 May 2010).

85 Benac, Nancy. "Kagan's Life an Undeviating Course to High Court." San Diego Union-Tribune (26 June 2010).

86 Greene, Meg. *Sonia Sotomayor: A Biography*. Santa Barbara, CA: Greenwood, 2012, p. 21.

87 Ibid., p. 37.

88 Epps, *American Justice*, p. 38.

89 Ibid., p. 44.

90 Toobin. *The Nine*, p. 69.

91 Peppers and Ward, *In Chambers*, p. 400.

92 Lithwick, Dahlia. "What the Women of SCOTUS Know." Slate (15 Dec. 2016). Available at: www.slate.com/articles/double_x/doublex/2016/12/in_troubled_times_the_women_of_the_supreme_court_are_the_role_models_we.html

93 Toobin, *The Oath*, p. 278.

94 Toobin, *The Nine*, p. 332.

95 Vianello, Michelangelo et al. "Gender Differences in Implicit and Explicit Personality Traits." *Personality and Individual Differences* 55.8 (2013), pp. 994–999, see p. 994.

96 Sherry, Suzanna. "Civic Virtue and the Feminine Voice in Constitutional Adjudication." *Virginia Law Review* 73.3 (1986), pp. 543–616, see p. 613.

97 None of the bivariate correlations between traits exceed .41.

98 Murphy, *Fortas*, p. 5.

99 Ferren, *Salt of the Earth, Conscience of the Court*, p. 227.

100 Gerhart, Eugene C. *America's Advocate: Robert H. Jackson*. Indianapolis, IN: Bobbs Merrill Company, 1958, p. 40, 300.

101 Ball, Howard. *Hugo L. Black: Cold Steel Warrior*. Oxford: Oxford University Press, 2006, pp. 15, 25.

102 Gerhart, *America's Advocate*, p. 236.

103 Ball, *Hugo L. Black*, p. 126.

104 Smith, Craig Alan. *Failing Justice: Charles Evans Whittaker on the Supreme Court*. Jefferson, NC: MacFarland & Companny, Inc., 2005, p. 16.

105 Schwartz, Bernard. *A History of the Supreme Court*. Oxford: Oxford University Press, 1993, p. 31.

106 Kalman, Laura. *Abe Fortas: A Biography*. New Haven, CT: Yale University Press, 1990, p. 45; Murphy, *Fortas: The Rise and Ruin of a Supreme Court Justice*, p. 99; Cushman, *The Supreme Court Justices*, pp. 474–475.

107 Murphy, *Fortas*, p. 219.

108 Toobin, *The Oath*, pp. 176–178.

109 Weinberg, "Elena Kagan's Management Style Amped Up Pressure at Harvard Law School."

110 Toobin, *The Oath*, p. 254.

111 Bailey and Maltzman, *The Constrained Court*, p. 72.

112 Woodward and Armstrong, *The Brethren*, pp. 306–307, 360.

113 Toobin, *The Nine*, p. 336; Toobin, *The Oath*, p. 279.

114 Gerber et al., "The Big Five Personality Traits in the Political Arena"; Hall et al., "Attributes Beyond Attitudes."

115 Mondak et al., "Personality and Civic Engagement."

116 Ramey, Klingler, and Hollibaugh, Jr. *More Than a Feeling*.

117 Martin, Andrew D. and Quinn, Kevin M. "Dynamic Ideal Point Estimation via Markov Chain Monte Carlo for the U.S. Supreme Court, 1953–1999." *Political Analysis* 10.2 (2002), pp. 134–153.

118 Spaeth et al., *Supreme Court Database, Version 2016 Release 01*.

119 Technically speaking, the dependent variable in our "liberal direction" model is a binomial variable, where the number of trials is the number of "votes" in that term, and the number of "successes" is the number of times the justice voted in the "liberal" direction.

4 Agenda Setting

1 Klarman, Michael J. *From Jim Crow to Civil Rights: The Supreme Court and the Struggle for Racial Equality*. New York: Oxford University Press, 2004, pp. 358–359.

2 *Hood v. Board of Trustees of Sumter City*. 232 F.2d 626 (4th Cir.). 1956.

3 Yarbrough, Tinsley E. *John Marshall Harlan: Great Dissenter of the Warren Court*. New York: Oxford University Press, 1992, p. 152.

4 Ibid., pp. 152–153.

5 The sentence was: "[I]t should go without saying that the vitality of these constitutional principles cannot be allowed to yield simply because of disagreement with them." Ibid., p. 235.

6 *NAACP v. Alabama*. 357 U.S. 449. 1958.

7 Cushman, *The Supreme Court Justices*, p. 445.

8 Yarbrough, *John Marshall Harlan*, p. 152.

9 Ibid.

10 Ibid., p. 153.

11 Provine, C. Herman. *Case Selection in the United States Supreme Court*. Chicago: University of Chicago Press, 1980, p. 60.

12 "Federal Judicial Caseload Statistics." Available at www.uscourts.gov/statistics-reports/judicial-facts-and-figures-2016. Judicial Facts and Figures, table 6.1.

13 Ibid., Judicial Facts and Figures, table 2.1.

14 Perry, H.W., Jr. *Deciding to Decide: Agenda Setting in the U.S. Supreme Court*. Cambridge, MA: Harvard University Press, 1991.

15 Black, Ryan C. and Owens, Ryan J. "Agenda Setting in the Supreme Court: The Collision of Policy and Jurisprudence." *Journal of Politics* 71.3 (2009), pp. 1062–1075.

16 *Rules of the Supreme Court of the United States*, 2013. Available at www .supremecourt.gov/ctrules/2013RulesoftheCourt.pdf.

17 Black and Owens, "Agenda Setting in the Supreme Court."

18 Ibid.

19 Ibid.

20 Ibid.

21 Black and Owens collected the justices' cert votes from the docket sheets of Justice Harry A. Blackmun. Their models include 13 justices; however, I exclude the votes by Justice Ginsburg because I am primarily interested in justice-level variables, and Justice Ginsburg cast only 22 of the 3,024 votes in their data set.

22 The differences between the absolute values of each of the personality marginal effects and the ideology marginal effect are all statistically insignificant.

23 DeYoung, Quilty, and Peterson, "Between Facets and Domains," p. 884.

24 Agreeable justices should be more likely to vote to grant cert for unpaid petitions due to their interest in helping the disadvantaged. However, because the Black and Owens data includes only paid petitions, I am unable to test this hypothesis.

25 Epstein and Knight, *The Choices Justices Make*.

26 Epstein, Landes, and Posner, "Why (and When) Judges Dissent."

27 I calculate the number of other grant votes by subtracting one from the total number of grant votes cast in each case if the justice in question voted to grant cert.

28 The difference between these statistics and the statistics reported in Figure 4.1 is due to rounding.

29 Gulati and McCauliff, "On 'Not' Making Law"; Clark, Tom S. "The Separation of Powers, Court Curbing, and Judicial Legitimacy." *American Journal of Political Science* 53.4 (2009), pp. 971–989; Rosenberg, Gerald N. "Judicial Independence and the Reality of Political Power." *Review of Politics* 54.3 (1992), pp. 369–398; Collins Paul M., Jr. "Lobbyists before the U.S. Supreme Court: Investigating the Influence of Amicus Curiae Briefs." *Political Research Quarterly* 60.1 (2007), pp. 55–70.

30 Durr, Robert H., Martin, Andrew D., and Wolbrecht, Christina. "Ideological Divergence and Public Support for the Supreme Court." *American Journal of Political Science* 44.4 (2000), pp. 768–776; Gibson, James L., Caldeira, Gregory A., and Spence, Lester Kenyatta. "The Supreme Court and the U.S. Presidential Election of 2000: Wounds, Self-Inflicted or Otherwise?" *British Journal of Political Science* 33.4 (2003), pp. 535–556; Grosskopf, Anke and Mondak, Jeffrey J. "Do Attitudes Toward Specific Supreme Court Decisions Matter? The Impact of *Webster* and *Texas v. Johnson* on Public Confidence in the Supreme Court." *Political Research Quarterly* 51.3 (1998), pp. 633–

654; Hoekstra, Valerie J. "The Supreme Court and Local Public Opinion." *American Political Science Review* 94.1 (2000), pp. 89–100.

31 Epstein, Landes, and Posner, *The Behavior of Federal Judges*; Baum, *The Puzzle of Judicial Behavior*; Schauer, "Incentives, Reputation, and the Inglorious Determinants of Judicial Behavior."

32 Johnson, Timothy R. and Martin, Andrew D. "The Supreme Court, the Solicitor General, and the Separation of Powers." *American Politics Research* 31.4 (2003), pp. 426–451; Epstein and Knight, *The Choices Justices Make.*

33 Cameron, Charles M. *The Tenth Justice: The Solicitor General and the Rule of Law.* New York: Vintage, 1988; Salokar, Rebecca Mae. *The Solicitor General: The Politics of Law.* Philadelphia: Temple University Press, 1992

34 Although not the focus of my theory, others have argued that the solicitor general is influential because he or she is uniquely positioned to provide credible ideological signals to the justices (Bailey, Michael A., Kamoie, Brian, and Maltzman, Forrest. "Signals from the Tenth Justice: The Political Role of the Solicitor General in Supreme Court Decision Making." *American Journal of Political Science* 49.1 (2005), pp. 72–85) or because the solicitor has special expertise as a frequent litigant before the Court (Pacelle, Richard L., Jr. *Between Law and Politics: The Solicitor General and the Structuring of Race, Gender, and Reproductive Rights Litigation.* College Station: Texas A&M University Press, 2003).

5 Opinion Assignments

1 O'Brien, David M. *Storm Center: The Supreme Court in American Politics.* 5th ed. New York: Norton, 2000, p. 282.

2 Wrightsman, Lawrence S. *The Psychology of the Supreme Court.* Oxford: Oxford University Press, 2006, p. 188.

3 Howard, J. Woodford. *Mr. Justice Murphy: A Political Biography.* Princeton, NJ: Princeton University Press, 1968, p. 491; Wrightsman. *The Psychology of the Supreme Court*, p. 187.

4 Howard, *Mr. Justice Murphy*, pp. 476, 491.

5 O'Brien, *Storm Center*, p. 282.

6 Johnson, Timothy R. *The Supreme Court Decision Making Process.* Oxford Research Encyclopedia of Politics. 2016. Available at: http://politics.oxfordre.com.

7 Throughout this chapter, I refer to the opinion of the Court as the "majority opinion" whether that opinion ultimately attracted majority support or not. If no single opinion attracts majority support, the opinion that received the most support among members of the majority coalition (the "plurality opinion") is the opinion of the Court.

8 Maltzman, Forrest and Wahlbeck, Paul J. "May It Please the Chief? Opinion Assignment in the Rehnquist Court." *American Journal of Political Science* 40.2 (1996), pp. 421–443, see p. 421.

9 Lax, Jeffrey R. and Cameron, Charles M. "Bargaining and Opinion Assignment on the U.S. Supreme Court." *Journal of Law, Economics, and Organization* 23.2 (2007), pp. 276–302; Bonneau, Chris W. et al. "Agenda Control,

the Median Justice, and the Majority Opinion on the U.S. Supreme Court." *American Journal of Political Science* 51.4 (2007), pp. 890–905.

10 Owens, Ryan J. and Wedeking, Justin. "Justices and Legal Clarity." *Law & Society Review* 45.4 (2011), pp. 1027–1061; Maltzman, Spriggs, and Wahlbeck, *Crafting Law on the Supreme Court*.

11 Some scholars argue that the median member of the majority coalition actually controls the content of the majority opinion. Carrubba, Cliff et al. "Who Controls the Content of Supreme Court Opinions?" *American Journal of Political Science* 56.2 (2012), pp. 400–412. However, others claim that the median member of the majority coalition controls the legal holding, while the majority opinion author controls the dicta. Khun, James, Hall, Matthew E.K., and Macher, Kristen. "Holding versus Dicta: Divided Control of Opinion Content on the U.S. Supreme Court." *Political Research Quarterly* 70.2 (2017), pp. 257–268.

12 Maltzman and Wahlbeck, "May It Please the Chief?"; Cross, Frank B. and Lindquist, Stefanie. "Doctrinal and Strategic Influences of the Chief Justice: The Decisional Significance of the Chief Justice." *University of Pennsylvania Law Review* 154 (2006), pp. 1665–1707; Davis, Sue. "The Chief Justice and Judicial Decision-Making: The Institutional Basis for Leadership on the Supreme Court." *In Supreme Court Decision-Making: New Institutionalist Approaches.* Ed. by Clayton, Cornell W. and Gillman, Howard. Chicago: University Of Chicago Press, 1999; Langer, Laura et al. "Recruitment of Chief Justices on State Supreme Courts: A Choice between Institutional and Personal Goals." *Journal of Politics* 65.3 (2003), pp. 656–675.

13 Maltzman, Forrest and Wahlbeck, Paul J. "A Conditional Model of Opinion Assignment on the Supreme Court." *Political Research Quarterly* 57.4 (2004), pp. 551–563, see p. 561.

14 Ibid., p. 552.

15 Ibid.

16 Ibid., p. 553.

17 Ambady, Nalini and Rosenthal, Robert. "Thin Slices of Expressive Behavior as Predictors of Interpersonal Consequences: A Meta-Analysis." *Psychological Bulletin* 111.2 (1992), pp. 256–274; Back, M and Nestler, S. "Accuracy of Judging Personality." In *The Social Psychology of Perceiving Others Accurately.* Ed. by Hall, Judith A., Mast, Marianne Schmid, and West, Tessa V. Cambridge University Press, 2016, pp. 98–124.

18 Unless noted otherwise, the data were obtained from the Supreme Court Database. Spaeth et al., *Supreme Court Database, Version 2016 Release 01.* I exclude Chief Justice Vinson and Justice Minton because SCIPEs are not available for those justices. I also exclude cases in which the Court issued a per curium opinion.

19 For all of my analyses, I assume that the author who ultimately authored the opinion of the Court was originally assigned to do so. This assumption is not strictly true. In a small percentage of cases, another author writes a competing opinion that eventually attracts majority support. Accordingly, some prior studies of opinion assignments limit their analyses to data derived from the chief's assignment sheets. Maltzman, Forrest and Wahlbeck, Paul J.

"May It Please the Chief?" *American Journal of Political Science* 40.2 (1996), pp. 421–443. I do not adopt this approach for three reasons. First, relying solely on data from assignment sheets would force me to restrict my analyses to the terms for which that data is available and, more importantly, the justices who served during those terms. Second, I believe the small number of cases in which the majority opinion author changes between the time of assignment and the time of publication is too small to warrant excluding decades of data and more than a dozen justices from my analyses. Finally, readers who are not persuaded by this methodological choice might find solace in reinterpreting my models as predicting which justice ultimately authored the majority opinion (either by initially receiving the assignment and preserving the majority coalition or by offering a new opinion that supplanted the opinion authored by the initial assignee). Interpreted in this light, my findings still shed valuable light on the factors influencing which justices ultimately author majority opinions.

20 Maltzman and Wahlbeck, "A Conditional Model of Opinion Assignment on the Supreme Court."

21 The differences between the absolute values of each of the personality marginal effects and the ideological distance marginal effect are all statistically insignificant, except for conscientiousness, which is significantly larger ($p < .05$; two-tailed test).

22 I have also conducted several exploratory analyses testing the possibility that chiefs prefer conscientious justices to author opinions in particularly complex, important, or salient cases, but I find no evidence to support these possibilities.

23 Maltzman and Wahlbeck, "A Conditional Model of Opinion Assignment on the Supreme Court."

24 The positive effect of agreeableness for cases with a winning margin of four is statistically significant ($p < .05$, one-tailed test), but the negative effect of agreeableness for cases with a winning margin of zero falls short of conventional levels of statistical significance ($p = .08$, one-tailed test).

25 Ibid.

26 Ibid.

27 Because I do not include a separate indicator variable for self-assignments, I conceptualize ideologically proximate justices as including the SAJ him- or herself. I exclude a self-assignment indicator because it confounds the interpretation of the ideological distance variable. However, the interaction between conscientiousness and ideological distance to the SAJ is still statistically significant and signed in the expected direction after including an indicator for self-assignments. In other words, the ideological effect is not solely driven by self-assignments.

28 Segal, Jeffrey A. and Cover, Albert D. "Ideological Values and the Votes of U.S. Supreme Court Justices." *American Political Science Review* 83.2 (1989), pp. 557–565.

29 I use Segal–Cover scores rather than Martin–Quinn scores throughout this book in order to avoid problems of circularity inherent in using vote-based ideology scores. However, all of my key findings are robust to the use of

Martin–Quinn scores. Martin and Quinn, "Dynamic Ideal Point Estimation via Markov Chain Monte Carlo for the U.S. Supreme Court, 1953–1999."

6 Intra-Court Bargaining

1 O'Brien, David M. *Storm Center*, p. 276; Woodward and Armstrong, *The Brethren*, p. 117.
2 Toobin, *The Nine*, p. 31.
3 Schwartz, *A History of the Supreme Court*, pp. 313–314.
4 *Swann v. Charlotte-Mecklenburg Board of Education.* 402 U.S. 1. 1971.
5 Woodward and Armstrong, *The Brethren*, p. 117.
6 Ibid., p. 118.
7 Ibid.
8 Ibid., p. 122.
9 Ibid.
10 Ibid.
11 Thomas, Evan. "Reagan's Mr. Right." *Time Magazine,* (30 June 1986).
12 Woodward and Armstrong, *The Brethren*, p. 210.
13 Ibid., p. 173.
14 Ibid., p. 127.
15 Ibid., p. 128.
16 Ibid., p. 127.
17 Wahlbeck, Paul J., Spriggs James F., II, and Maltzman, Forrest. *The Burger Court Opinion-Writing Database.* 2011. Available at: http://supremecourtopinions.wustl.edu January 11, 1971 draft opinion from Warren Burger.
18 Ibid., p. 131.
19 Ibid., p. 131.
20 Wahlbeck, Spriggs, and Maltzman, *The Burger Court Opinion-Writing Database.* March 16, 1971, memorandum from Warren Burger in *Swann v. Charlotte-Mecklenburg Board of Education.*
21 Ibid., March 22, 1971, memorandum from Warren Burger in *Swann v. Charlotte-Mecklenburg Board of Education.*
22 Ibid., March 23, 1971, memorandum from Thurgood Marshall to Warren Burger in *Swann v. Charlotte-Mecklenburg Board of Education.*
23 Ibid., p. 136.
24 Ibid., p. 137.
25 Ibid., p. 138.
26 In less than 1% of cases, the justice who ended up as the majority opinion author never actually circulated a draft majority opinion.
27 The original documents were obtained from the personal papers of justices who served on the Burger Court. See Wahlbeck, Spriggs, and Maltzman. *The Burger Court Opinion-Writing Database.* 2009.
28 I code opinion suggestions based on the coding scheme developed for the *Burger Court Opinion Writing Database.* I code category 100 as majority opinion drafts, categories 110–140 as separate opinion drafts, categories

400–460 as opinion suggestions, categories 500–510 as wait statements, and categories 300–313 as join statements.

29 I used either negative binomial regression models or Poisson models, depending on which model was appropriate for the data (specifically, whether a likelihood ratio test indicated the presence of overdispersion). I also included random intercepts for justice unless a likelihood ratio test indicated that random intercepts were not appropriate.

30 I include the time trend to account for the rise in opinions dissenting from denial of certiorari, word processing and electronic research, and the number of law clerks. (Epstein, Landes, and Posner, "Why (and When) Judges Dissent.")

31 The differences between the absolute values of the conscientiousness and openness marginal effects and the ideological distance marginal effect are both statistically significant ($p < .01$; two-tailed test).

32 Segal and Cover, "Ideological Values and the Votes of U.S. Supreme Court Justices."

7 Voting on the Merits

1 *Brown v. Board of Education.* 347 U.S. 483. 1954.

2 Pollak, Louis H. "Mr. Justice Frankfurter: Judgment and the Fourteenth Amendment." *Yale Law Journal* 67.2 (1957), pp. 304–323, p. 304.

3 Hutchinson, Dennis J. "Unanimity and Desegregation: Decisionmaking in the Supreme Court, 1948–1958." *Georgetown Law Journal* 68 (1979), pp. 1–96, p. 2.

4 Kluger, *Simple Justice*, p. 683.

5 See ibid., pp. 701–702; Considerable uncertainty exists regarding the details of this narrative. See Ellman, Stephen. "The Rule of Law and the Achievement of Unanimity in *Brown*." *New York Law School Law Review* 49 (2005), pp. 741–784.

6 Ferren, *Salt of the Earth, Conscience of the Court*, p. 233.

7 U.S. Supreme Court. *In Memoriam, Honorable Stanley Forman Reed: Proceedings of the Bar and Officers of the Supreme Court of the United States.* Washington, DC: U.S. Supreme Court, 1980, p. 11; "Stanley Reed Goes to the Supreme Court." *New York Times* (16 Jan. 1938). Reed has the 7th-highest SCIPE on conscientiousness.

8 U.S. Supreme Court, *In Memoriam, Honorable Stanley Forman Reed*, p. 37.

9 Klarman, *From Jim Crow to Civil Rights*, p. 302.

10 Kluger, *Simple Justice*, p. 702.

11 Klarman, *From Jim Crow to Civil Rights*.

12 Kluger, *Simple Justice*, p. 702.

13 Note that a majority of justices may vote for one party to win but not agree on the rationale for why that party should win. In such cases, the Court issues a plurality opinion rather than a majority opinion. If a justice recuses him- or herself, a seat is vacant, or a justice is unable to participate, the Court can split four-to-four. In these rare cases, the lower court's decision is left in place, but the decision does not set national precedent.

14 Epstein, Segal, and Spaeth, "The Norm of Consensus on the U.S. Supreme Court."

15 Walker, Epstein, and Dixon, "On the Mysterious Demise of Consensual Norms in the United States Supreme Court."

16 Epstein and Knight, *The Choices Justices Make*; Murphy, Walter F. *Elements of Judicial Strategy*. Chicago: University of Chicago Press, 1964, p. 63.

17 Epstein, Landes, and Posner, "Why (and When) Judges Dissent."

18 Seitz, Collins J. "Collegiality and the Court of Appeals: Appeals: What Is Important to the Court as an Institution is the Quality of the Working Relationship among Its Members." *Judicature* 75.1 (1991), pp. 26–27; Epstein, Landes, and Posner, "Why (and When) Judges Dissent."

19 Spriggs, James F. and Hansford, Thomas G. "Explaining the Overruling of U.S. Supreme Court Precedent." *Journal of Politics* 63.4 (2001), pp. 1091–1111.

20 Epstein, Landes, and Posner, *The Behavior of Federal Judges*, p. 266.

21 Murphy, *Elements of Judicial Strategy*; Pritchett, C. Herman. *Civil Liberties and the Vinson Court*. Chicago: University of Chicago Press, 1954; Sheldon, Charles H. "The Incidence and Structure of Dissensus on a State Supreme Court." *Supreme Court Decision-Making: New Institutionalist Approaches*. Ed. by Clayton, Cornell W. and Gillman, Howard. Chicago: University of Chicago Press, 1999.

22 Bartels, "The Constraining Capacity of Legal Doctrine on the U.S. Supreme Court"; Bailey and Maltzman, "Does Legal Doctrine Matter?"; Knight, Jack and Epstein, Lee. "The Norm of Stare Decisis." *American Journal of Political Science* 40.4 (1996), pp. 1018–1035; Hansford and Spriggs, *The Politics of Precedent on the U.S. Supreme Court*.

23 Epstein and Knight, *The Choices Justices Make*; Epstein, Landes, and Posner, "Why (and When) Judges Dissent"; Epstein, Landes, and Posner, *The Behavior of Federal Judges*.

24 For a complete description of the coding scheme, see Spaeth et al., *Supreme Court Database, Version 2016 Release 01*.

25 Segal and Spaeth, *The Supreme Court and the Attitudinal Model Revisited*; Epstein and Knight, *The Choices Justices Make*; Hall, Matthew E.K. "Experimental Justice: Random Judicial Assignment and the Partisan Process of Supreme Court Review." *American Politics Research* 37.2 (2009), pp. 195–226.

26 McGuire, Kevin T. and Stimson, James A. "The Least Dangerous Branch Revisited: New Evidence on Supreme Court Responsiveness to Public Preferences." *Journal of Politics* 66.4 (2004), pp. 1018–1035; Mishler, William and Sheehan, Reginald S. "Public Opinion, the Attitudinal Model, and Supreme Court Decision-Making: A Micro-Analytic Perspective." *Journal of Politics* 58.1 (1996), pp. 169–200; Flemming, Roy B. and Wood, B. Dan. "The Public and the Supreme Court: Individual Justice Responsiveness to American Policy Mood." *American Journal of Political Science* 41.2 (1997), pp. 468–498

27 Norpoth, Helmut and Segal, Jeffrey A. "Popular Influence on Supreme Court Decisions." *American Political Science Review* 88.3 (1994), pp. 711–724.

28 Giles, Micheal W., Blackstone, Bethany, and Vining, Richard L. "The Supreme Court in American Democracy: Unraveling the Linkages between Public Opinion and Judicial Decision Making." *Journal of Politics* 70.2 (2008), pp. 293–306; Casillas, Christopher, Enns, Peter K., and Wohlfarth, Patrick C. "How Public Opinion Constrains the U.S. Supreme Court." *American Journal of Political Science* 55.1 (2011), pp. 74–88.

29 Ferejohn, John and Shipan, Charles. "Congressional Influence on Bureaucracy." *Journal of Law, Economics, & Organization* 6.Special Issue (1990), pp. 1–20; Gely, Rafael and Spiller, Pablo T. "A Rational Choice Theory of Supreme Court Statutory Decisions with Applications to the *State Farm* and *Grove City* Cases." *Journal of Law, Economics & Organization* 6.2 (1990), pp. 263–300; Spiller, Pablo T. and Gely, Rafael. "Congressional Control or Judicial Independence: The Determinants of U.S. Supreme Court Labor-Relations Decisions." *Rand Journal of Economics* 23.4 (1992), pp. 463–492.

30 Rosenberg, "Judicial Independence and the Reality of Political Power"; Clark, "The Separation of Powers, Court Curbing, and Judicial Legitimacy" Segal, Jeffrey A.,Westerland, Chad, and Lindquist, Stephanie A. "Congress, the Supreme Court, and Judicial Review: Testing a Constitutional Separation of Powers Model." *American Journal of Political Science* 55.1 (2011), pp. 89–104.

31 Hall, Matthew E.K. *The Nature of Supreme Court Power*. New York: Cambridge University Press, 2011; Hall, Matthew E.K. "The Semi-Constrained Court: Public Opinion, the Separation of Powers, and the U.S. Supreme Court's Fear of Nonimplementation." *American Journal of Political Science* 58.2 (2014), pp. 352–366.

32 Black, Ryan C. and Owens, Ryan J. "Solicitor General Influence and Agenda Setting on the U.S. Supreme Court." *Political Research Quarterly* 64.4 (2011), pp. 765–778; Black, Ryan C. and Owens, Ryan J. *The Solicitor General and the United States Supreme Court: Executive Influence and Judicial Decisions*. New York: Cambridge University Press, 2012; Segal, Westerland and Lindquist, "Congress, the Supreme Court, and Judicial Review"; Harvey, Anna and Friedman, Barry. "Ducking Trouble: Congressionally Induced Selection Bias in the Supreme Court's Agenda." *Journal of Politics* 71.2 (2009), pp. 574–592; Harvey, Anna and Friedman, Barry. "Pulling Punches: Congressional Constraints on the Supreme Court's Constitutional Rulings, 1987–2000." *Legislative Studies Quarterly* 31.4 (2006), pp. 533–562.

33 Hall, "The Semi-Constrained Court."

34 Unless noted otherwise, the data were obtained from the Supreme Court Database. Spaeth et al., *Supreme Court Database, Version 2016 Release 01*. I exclude Chief Justice Vinson and Justice Minton because SCIPEs are not available for those justices. I limit my analysis to those terms for which the Stimson Mood Indicator is available (Stimson, James A. *Public Opinion in America: Moods, Cycles, and Swings*. 2nd ed. Boulder, CO: Westview Press, 1999) and those cases in which the Supreme Court Database coded the ideological direction of the decision.

35 I use Segal–Cover ideology scores rather than Martin–Quinn ideology scores because Martin–Quinn scores are based on merits votes and, therefore, do not provide an exogenous measure of the justices' ideology for this analysis.

36 I include the time trend to account for the rise in opinions dissenting from denial of certiorari, word processing and electronic research, and the number of law clerks. Epstein, Landes, and Posner, "Why (and When) Judges Dissent."

37 All of the marginal effects for opinion author traits are a one percentage point change or less. Furthermore, for purposes of model efficiency, I do not include crossed random intercepts for opinion author. (Models with these crossed random effects have a great deal of difficulty converging.) Therefore, the statistical significance of these findings should be interpreted with extreme caution.

38 The differences between the absolute values of the personality marginal effects and the ideological distance marginal effect are all statistically insignificant.

39 Schauer, "Incentives, Reputation, and the Inglorious Determinants of Judicial Behavior"; Gulati and McCauliff, "On 'Not' Making Law."

40 Epstein and Knight, "Reconsidering Judicial Preferences," p. 21.

41 Casillas, Enns, and Wohlfarth, "How Public Opinion Constrains the U.S. Supreme Court"; McGuire and Stimson, "The Least Dangerous Branch Revisited"; Durr, Martin, and Wolbrecht, "Ideological Divergence and Public Support for the Supreme Court"; Hoekstra, "The Supreme Court and Local Public Opinion."

42 Stimson, *Public Opinion in America: Moods, Cycles, and Swings.*

43 Casillas, Enns, and Wohlfarth, "How Public Opinion Constrains the U.S. Supreme Court"; McGuire, Kevin T. and Stimson, James A. "The Least Dangerous Branch Revisited." *Journal of Politics* 66.4 (2004), pp. 1018–1035; Hall, "The Semi-Constrained Court."

44 Clark, Tom S., Lax, Jeffrey R., and Rice, Douglas. "Measuring the Political Salience of Supreme Court Cases." *Journal of Law and Courts* 3.1 (2015), pp. 37–65.

45 Liptak, *The End of an Era, for Court and Nation.*

46 Danelski, "The Influence of the Chief Justice in the Decisional Process"; Haynie, "Leadership and Consensus on the U.S. Supreme Court"; Caldeira and Zorn, "Of Time and Consensual Norms in the Supreme Court"; Walker, Epstein, and Dixon, "On the Mysterious Demise of Consensual Norms in the United States Supreme Court."

47 Segal and Spaeth, *The Supreme Court and the Attitudinal Model Revisited.*

48 Segal and Cover, "Ideological Values and the Votes of U.S. Supreme Court Justices."

49 Keck, "Party, Policy, or Duty: Why Does the Supreme Court Invalidate Federal Statutes?" p. 321.

50 Gillman, Howard. "The Court as an Idea, Not a Building (or a Game): Interpretive Institutionalism and the Analysis of Supreme Court Decision-Making." *Supreme Court Decision-Making: New Institutionalist Approaches.*

Ed. by Clayton, Cornell W. and Gillman, Howard. Chicago: University of Chicago Press, 1999, pp. 65–90.

51 Another way to think about this figure is to note that the probability of a justice dissenting is very high for all justices who disagree with the ideological direction of the Court's ruling regardless of conscientiousness. However, when justices are ideologically predisposed to agree with the Court's ruling (i.e., low justice disagreement), the probability of dissent is very low for less-conscientious justices, but still fairly high for more-conscientious justices. This finding suggests that more-conscientious justices are willing to dissent, even when they are ideologically inclined to agree with the Court's ruling.

52 Epstein and Jacobi, "The Strategic Analysis of Judicial Decisions," p. 341.

53 Maltzman, Spriggs, and Wahlbeck, *Crafting Law on the Supreme Court*; Epstein and Knight, *The Choices Justices Make*; Edwards, "The Effects of Collegiality on Judicial Decision Making."

54 Epstein, Landes, and Posner, "Why (and When) Judges Dissent."

55 Ibid.

56 Spriggs and Hansford, "Explaining the Overruling of U.S. Supreme Court Precedent."

57 The behavior of other justices may also reflect unobserved factors that favor dissent; however, if the influence of other dissents were solely driven by unobserved factors, there is no reason why agreeableness would moderate this effect unless such factors were also related to social harmony or altruism.

58 Dahl, Robert A. "Decision-Making in a Democracy: The Supreme Court as a National Policy-Maker." *Journal of Public Law* 6 (1957), pp. 279–295, see pp. 282, 291.

59 Black and Owens, *The Solicitor General and the United States Supreme Court*.

60 Cameron, *The Tenth Justice*.

61 Rosenberg, "Judicial Independence and the Reality of Political Power."

62 Hall, Matthew E.K. and Ura, Joseph Daniel. "Judicial Majoritarianism." *Journal of Politics* 77.3 (2015), pp. 818–831; Hall, "The Semi-Constrained Court"; Segal, Westerland, and Lindquist, "Congress, the Supreme Court, and Judicial Review"; Harvey, Anna and Friedman, Barry. "Pulling Punches."

63 Hansford and Spriggs, *The Politics of Precedent on the U.S. Supreme Court*.

8 Separate Opinions

1 Woodward and Armstrong, *The Brethren*, p. 74.

2 Ibid., p. 75.

3 Cushman, *The Supreme Court Justices*, p. 445.

4 Wrightsman, *The Psychology of the Supreme Court*, p. 189.

5 Woodward and Armstrong, *The Brethren*, p. 59.

6 Ibid., p. 75.

7 Ibid.

8 Ibid., p. 76.

9 These two opinion types are also known as general concurrences and special concurrences, respectively.

10 For example, in 11% of cases with only one dissenting vote, the dissenter chose not to write a dissenting opinion. This statistic was calculated based on data from the Supreme Court Database. First, I counted the number of opinions with only one dissenting vote during the 1946–2015 terms (7,071). Then, I counted the number of lone dissents (i.e., individual justice votes) in these cases (845). Finally, I counted the number of times a justice cast a lone dissenting vote and did not file a dissenting opinion (95). 95 is 11% of 845.

11 Wahlbeck, Paul J., Spriggs II, James F., and Maltzman, Forrest. "The Politics of Dissents and Concurrences on the U.S. Supreme Court." *American Politics Quarterly* 27.4 (1999), pp. 488, 490.

12 Murphy, *Elements of Judicial Strategy*, pp. 60, 66; Segal and Spaeth, *The Supreme Court and the Attitudinal Model Revisited*, p. 261; Ulmer. "Dissent Behavior and the Social Background of Supreme Court Justices."

13 Johnson, Charles A. "Law, Politics, and Judicial Decision Making: Lower Federal Court Uses of Supreme Court Decisions." *Law & Society Review* 21.2 (1987), pp. 325–340; Ulmer. "Dissent Behavior and the Social Background of Supreme Court Justices," p. 581.

14 Baird, Vanessa and Jacobi, Tonja. "How the Dissent Becomes the Majority: Using Federalism to Transform Coalitions in the U.S. Supreme Court." *Dule Law Journal* 59.2 (2009), pp. 183–238.

15 Warren's aversion to filing separate opinions may have been related to his role as chief justice; however, many associate justices tend to avoid separate opinions. For example, during this time period, Justice Kagan filed separate opinions in only 6% of cases.

16 Wahlbeck, Spriggs, and Maltzman, "The Politics of Dissents and Concurrences on the U.S. Supreme Court." Collins, Paul M., Jr. "Cognitive Dissonance on the U.S. Supreme Court." *Political Research Quarterly* 64.2 (2011), pp. 362–376.

17 Epstein, Landes, and Posner, "Why (and When) Judges Dissent"; Collins, "Cognitive Dissonance on the U.S. Supreme Court."

18 Wahlbeck, Spriggs, and Maltzman, "The Politics of Dissents and Concurrences on the U.S. Supreme Court." Collins, "Cognitive Dissonance on the U.S. Supreme Court."

19 Wahlbeck, Spriggs, and Maltzman, "The Politics of Dissents and Concurrences on the U.S. Supreme Court."

20 Collins, "Cognitive Dissonance on the U.S. Supreme Court."

21 Unless noted otherwise, the data were obtained from the Supreme Court Database. Spaeth et al., *Supreme Court Database, Version 2016 Release 01*. As in prior chapters, I exclude Chief Justice Vinson and Justice Minton because SCIPEs are not available for those justices. I limit my analysis to those cases in which the Supreme Court Database coded the ideological direction of the decision.

22 I include the time trend to account for the rise in opinions dissenting from denial of certiorari, word processing and electronic research, and the number of law clerks. Epstein, Landes, and Posner, "Why (and When) Judges Dissent."

23 All of the marginal effects for opinion author traits are a less than a one percentage point change. Furthermore, for purposes of model efficiency, I do not include crossed random intercepts for opinion author. (Models with these crossed random effects have a great deal of difficulty converging.) Therefore, the statistical significance of these findings should be interpreted with extreme caution.

24 The differences between the absolute values of each of the personality marginal effects and the ideological distance marginal effect are all statistically insignificant.

25 Cooke, Molly. "Justice Scalia Addresses First-Year Law Students." *Hoya* (7 Nov. 2015).

26 In fact, amicus participation is often described as a proxy for "political salience." Wahlbeck, Spriggs, and Maltzman, "The Politics of Dissents and Concurrences on the U.S. Supreme Court." Collins, "Cognitive Dissonance on the U.S. Supreme Court."

27 Liptak, *The End of an Era, for Court and Nation.*

28 The marginal effect is statistically significant ($p < .05$; one-tailed test) but not substantively significant (the predicted probability of dissent for more conscientious justices rounds to .12, regardless of justice disagreement).

29 Gulati and McCauliff, "On 'Not' Making Law."

9 Behind the Black Robes

1 Epstein, Landes, and Posner, "Why (and When) Judges Dissent"; Epstein, Landes, and Posner, *The Behavior of Federal Judges*; Baum, *Judges and Their Audiences.*

2 Specifically, I found no evidence to support my hypotheses related to chief assignments and conscientiousness in Chapter 5, my hypotheses related to opinion suggestions and either extraversion or openness in Chapter 6, or my hypothesis related to concurrences and extraversion in Chapter 8.

3 Epstein, Segal, and Spaeth, "The Norm of Consensus on the U.S. Supreme Court"; Walker, Epstein, and Dixon, "On the Mysterious Demise of Consensual Norms in the United States Supreme Court"; Epstein, Landes, and Posner, "Why (and When) Judges Dissent."

4 Edwards, "The Effects of Collegiality on Judicial Decision Making"; Edwards and Livermore, "The Pitfalls of Empirical Studies That Attempt to Understand the Factors Affecting Appellate Decisionmaking."

5 Hall, "Experimental Justice"; Hall, Matthew E.K. "Randommess Reconsidered: Modeling Random Judicial Assignment in the U.S. Courts of Appeals." *Journal of Empirical Legal Studies* 7.3 (2010), pp. 574–589.

6 Ramey, Klingler, and Hollibaugh, Jr. *More Than a Feeling.*

A Agenda-Setting Analysis

1 Black and Owens collected the justices' cert votes from the docket sheets of Justice Blackmun. Their models include 13 justices; however, I exclude the votes by Justice Ginsburg because I am primarily interested in

justice-level variables, and Justice Ginsburg cast only 22 of the 3,024 votes in their data set.

2 See Black and Owens for further details regarding the control variables. Black and Owens, "Agenda Setting in the Supreme Court."

3 Epstein, Lee, Knight, Jack, and Martin, Andrew D. "The Judicial Common Space." *Journal of Law, Economics, & Organization* 23 (2007), pp. 305–325.

4 Black and Owens, "Agenda Setting in the Supreme Court."

B Opinion Assignment Analysis

1 I exclude Chief Justice Vinson and Justice Minton because SCIPEs are not available for those justices.

2 Spaeth et al., *Supreme Court Database, Version 2016 Release 01.*

3 Maltzman and Wahlbeck, "A Conditional Model of Opinion Assignment on the Supreme Court," p. 555.

4 Ibid., p. 556.

5 Martin and Quinn, "Dynamic Ideal Point Estimation via Markov Chain Monte Carlo for the U.S. Supreme Court, 1953–1999."

C Intra-Court Bargaining Analysis

1 The original documents were obtained from the personal papers of justices who served on the Burger Court. See Wahlbeck, Spriggs, II, and Maltzman. *The Burger Court Opinion-Writing Database.* 2009 for further details regarding the data.

2 Note that, unlike Johnson et al., I do not incorporate the number of separate opinions filed by the justices into this measure in order to avoid circularity (because I use complexity to predict the number of separate opinion drafts circulated by the justices). Johnson, Timothy R., Spriggs, James F., II, Wahlbeck, Paul J. "Passing and Strategic Voting on the U.S. Supreme Court." *Law & Society Review* 39.2 (2005), pp. 349–378.

3 Maltzman and Wahlbeck, "A Conditional Model of Opinion Assignment on the Supreme Court," p. 556.

4 Segal and Cover, "Ideological Values and the Votes of U.S. Supreme Court Justices."

D Voting on the Merits Analysis

1 Spaeth et al., *Supreme Court Database, Version 2016 Release 01.*

2 Stimson, *Public Opinion in America.*

3 Clark, Lax, and Rice, "Measuring the Political Salience of Supreme Court Cases."

4 Segal and Cover, "Ideological Values and the Votes of U.S. Supreme Court Justices."

5 Note that, again, I do not incorporate the number of separate opinions filed by the justices into this measure in order to avoid circularity (because I use complexity to predict dissents, which may induce filing separate opinions).

E Separate Opinion Analysis

1 Spaeth et al., *Supreme Court Database, Version 2016 Release 01.*
2 Segal and Cover, "Ideological Values and the Votes of U.S. Supreme Court Justices."
3 Note that, again, I do not incorporate the number of separate opinions filed by the justices into this measure in order to avoid circularity.
4 Maltzman and Wahlbeck, "A Conditional Model of Opinion Assignment on the Supreme Court," p. 556.

Index